JUMP Math 8.1

Book 8 Part 1 of 2

Contents

jump math™

MULTIPLYING POTENTIAL.

JUMP Math
Toronto, Canada
www.jumpmath.org

Writers: Dr. John Mighton, Dr. Sindi Sabourin, Dr. Anna Klebanov
Contributing Writer: Margaret McClintock
Cover Design: Blakeley Words+Pictures
Text Design: Pam Lostracco
Layout: Pam Lostracco, Rita Camacho, Ilyana Martinez
Cover Photograph: © NASA, ESA, S. Beckwith (STScI), and The Hubble Heritage Team (STScI/AURA)

ISBN: 978-1-897120-60-6

Fourteenth printing July 2020

Printed and bound in Canada

Welcome to JUMP Math

Entering the world of JUMP Math means believing that every child has the capacity to be fully numerate and to love math. Founder and mathematician John Mighton has used this premise to develop his innovative teaching method. The resulting materials isolate and describe concepts so clearly and incrementally that everyone can understand them.

JUMP Math is comprised of workbooks, teacher's guides, evaluation materials, outreach programs, tutoring support through schools and community organizations, and provincial curriculum correlations. All of this is presented on the JUMP Math website: **www.jumpmath.org**.

Teacher's guides are available on the website for free use. Read the introduction to the teacher's guides before you begin using these materials. This will ensure that you understand both the philosophy and the methodology of JUMP Math. The workbooks are designed for use by students, with adult guidance. Each student will have unique needs and it is important to provide the student with the appropriate support and encouragement as he or she works through the material.

Allow students to discover the concepts on the worksheets by themselves as much as possible. Mathematical discoveries can be made in small, incremental steps. The discovery of a new step is like untangling the parts of a puzzle. It is exciting and rewarding.

Students will need to answer the shaded questions using a notebook. Grid paper and notebooks should always be on hand for answering extra questions or when additional room for calculation is needed. Grid paper is also available in the BLM section of the Teacher's Guide.

Contents

Unit 2: Patterns and Algebra

Unit 3: Number Sense

Unit 4: Probability and Data Management

Unit 5: Geometry

Unit 6: Measurement

Unit 7: Number Sense

Unit 8: Geometry

NS8-1 Factors and Multiples

The **multiples** of a number are the numbers you say when counting by that number.

15 is a **multiple** of both 3 and 5

$3 \times 5 = 15$

3 and 5 are both **factors** of 15

0 is a **multiple** of both 0 and 4

$0 \times 4 = 0$

0 and 4 are both **factors** of 0

1. List the first few multiples of these numbers.

    a) 3: __0__ , __3__ , __6__ , ____ , ____ , ____ , ____

    b) 4: ____ , ____ , ____ , ____ , ____ , ____ , ____

    c) 5: ____ , ____ , ____ , ____ , ____ , ____ , ____

2. Look at the lists you made in Question 1.

    a) Is 12 a multiple of 4? _____ How do you know? _____

    b) Is 17 a multiple of 5? _____ How do you know? _____

    c) Is 0 a multiple of 3? _____ Of 4? _____ Of 5? _____

3. a) Write 0 as a multiple of 17: $0 = 17 \times$ _____

    b) Which whole numbers is 0 a multiple of? Explain. _____

    _____

4. Rewrite each statement in a way that means the same thing but uses the word "factor."

    a) 20 is a multiple of 5.   _____

    b) 9 is a multiple of 1.   _____

    c) 0 is a multiple of 8.   _____

    d) 8 is a multiple of 8.   _____

    e) 11 is not a multiple of 4.   _____

    f) Every number is a multiple of 1.   _____

    g) Every number is a multiple of itself.   _____

    h) 0 is a multiple of any number.   _____

5. Rewrite each statement in a way that means the same thing but uses the word "multiple."

    a) 5 is a factor of 15.   b) 2 is a factor of 18.
    c) 3 is a factor of 0.   d) Every number is a factor of 0.
    e) 1 is a factor of 7.   f) 1 is a factor of every number.
    g) 6 is a factor of 6.   h) Any number is a factor of itself.

6. Alana wants to find all pairs of numbers that multiply to give 10.

She lists each number from 1 to 10 in a chart. She looks for a second number that multiplies with the first to give 10.

a) Why didn't Alana list any number greater than 10 in the first column of her table?

b) Why didn't Alana list 0 in the first column of her table?

1st	2nd
1	10
2	5
3	
4	
5	2
6	
7	
8	
9	
10	1

7. Use Alana's method to find all pairs of numbers that multiply to give the number in bold.

a) **6**

1st	2nd
1	
2	
3	
4	
5	
6	

b) **8**

1st	2nd
1	
2	
3	
4	
5	
6	
7	
8	

c) **9**

1st	2nd
1	
2	
3	
4	
5	
6	
7	
8	
9	

8. Cross out the pairs that are repeated in Question 7.

9. Connor makes a chart to list all the factors of 20. He doesn't want to write and check all the numbers from 1 to 20. He starts his list as follows:

a) Connor knows that $5 \times 4 = 20$. He thinks that if $6 \times \blacksquare = 20$, then $\blacksquare$ must be less than 4. Explain his thinking.

b) Explain why Connor's list is complete.

1st	2nd
1	20
2	10
3	
4	5
5	4

10. Connor used this chart to help him identify pairs that multiply to 36. Why did he know that his search was complete as soon as he found a pair with both numbers the same?

11. Find all pairs of numbers that multiply to 120.

1st	2nd
1	36
2	18
3	12
4	9
5	
6	6

NS8-2 LCMs and GCFs

1. Mark the multiples of each number on the number lines.

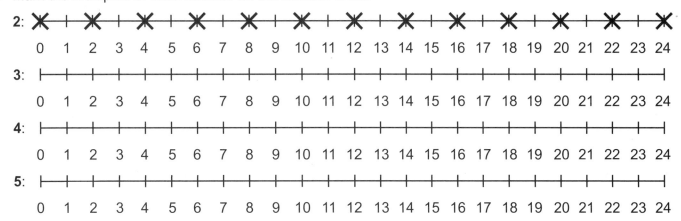

2: ✗ ✗ ✗ ✗ ✗ ✗ ✗ ✗ ✗ ✗ ✗ ✗ ✗
   0 1 2 3 4 5 6 7 8 9 10 11 12 13 14 15 16 17 18 19 20 21 22 23 24

3:
   0 1 2 3 4 5 6 7 8 9 10 11 12 13 14 15 16 17 18 19 20 21 22 23 24

4:
   0 1 2 3 4 5 6 7 8 9 10 11 12 13 14 15 16 17 18 19 20 21 22 23 24

5:
   0 1 2 3 4 5 6 7 8 9 10 11 12 13 14 15 16 17 18 19 20 21 22 23 24

2. 0 is a multiple of every number. Not counting 0, find the first 2 common multiples of:

   a) 2 and 5 ____ , ____   b) 2 and 3 ____ , ____   c) 3 and 4 ____ , ____   d) 2 and 4 ____ , ____

> The **lowest common multiple (LCM)** of two or more numbers is the smallest number (not 0) that is a multiple of the numbers.

3. Look at your answers to Question 2. What is the LCM of:

   a) 2 and 5 ____   b) 2 and 3 ____   c) 3 and 4 ____   d) 2 and 4 ____

4. Find the lowest common multiple of each pair of numbers.

   a) 3 and 5   b) 6 and 10   c) 9 and 12   d) 2 and 6

   3: *3, 6, 9, 12, 15, 18*   **6:**   **9:**   **2:**

   5: *5, 10, 15, 20*   **10:**   **12:**   **6:**

   LCM = __15__   LCM = ____   LCM = ____   LCM = ____

   e) 2 and 10   f) 2 and 9   g) 3 and 15   h) 4 and 8   i) 8 and 8

   j) 5 and 15   k) 5 and 10   l) 3 and 10   m) 6 and 15   n) 6 and 8

5. a) How can you find the second common multiple of two numbers from the first?

   b) The first common multiple of 18 and 42 is 126. What is the second common multiple? _____

6. Find all the factors of each number by dividing the number by the whole numbers in increasing order—divide by 1, 2, 3, 4, 5, and so on. How do you know when you can stop dividing?

   a) 33   b) 55   c) 65   d) 66   e) 90

      1, 3, 11, 33

The greatest number that is a factor of two or more numbers is called the **greatest common factor (GCF)** of the numbers.

7. Use your answers to Question 6. Find the greatest common factor of:

   a) 33 and 55   b) 33 and 66   c) 33 and 90   d) 65 and 66

   e) 33 and 65   f) 55 and 65   g) 33, 55 and 65   h) 55, 65 and 90

Two numbers are called **consecutive** if one number is the next number after the other.

Example: 13 and 14 are consecutive because 14 is the next number after 13.

INVESTIGATION 1 ▶ What is the GCF of two consecutive numbers?

A. Find the factors of each number and then the GCF of each pair.

   a) 14 and 15   b) 24 and 25   c) 27 and 28   d) 44 and 45

   14: 1, 2, 7, 14   **24**:   **27**:   **44**:

   15: 1, 3, 5, 15   **25**:   **28**:   **45**:

   GCF: _1_   GCF: ____   GCF: ____   GCF: ____

B. Make a conjecture about the GCF of any two consecutive numbers.

   _____

C. Test your conjecture on two consecutive numbers of your choice: ____ and ____ GCF: ____

9 and 15 are multiples of 3.   So 15 + 9 and 15 − 9 are multiples of 3, too!

9 = ○○○   15 = ○○○○○   15 + 9 = ○○○○○○○○   15 − 9 = ○○○○○
    ○○○   ○○○○○   ○○○○○○○○   ○○○○○
    ○○○   ○○○○○   ○○○○○○○○   ○○○○○

8. a) Rewrite the conclusion in the box using the word factor instead of multiple:

   3 is a factor of both 9 and 15, so 3 is a factor of both _____ *and* _____

   b) Draw pictures to show that any factor of both 8 and 20 is also a factor of both 20 + 8 and 20 − 8.

   c) Explain why any common factor of 99 and 100 must divide the sum 99 + 100.

   d) Explain why any common factor of 99 and 100 must divide the difference 100 − 99.

   e) Without finding the factors of 99 and 100, explain why their GCF is 1.

INVESTIGATION 2 ▶ How are the GCF, the LCM, and the product of two numbers related?

A. Complete the chart. Include three more values of your choice for *a* and *b*.

a	*b*	*a* × *b*	GCF	LCM	GCF × LCM
3	4				
2	5				
4	6				
10	15				
5	10				
3	5				
4	5				
6	9				
12	15				

B. Which two columns are the same in every row?

_____ and _____

C. Write an expression for the LCM in terms of *a* × *b* and GCF.

LCM = _____

D. When the LCM is the same as the product, what is the GCF? _____

E. Choose two more pairs of numbers *a* and *b* where *a* is a factor of *b*, and complete the chart.

a	*b*	*a* × *b*	GCF	LCM	GCF × LCM
2	6				

Which columns are equal? GCF = _____, LCM = _____ and GCF × LCM = _____ × _____

NS8-3 Prime Numbers

> A **prime** number has **exactly two** distinct factors: itself and 1.
>
> A **composite** number has **more than two** distinct factors: itself, at least one number other than itself, and 1.

1. How many distinct factors does the number 1 have? _____ Is 1 a prime number? _____

2. List all prime numbers less than 10: _____

3. List all composite numbers between 10 and 20: _____

4. What is the greatest prime number less than 30? _____

5. Circle the prime numbers in each list.

   a) 5   4   2   8   9   1   b) 6   2   3   4   7   10

   c) 11   25   14   13   17   20   d) 27   15   12   18   29   33

6. List all the factors of each number.

   a) 25: _____*1, 5, 25*_____   b) 8: _____

   c) 12: _____   d) 16: _____

   e) 9: _____   f) 18: _____

   g) 50: _____   h) 45: _____

   i) 60: _____   j) 42: _____

7. Put a check mark in front of the numbers that are composite numbers.

   _____ 30   _____ 31   _____ 32   _____ 33   _____ 34   _____ 35   _____ 36   _____ 37

8. Write a number between 0 and 20 that has…

   a) two factors _____   b) four factors _____   c) five factors _____

9. The prime numbers 3 and 5 differ by 2. Find three other pairs of prime numbers less than 20 that differ by 2:

10. Write three consecutive numbers which are also all composite numbers:

11. Eratosthenes was a Greek scholar who was born over 2 000 years ago in what is now Libya. He developed a method to systematically identify prime numbers. It is called **Eratosthenes' Sieve**.

Follow these directions to use Eratosthenes' Sieve:

a) Shade the number 1 (it is not prime).

b) Circle 2, 3, 5, and 7—all the primes less than 10.

c) Shade all the remaining multiples of 2.

d) Shade all the remaining multiples of 3.

e) Shade all the remaining multiples of 5.

f) Shade all the remaining multiples of 7.

g) Circle the next uncircled number (11).

Note that all multiples of 11 less than 100 (11 × 2, 11 × 3, ..., 11 × 9) are **already shaded** because they have a factor less than 10.

h) Circle the next uncircled number. How do you know all multiples of that number less than 100 are already shaded?

1	2	3	4	5	6	7	8	9	10
11	12	13	14	15	16	17	18	19	20
21	22	23	24	25	26	27	28	29	30
31	32	33	34	35	36	37	38	39	40
41	42	43	44	45	46	47	48	49	50
51	52	53	54	55	56	57	58	59	60
61	62	63	64	65	66	67	68	69	70
71	72	73	74	75	76	77	78	79	80
81	82	83	84	85	86	87	88	89	90
91	92	93	94	95	96	97	98	99	100

_____

_____

i) Now circle all the remaining numbers.

You've just used Eratosthenes' Sieve to circle all the prime numbers from 1 to 100!

12. How many prime numbers are there between 30 and 50? _____

13. Solve these riddles.

a) I am a prime number less than 100. If you add 10 or 20 to me, the result is prime. What number am I?

b) I am a prime number less than 100. My digits add to 13. What number am I?

c) I am a prime number less than 100. My tens digit is one more than my ones digit. What number am I?

d) I am a prime number between 20 and 70. If you reverse my digits, the result is a larger prime number. What number am I?

NS8-4 Prime Factorizations

Any **composite** number can be written as a product of prime numbers. This product is called the **prime factorization** of the original number.

10 × 2 **is not** a prime factorization of 20 because the number 10 is composite

5 × 2 × 2 **is** a prime factorization of 20

You can find a prime factorization for a number by using a **factor tree**.

Here is how you can make a factor tree for the number 20:

Step 1: Find any pair of numbers (not including 1) that multiply to give 20.

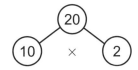

Step 2: Repeat Step 1 for the numbers on the "branches" of the tree.

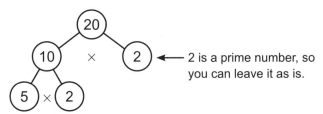
2 is a prime number, so you can leave it as is.

1. Complete the factor trees.

a) 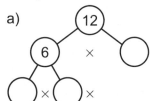   b) 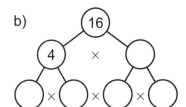   c)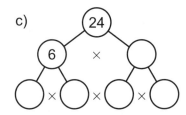

2. Write a prime factorization for each number.

a) 20 = *10 × 2 = 2 × 5 × 2*   b) 18 =   c) 8 =   d) 14 =

3. Use a factor tree to find a prime factorization for each number.

a) 30   b) 36   c) 27   d) 28   e) 75

4. Here are some **branching patterns** for factor trees:

Can you find a factor tree for the number 24 that has a different branching pattern from the tree in Question 1 c)?

NS8-5 Prime Factorizations and GCFs

INVESTIGATION ▶ How does the prime factorization of a number compare to the prime factorization of its factors?

A. Write the prime factorization of 72 and all its factors:

Factors of 72	Prime Factorization
1	____
2	2
3	3
4	2×2
6	
8	
9	
12	
18	
24	
36	
72	

B. How many 2s are in the prime factorization of 72? _____

Does any factor of 72 have more 2s in its prime factorization than 72 does? _____

C. How many 3s are in the prime factorization of 72? _____

Does any factor of 72 have more 3s in its prime factorization than 72 does? _____

D. Finish the sentences below by writing **at least** or **at most**.

Any factor of 72 must have _____ as many 2s in its prime factorization as 72 does.

Any factor of 72 must have _____ as many 3s in its prime factorization as 72 does.

E. Does 72 have a 5 in its prime factorization?

Does any factor of 72 have a 5 in its prime factorization? Explain why this is so.

---

1. The prime factorization of 180 is $2 \times 2 \times 3 \times 3 \times 5$. Without doing any calculations, circle the products that show factors of 180:

$2 \times 3 \times 5$ $2 \times 3 \times 7$ $2 \times 3 \times 3 \times 5$ $3 \times 3 \times 3$ 5×5

How did you decide which products to circle?

2. a) Find the prime factorizations of 84 and 96. Do the rough work in your notebook.

84 = __2__ × __2__ × __3__ × __7__

96 = _____ × _____ × _____ × _____ × _____ × _____

b) Any factor of 84 must have in its prime factorization **at most**:

____*two*____ 2s, ____*one*____ 3s, ____*one*____ 7s

c) Any factor of 96 must have in its prime factorization **at most**:

_____ 2s, _____ 3s

d) Can a common factor of 84 and 96 have any 7s in its prime factorization? _____

How do you know? _____

e) Any common factor of 84 and 96 must have in its prime factorization **at most**:

_____ 2s, _____ 3s

f) The prime factorization of the **greatest common factor (GCF)** of 84 and 96 is:

_____ × _____ × _____ So the GCF of 84 and 96 is _____.

3. The prime factorization of each number is given. Match up as many pairs of common prime factors as you can. Then find the prime factorization of the GCF and calculate the GCF.

a) 36 = 2 × 2 × 3 × 3

24 = 2 × 2 × 2 × 3

GCF = __2__ × __2__ × __3__ = __12__

b) 60 = 2 × 2 × 3 × 5

50 = 2 × 5 × 5

GCF = _____ × _____ = _____

c) 42 = 2 × 3 × 7

72 = 2 × 2 × 2 × 3 × 3

GCF = _____ × _____ = _____

d) 90 = 2 × 3 × 3 × 5

140 = 2 × 2 × 5 × 7

GCF = _____ × _____ = _____

4. Write a prime factorization for each number, then find the GCF of each pair.

a) 24 and 32   **b)** 24 and 30   **c)** 16 and 40   **d)** 27 and 39   **e)** 70 and 56

5. Find the GCF of the numbers.

a) 24, 30, 54   **b)** 84, 210, 300   **c)** 45, 72, 120

INVESTIGATION ▶ How does the prime factorization of a number compare to the prime factorization of its multiples?

A. Write the prime factorizations of the first ten multiples of 90 (don't include zero).

Multiples of 90	Prime factorizations
1 × 90	2 × 3 × 3 × 5
2 × 90	**2** × 2 × 3 × 3 × 5
3 × 90	**3** × 2 × 3 × 3 × 5
4 × 90	**2 × 2** × 2 × 3 × 3 × 5
5 × 90	
6 × 90	
7 × 90	
8 × 90	
9 × 90	
10 × 90	

B. How many 2s are in the prime factorization of 90? _____

Does any multiple of 90 have fewer 2s in its prime factorization than 90 does? _____

C. How many 3s are in the prime factorization of 90? _____

Does any multiple of 90 have fewer 3s in its prime factorization than 90 does? _____

D. How many 5s are in the prime factorization of 90? _____

Does any multiple of 90 have fewer 5s in its prime factorization than 90 does? _____

E. Finish the sentences below by writing **at least** or **at most**.

Any multiple of 90 must have _____ as many 2s in its prime factorization as 90 does.

Any multiple of 90 must have _____ as many 3s in its prime factorization as 90 does.

Any multiple of 90 must have _____ as many 5s in its prime factorization as 90 does.

F. Does 90 have a 7 in its prime factorization? _____

Does any multiple of 90 have a 7 in its prime factorization? _____

---

1. The prime factorization of 60 is 2 × 2 × 3 × 5.

Without doing any calculations, circle the products that show multiples of 60:

2 × 2 × 3 × 3 × 5   2 × 3 × 5 × 7 × 7   2 × 2 × 5 × 5 × 5   2 × 2 × 2 × 2 × 3 × 5 × 11

How did you decide which products to circle?

2. a) Find the prime factorizations of 90 and 168. Do the rough work in your notebook.

$90 = \underline{\quad 2 \quad} \times \underline{\quad 3 \quad} \times \underline{\quad 3 \quad} \times \underline{\quad 5 \quad}$

$168 = \underline{\qquad} \times \underline{\qquad} \times \underline{\qquad} \times \underline{\qquad} \times \underline{\qquad}$

b) Any multiple of 90 must have in its prime factorization **at least**:

$\underline{\quad one \quad}$ 2s, $\underline{\quad two \quad}$ 3s, $\underline{\quad one \quad}$ 5s

c) Any multiple of 168 must have in its prime factorization **at least**:

$\underline{\qquad\qquad}$ 2s, $\underline{\qquad\qquad}$ 3s, $\underline{\qquad\qquad}$ 7s

d) Any common multiple of 90 and 168 must have in its prime factorization **at least**:

$\underline{\qquad\qquad}$ 2s, $\underline{\qquad\qquad}$ 3s, $\underline{\qquad\qquad}$ 5s, and $\underline{\qquad\qquad}$ 7s.

e) The **lowest common multiple (LCM)** of 90 and 168 must be:

$\underline{\qquad} \times \underline{\qquad} \times \underline{\qquad} \times \underline{\qquad} \times \underline{\qquad} \times \underline{\qquad} \times \underline{\qquad} = \underline{\qquad}$

3. a) Find the prime factorizations of 100 and 126.

$100 = \underline{\qquad} \times \underline{\qquad} \times \underline{\qquad} \times \underline{\qquad}$

$126 = \underline{\qquad} \times \underline{\qquad} \times \underline{\qquad} \times \underline{\qquad}$

b) Any multiple of 100 must have in its prime factorization **at least**:

$\underline{\qquad\qquad}$ 2s, and $\underline{\qquad\qquad}$ 5s

c) Any multiple of 126 must have in its prime factorization **at least**:

$\underline{\qquad\qquad}$ 2s, $\underline{\qquad\qquad}$ 3s, and $\underline{\qquad\qquad}$ 7s

d) Any common multiple of 100 and 126 must have in its prime factorization **at least**:

$\underline{\qquad\qquad}$ 2s, $\underline{\qquad\qquad}$ 3s, $\underline{\qquad\qquad}$ 5s, and $\underline{\qquad\qquad}$ 7s.

e) The **lowest common multiple (LCM)** of 100 and 126 must be:

$\underline{\qquad} \times \underline{\qquad} \times \underline{\qquad} \times \underline{\qquad} \times \underline{\qquad} \times \underline{\qquad} \times \underline{\qquad} = \underline{\qquad}$

4. The prime factorization of each number is given. Find the prime factorization of the LCM. Then calculate the LCM.

a) $90 = 2 \times 3 \times 3 \times 5$ and $140 = 2 \times 2 \times 5 \times 7$

So LCM $= \underline{\qquad} \times \underline{\qquad} \times \underline{\qquad} \times \underline{\qquad} \times \underline{\qquad} \times \underline{\qquad} = \underline{\qquad}$

b) $120 = 2 \times 2 \times 2 \times 3 \times 5$ and $180 = 2 \times 2 \times 3 \times 3 \times 5$

So LCM $= \underline{\qquad} \times \underline{\qquad} \times \underline{\qquad} \times \underline{\qquad} \times \underline{\qquad} \times \underline{\qquad} = \underline{\qquad}$

5. Find the prime factorizations of each number. Then find the prime factorization of the LCM and calculate the LCM.

a) 35 and 84   **b)** 15 and 21   **c)** 50 and 60   **d)** 42 and 72   **e)** 24 and 48

Number Sense 8-6

NS8-7 Order of Operations

> Addition and subtraction are done from left to right. If there are brackets, do the operations in brackets first. Example: $7 - 3 + 2 = 4 + 2 = 6$ but $7 - (3 + 2) = 7 - 5 = 2$

1. a) Calculate each expression using the correct order of operations.

$(12 + 9) - 2 - 1$	$12 + (9 - 2) - 1$	$12 + 9 - (2 - 1)$
$(12 + 9 - 2) - 1$	$12 + (9 - 2 - 1)$	$(12 + 9) - (2 - 1)$

b) How many different answers did you get in part a)? _____

2. a) Add brackets in different ways to get as many different answers as you can.

    i) $12 + 9 + 2 + 1$ ii) $12 - 9 + 2 - 1$ iii) $12 - 9 - 2 - 1$

b) How many different answers did you get in part a)? i) _____ ii) _____ iii) _____

c) Check all that apply. The order of operations affects the answer when the expression consists of…

   ☐ addition only   ☐ subtraction only   ☐ addition and subtraction

> Multiplication and division are done from left to right. If there are brackets, do the operations in brackets first. Example: $15 \div 5 \times 3 = 3 \times 3 = 9$ but $15 \div (5 \times 3) = 15 \div 15 = 1$

3. Evaluate each expression.

   a) $4 \times 3 \div 6 \times 7$ b) $6 \times 4 \div 2 \div 3$ c) $30 \div 5 \div (2 \times 3)$ d) $16 \times 2 \div (4 \times 2)$

4. a) Add brackets in different ways to get as many different answers as you can.

    i) $2 \times 3 \times 2 \times 5$ ii) $64 \div 8 \div 4 \div 2$ iii) $90 \div 5 \times 6 \div 3$

b) Which expressions in part a) give the same answer, no matter where you place the brackets?

5. Do the operation in brackets first.

   a) $18 + (6 \times 3)$ b) $(18 + 6) \times 3$ c) $(18 + 6) \div 3$ d) $18 + (6 \div 3)$

     $= 18 + 18 = 36$

   e) $18 - (6 \times 3)$ f) $(18 - 6) \times 3$ g) $(18 - 6) \div 3$ h) $18 - (6 \div 3)$

6. Check all that apply. The order of operations affects the answer when the expression combines…

   ☐ addition and multiplication   ☐ addition and division

   ☐ subtraction and multiplication   ☐ subtraction and division

   ☐ addition and subtraction   ☐ multiplication and division

Mathematicians have ordered the operations to avoid writing brackets all the time. The order is:

1. Operations in brackets.
2. Multiplication and division, from left to right.
3. Addition and subtraction, from left to right

Example: $3 \times 5 + 3 \times 6 = (3 \times 5) + (3 \times 6)$ but $3 \times (5 + 3) \times 6$
$$= 15 + 18$$
$$= 33$$

$$= 3 \times 8 \times 6$$
$$= 144$$

Notice that the brackets in the first expression are not necessary.

7. Evaluate each expression. Use the correct order of operations.

a) $4 \times 2 - 7$ b) $3 + 6 \div 3$ c) $9 - 2 \times 4$ d) $70 \div 7 + 4$

e) $9 + 9 \div 3 - 5$ f) $3 \times 7 - 6 \div 2$ g) $(9 - 5) \times 3$ h) $(17 - 9) \div 4$

8. Translate the instructions into mathematical expressions.

a) Add 8 and 3. Then subtract 4. Then multiply by 3.   _____ $(8 + 3 - 4) \times 3$ _____

b) Subtract 6 from 9. Then multiply by 2. Then add 4.   _____

c) Multiply 6 and 5. Then subtract from 32. Then add 5.   _____

9. Write the expressions in words.

a) $(6 + 2) \times 3$ Add _____ and _____ . Then multiply by _____ . _____

b) $(24 - 2 \times 6) \div 4$ Multiply _____ and _____ . Then subtract from _____ . Then _____

c) $4 \times (3 - 1 + 5)$ _____

d) $(3 + 2 \times 6) \div 5$ _____

10. Calculate the expression in the box in your notebook. Which expression without brackets gives the same answer?

a) $\boxed{8 - (5 + 2)}$ $=$ $8 - 5 - 2$ or $8 - 5 + 2$ b) $\boxed{7 - (3 - 2)}$ $=$ $7 - 3 - 2$ or $7 - 3 + 2$

c) $\boxed{7 + (5 - 2)}$ $=$ $7 + 5 - 2$ or $7 + 5 + 2$ d) $\boxed{6 + (2 + 4)}$ $=$ $6 + 2 + 4$ or $6 + 2 - 4$

11. a) Add brackets in different ways to get as many different answers as you can.

i) $3 + 1 \times 7 - 2$ ii) $16 - 4 \times 2 + 8$ iii) $16 \div 4 \times 2 + 8$

b) How many different answers did you get in part a)? i) _____ ii) _____ iii) _____

12. Rewrite each expression without brackets by changing only operations symbols.
Keep the answer the same.

a) $5 \times 8 \div (4 \div 2)$ b) $5 \times 8 \div (4 \times 2)$ c) $5 \times 8 \times (4 \div 2)$

INVESTIGATION 1 ▶ What types of expressions can be written without brackets?

A. Write the dimensions of the two smaller rectangles in the blanks.

Write the area of the large rectangle in two ways: one with brackets and one without.

Then write an equation.

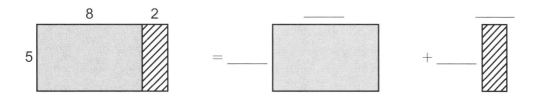

Area = 5 × (_____ + _____) and Area = _____ × _____ + _____ × _____

So   5 × (_____ + _____) = _____ × _____ + _____ × _____

B. Write these expressions without brackets. Draw a picture if it helps.

   a) 7 × (10 + 2) = _____ × _____ + _____ × _____

   b) 4 × (20 + 3) = _____ × _____ + _____ × _____

C. Use your answers in B. to find 7 × 12 and 4 × 23.

D. Write the dimensions of the four smaller rectangles in the blanks.

Write the area of the large rectangle in two ways, one with brackets and one without.

Then write an equation.

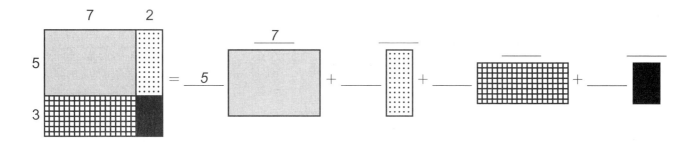

Area = (__5__ + __3__) × (_____ + _____) and

Area = __5__ × __7__ + _____ × _____ + _____ × _____ + _____ × _____

So (5 + 3) × (7 + 2) = _____ .

E. Write these expressions without brackets. Draw pictures in your notebook to show your answers.

a) $(10 + 2) \times (10 + 3) =$ _____ × _____ + _____ × _____ + _____ × _____ + _____ × _____

b) $(20 + 7) \times (40 + 5) =$ _____ × _____ + _____ × _____ + _____ × _____ + _____ × _____

c) $(3 + 4 + 5) \times 2 =$ _____ × _____ + _____ × _____ + _____ × _____

d) $2 \times (3 + 4 + 5) =$ _____ × _____ + _____ × _____ + _____ × _____

F. Use your answers to part E to find 12×13 and 27×45.

G. Calculate both sides to determine which equations are true.

a) $6 \div (2 + 1) = 6 \div 2 + 6 \div 1$

$6 \div (2 + 1) =$ _____ ÷ _____ = _____

$6 \div 2 + 6 \div 1 =$ _____ + _____ = _____

Is the equation true? _____

b) $(6 + 4) \div 2 = 6 \div 2 + 4 \div 2$

$(6 + 4) \div 2 =$ _____ ÷ _____ = _____

$6 \div 2 + 4 \div 2 =$ _____ + _____ = _____

Is the equation true? _____

c) $(5 - 2) \times 4 = 5 \times 4 - 2 \times 4$

$(5 - 2) \times 4 =$ _____ × _____ = _____

$5 \times 4 - 2 \times 4 =$ _____ − _____ = _____

Is the equation true? _____

d) $(8 - 2) \times (8 - 3) = 8 - 2 \times 3$

$(8 - 2) \times (8 - 3) =$ _____ × _____ = _____

$8 - 2 \times 3 =$ _____ − _____ = _____

Is the equation true? _____

e) $10 \div (4 - 2) = 10 \div 4 - 10 \div 2$

$10 \div (4 - 2) =$ _____ ÷ _____ = _____

$10 \div 4 - 10 \div 2 =$ _____ − _____ = _____

Is the equation true? _____

f) $5 \times (8 - 3) = 5 \times 8 - 5 \times 3$

$5 \times (8 - 3) =$ _____ × _____ = _____

$5 \times 8 - 5 \times 3 =$ _____ − _____ = _____

Is the equation true? _____

H. Match each expression with its description.

$8 \div (4 + 3)$ Can be written without brackets and does not require writing more numbers.

$8 - (4 + 3)$ Can be written without brackets but requires writing more numbers.

$8 \times (4 + 3)$ Cannot be written without brackets (using only $+, -, \times, \div$).

NS8-8 Fractions

> **Fractions** name equal parts of a whole.
>
> This pie is cut into 4 equal parts, and
> 3 of the parts are shaded.
>
> So $\frac{3}{4}$ of the pie is shaded.
>
>
>
> $\frac{3}{4}$
>
> The **numerator** tells you how many parts are counted.
>
> The **denominator** tells you how many equal parts are in a whole.

1. Name the following fractions.

    a)   b) 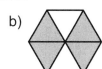   c)

2. Draw lines to divide each figure into equal parts. Then say what fraction of each figure is shaded.

    a)    b)    c) 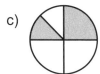   d)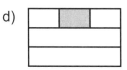

3. Divide each line into the given parts, as done in part a).

    a) Thirds

    b) Halves

    c) Thirds

    d) Quarters

    e) Fifths

Fractions can name parts of a set. In this set, $\frac{3}{5}$ of the figures are pentagons, $\frac{1}{5}$ are squares, and $\frac{1}{5}$ are circles:

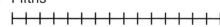

---

4. Fill in the blanks for this set:

    a) $\frac{4}{10}$ of the figures are _____.

    b) $\frac{3}{10}$ of the figures are _____.

    c) _____ of the figures are squares.

    d) _____ of the figures are triangles.

5.

	Whole Numbers from 2 to 9	Whole Numbers from 10 to 16
Prime Numbers	2, 3,	
Composite Numbers		

a) Fill in the chart.

b) What fraction of the whole numbers from 2 to 9 are composite?

c) What fraction of the whole numbers from 2 to 16 are prime?

NS8-9 Mixed Numbers

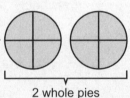

2 whole pies   and $\frac{3}{4}$ of another pie

1. Follow the example to find the **mixed number** for each picture.

   a)

   b)

   c)

   <u> 2 </u> whole pies and <u> $\frac{1}{3}$ </u>   ____ whole pie and ____   ____ whole pies and ____

   of another pie = <u> $2\frac{1}{3}$ </u> pies   of another pie = ____ pies   of another pie = ____ pies

2. Write each fraction as a **mixed number**.

   a)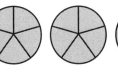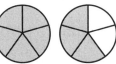

   b)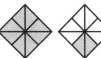

   c)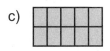

   d)

3. Shade the area given by the mixed number. Note: There may be more figures than you need.

   a) $2\frac{2}{3}$

   b) $3\frac{5}{6}$

   c) $1\frac{3}{4}$

   d) $2\frac{4}{5}$

4. Sketch:

   a) $2\frac{1}{3}$ pies   b) $3\frac{3}{4}$ squares   c) $1\frac{3}{5}$ pies   d) $2\frac{5}{6}$ rectangles   e) $3\frac{7}{8}$ circles

5. Order from smallest to largest: $4\frac{2}{3}$, $4\frac{1}{4}$, $3\frac{3}{4}$.

6. Which is closer to 5: $5\frac{3}{4}$ or $4\frac{2}{3}$? Explain.

NS8-10 Improper Fractions

 Huan-Yue and her friends ate **9** quarter-sized pieces of pizza:

Altogether, they ate $\frac{9}{4}$ pizzas.

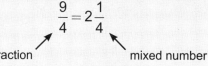

$$\frac{9}{4} = 2\frac{1}{4}$$

improper fraction   mixed number

When the numerator of a fraction is larger than the denominator, the fraction represents **more than a whole**. Such fractions are called **improper fractions**.

---

1. Write these fractions as **improper fractions**.

a)

b)

c)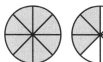

d)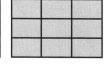

e)

f)

2. Shade one piece at a time until you have shaded the amount given by the improper fraction.

a) $\frac{13}{4}$

b) $\frac{5}{2}$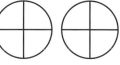

c) $\frac{8}{3}$

d) $\frac{15}{5}$

3. Sketch:

a) $\frac{7}{3}$ pies

b) $\frac{13}{4}$ squares

c) $\frac{9}{2}$ parallelograms

d) $\frac{11}{6}$ rectangles

e) $\frac{17}{8}$ circles

4. Order from smallest to largest: $\frac{7}{4}, \frac{9}{4}, \frac{9}{3}, \frac{10}{3}$.

5. Which fractions are improper fractions? How do you know?

a) $\frac{5}{7}$

b) $\frac{13}{11}$

c) $1\frac{9}{8}$

d) $\frac{8}{3}$

NS8-11 Mixed and Improper Fractions

1. Write these fractions as **mixed numbers** and as **improper fractions**.

a)   b)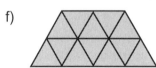

c)   d)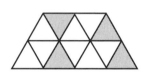

e)  f)

2. Shade the amount of pie given by the mixed fraction. Then write an improper fraction for the amount.

a) $4\frac{1}{2}$

Improper fraction: _____

b) $3\frac{3}{5}$

Improper fraction: _____

3. Shade the amount of area given by the improper fraction. Then write a mixed number for the amount.

a) $\frac{11}{3}$

Mixed number: _____

b) $\frac{11}{4}$

Mixed number: _____

c) $\frac{17}{6}$

Mixed number: _____

d) $\frac{21}{8}$

Mixed number: _____

4. Draw a picture to find out which fraction is greater.

a) $3\frac{1}{2}$, $2\frac{2}{3}$, $\frac{5}{3}$ b) $1\frac{4}{5}$, $2\frac{1}{4}$, $\frac{11}{5}$ c) $\frac{13}{4}$, $\frac{7}{2}$, $2\frac{2}{3}$ d) $\frac{15}{8}$, $\frac{13}{5}$, $\frac{7}{3}$

5. How could you use division to find out how many whole pies are in $\frac{24}{7}$ of a pie? Explain.

NS8-12 More Mixed Numbers

 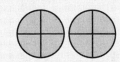 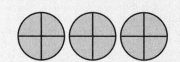

There are 4 quarter pieces
in 1 pie.

There are 8 (2 × 4) quarters
in 2 pies.

There are 12 (3 × 4) quarters
in 3 pies.

12 pieces (3 × 4) +1 extra piece

How many quarter pieces are in $3\frac{1}{4}$ pies? → $3\frac{1}{4}$ ← So there are 13 quarter pieces altogether.

1. Find the number of **halves** in each amount.

   a) 1 pie = _____ halves

   b) 3 pies = _____ halves

   c) 5 pies = _____ halves

   d) $2\frac{1}{2}$ pies = _____ halves

   e) $4\frac{1}{2}$ pies = _____ halves

   f) $6\frac{1}{2}$ pies = _____

2. Find the number of **thirds** in each amount.

   a) 1 pie = _____ thirds

   b) 2 pies = _____ thirds

   c) 3 pies = _____ thirds

   d) $1\frac{1}{3}$ pies = _____ thirds

   e) $3\frac{2}{3}$ pies = _____

   f) $5\frac{1}{3}$ pies = _____

3. A box holds 4 cans, so each can is a **fourth**. Find the number of cans in each amount.

   a) 2 boxes hold _____ cans

   b) $2\frac{1}{2}$ boxes hold _____ cans

   c) $4\frac{3}{4}$ boxes hold _____ cans

4. If a bag holds 16 peas, then…

   a) $1\frac{1}{16}$ bags hold _____ peas

   b) $2\frac{1}{2}$ bags hold _____ peas

   c) $3\frac{1}{4}$ bags hold _____ peas

5. Write the mixed numbers as improper fractions.

   a) $2\frac{2}{3} = \frac{}{3}$

   b) $3\frac{1}{2} = \frac{}{2}$

   c) $5\frac{4}{5} =$

   d) $4\frac{3}{4} =$

   e) $5\frac{2}{7} =$

6. Envelopes come in packs of 8. Alice used $3\frac{7}{8}$ packs. How many envelopes did she use? _____

7. Maia and her friends ate $2\frac{3}{4}$ pizzas. How many quarter-sized pieces did they eat? _____

BONUS ▶

8. How many quarters are there in $7\frac{1}{2}$ dollars? _____

9. Cindy needs $4\frac{2}{3}$ cups of flour.

   a) How many scoops of cup A would she need? _____

   b) How many scoops of cup B would she need? _____

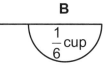

A $\frac{1}{3}$ cup

B $\frac{1}{6}$ cup

How many whole pies are there in $\frac{13}{4}$ pies?

There are 13 pieces altogether, and each pie has 4 pieces. So you can find the number of whole pies by dividing 13 by 4: **13 ÷ 4 = 3 remainder 1**

There are 3 whole pies and 1 quarter left over: $\frac{13}{4} = 3\frac{1}{4}$

1. Find the number of whole pies in each amount by dividing.

   a) $\frac{4}{2}$ pies = _____ whole pies   b) $\frac{15}{3}$ pies = _____ whole pies   c) $\frac{16}{4}$ pies = _____ whole pies

   d) $\frac{21}{7}$ pies = _____ whole pies   e) $\frac{25}{5}$ pies = _____ whole pies   f) $\frac{30}{6}$ pies = _____ whole pies

2. Find the number of whole pies and the number of pieces remaining by dividing.

   a) $\frac{5}{2}$ pies = ___2___ whole pies and ___1___ half pie = ___$2\frac{1}{2}$___ pies

   b) $\frac{11}{2}$ pies = _____ whole pies and _____ half pie = _____ pies

   c) $\frac{13}{3}$ pies = _____ whole pies and _____ third = _____ pies

   d) $\frac{17}{4}$ pies = _____ whole pies and _____ fourth = _____ pies

3. Write the following improper fractions as mixed numbers.

   a) $\frac{5}{2}$ b) $\frac{14}{3}$ c) $\frac{17}{6}$ d) $\frac{21}{4}$ e) $\frac{29}{5}$ f) $\frac{31}{7}$ g) $\frac{70}{9}$ h) $\frac{61}{8}$

4. Write a mixed number and improper fraction for the total number of litres:

5. Write a mixed number and improper fraction for the length of the rope:

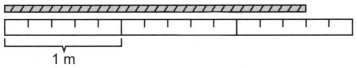

6. Order from smallest to largest: $\frac{7}{3}, \frac{9}{4}, \frac{5}{2}$.

7. Between which two whole numbers is $\frac{21}{8}$?

8. How much greater than a whole is each fraction?

   a) $\frac{11}{7}$ b) $\frac{8}{5}$ c) $\frac{5}{3}$ d) $\frac{19}{10}$

9. Which fractions are greater than 3 but less than 4?

   a) $\frac{17}{4}$ b) $\frac{5}{3}$ c) $\frac{16}{5}$ d) $\frac{5}{2}$ e) $\frac{11}{6}$

1. Shade the given amount in each pie. Then circle the greater fraction in each pair.

   a) $\frac{3}{8}$ $\left(\frac{5}{8}\right)$

   b) $\frac{7}{9}$ $\frac{5}{9}$

   c) $\frac{9}{10}$ $\frac{8}{10}$

2. Two fractions have the same denominators (bottoms) but different numerators (tops)?

   How can you tell which fraction is greater?

   _____

   _____

3. Shade the given amount in each pie. Then circle the greater fraction in each pair.

   a) $\left(\frac{1}{3}\right)$ $\frac{1}{4}$

   b) $\frac{1}{10}$ $\frac{1}{2}$

   c) $\frac{3}{5}$ $\frac{3}{10}$

4. Two fractions have the same numerators (tops) but different denominators (bottoms).

   How can you tell which fraction is greater?

   _____

   _____

5. Write the fractions in order from least to greatest.

   a) $\frac{1}{8}, \frac{1}{3}, \frac{1}{15}$

   b) $\frac{2}{9}, \frac{2}{6}, \frac{2}{8}, \frac{2}{12}$

   c) $\frac{4}{5}, \frac{1}{5}, \frac{3}{5}$

   _____ _____ _____

   _____ _____ _____ _____

   _____ _____ _____

   d) $\frac{9}{10}, \frac{2}{10}, \frac{1}{10}, \frac{5}{10}$

   e) $\frac{5}{8}, \frac{7}{8}, \frac{5}{9}$

   f) $\frac{4}{7}, \frac{3}{7}, \frac{4}{5}$

   _____ _____ _____ _____

   _____ _____ _____

   _____ _____ _____

   BONUS ▶ $\frac{15}{19}$ $\frac{9}{23}$ $\frac{11}{21}$ $\frac{11}{19}$ $\frac{6}{23}$ $\frac{9}{22}$ $\frac{15}{17}$ $\frac{9}{21}$

6. Which fraction is greater? How do you know?

   a) $\frac{7}{5}$ or $\frac{9}{5}$

   b) $4\frac{1}{4}$ or $4\frac{3}{4}$

NS8-15 Equivalent Fractions

1. Compare the fractions by shading to see which is more. Write > (more than), < (less than), or = (equal).

a)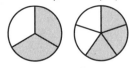

$\dfrac{2}{3}$ ⟦ > ⟧ $\dfrac{3}{5}$

b)

$\dfrac{2}{3}$ ⟦ ⟧ $\dfrac{4}{6}$

c)

$\dfrac{5}{9}$ ⟦ ⟧ $\dfrac{2}{3}$

d)

$\dfrac{6}{8}$ ⟦ ⟧ $\dfrac{3}{4}$

e)

$\dfrac{2}{3}$ ⟦ ⟧ $\dfrac{7}{10}$

f)

$\dfrac{3}{4}$ ⟦ ⟧ $\dfrac{6}{10}$

> Two fractions are said to be **equivalent** if they represent the same amount.

2. List two pairs of equivalent fractions from Question 1. _____ = _____ and _____ = _____

3. Group the squares to make an equivalent fraction. How many of the equal larger groups are shaded?

a)

$\dfrac{6}{10} = \dfrac{3}{5}$

b)

$\dfrac{4}{6} = \dfrac{}{3}$

c)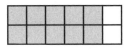

$\dfrac{10}{12} = \dfrac{}{6}$

4. Write three equivalent fractions for the amount shaded here: _____ _____ _____

5. a) Draw lines to cut the pies into:

4 equal pieces   6 equal pieces   8 equal pieces

b) Then fill in the numerators of the equivalent fractions:  $\dfrac{1}{2} = \dfrac{}{4} = \dfrac{}{6} = \dfrac{}{8}$

6. Make an equivalent fraction by cutting each piece into the same number of parts.

a) $\dfrac{1}{2} = \dfrac{3}{6}$

b) $\dfrac{2}{3} = \dfrac{4}{}$

c) $\dfrac{2}{3} = \dfrac{}{9}$

d) $\dfrac{2}{5} = \dfrac{}{15}$

NS8-16 Comparing Fractions Using Equivalent Fractions

1. Write six equivalent fractions by skip counting to find the numerators.

   a) $\dfrac{2}{3} = \dfrac{}{6} = \dfrac{}{9} = \dfrac{}{12} = \dfrac{}{15} = \dfrac{}{18} = \dfrac{}{21}$

   b) $\dfrac{3}{5} = \dfrac{}{10} = \dfrac{}{15} = \dfrac{}{20} = \dfrac{}{25} = \dfrac{}{30} = \dfrac{}{35}$

2. Find two fractions with the same denominators from the lists in Question 1. _____ and _____

   Which fraction is greater: $\dfrac{2}{3}$ or $\dfrac{3}{5}$? _____

   How do you know? _____

When you multiply the numerator and denominator of a fraction by the same number, you create an **equivalent fraction**.

$$\dfrac{1}{2} = \dfrac{1 \times 5}{2 \times 5} = \dfrac{5}{10}$$

   You are cutting each
piece into 5 parts

---

3. Create an equivalent fraction with denominator 36 by multiplying the numerator and denominator by the same number:

   a) $\dfrac{1 \times 18}{2 \times 18} = \dfrac{18}{36}$ b) $\dfrac{4}{9} = \dfrac{}{36}$ c) $\dfrac{5}{6} = \dfrac{}{36}$ d) $\dfrac{11}{18} = \dfrac{}{36}$

   e) $\dfrac{2}{3} = \dfrac{}{36}$ f) $\dfrac{3}{4} = \dfrac{}{36}$ g) $\dfrac{1}{6} = \dfrac{}{36}$ h) $\dfrac{5}{12} = \dfrac{}{36}$

4. Write the fractions from Question 3 in order from smallest to largest.

5. a) Write several fractions equivalent to $\dfrac{1}{2}$.

   $\dfrac{1}{2} = \dfrac{}{4} = \dfrac{}{6} = \dfrac{}{8} = \dfrac{}{10} = \dfrac{}{12} = \dfrac{}{14} = \dfrac{}{16} = \dfrac{}{18} = \dfrac{}{20}$

   b) How much more than a half is each fraction below?

   $\dfrac{3}{4}$ is _____ more than $\dfrac{1}{2}$ $\dfrac{4}{6}$ is _____ more than $\dfrac{1}{2}$ $\dfrac{5}{8}$ is _____ more than $\dfrac{1}{2}$

   $\dfrac{6}{10}$ is _____ more than $\dfrac{1}{2}$ $\dfrac{7}{12}$ is _____ more than $\dfrac{1}{2}$ $\dfrac{8}{14}$ is _____ more than $\dfrac{1}{2}$

   c) Write all the given fractions from part b) in order from smallest to largest.

---

1. Imagine moving the shaded pieces from pies A and B into pie plate C.
   Show how much of pie C would be filled, then write a fraction for pie C.

$$\frac{1}{4} \quad + \quad \frac{2}{4} \quad = \quad \underline{\hspace{1cm}}$$

2. Imagine pouring the liquid from cups A and B into cup C.

   Shade the amount of liquid that would be in C. Then complete the
   addition statements.

$$\frac{}{5} \quad + \quad \frac{}{5} \quad = \quad \underline{\hspace{1cm}} \qquad\qquad \frac{}{3} \quad + \quad \frac{}{3} \quad = \quad \underline{\hspace{1cm}}$$

3. Add.

   a) $\frac{3}{5} + \frac{1}{5} =$ b) $\frac{1}{4} + \frac{2}{4} =$ c) $\frac{2}{7} + \frac{4}{7} =$ d) $\frac{5}{8} + \frac{2}{8} =$

   e) $\frac{3}{11} + \frac{6}{11} =$ f) $\frac{10}{17} + \frac{6}{17} =$ g) $\frac{15}{24} + \frac{4}{24} =$ h) $\frac{18}{57} + \frac{13}{57} =$

4. Show how much pie would be left if you took away the amount shown.
   Then complete the fraction statement.

   a)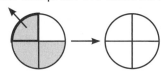

   $$\frac{3}{4} - \frac{1}{4} \quad = \quad \underline{\hspace{1cm}}$$

   b)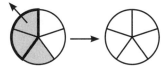

   $$\frac{3}{5} - \frac{2}{5} \quad = \quad \underline{\hspace{1cm}}$$

5. Subtract.

   a) $\frac{2}{3} - \frac{1}{3} =$ b) $\frac{3}{5} - \frac{2}{5} =$ c) $\frac{6}{7} - \frac{3}{7} =$ d) $\frac{5}{8} - \frac{2}{8} =$

   e) $\frac{10}{12} - \frac{3}{12} =$ f) $\frac{6}{19} - \frac{4}{19} =$ g) $\frac{9}{28} - \frac{3}{28} =$ h) $\frac{17}{57} - \frac{12}{57} =$

6. Calculate.

   a) $\frac{2}{7} + \frac{1}{7} + \frac{3}{7} =$ b) $\frac{4}{11} + \frac{5}{11} - \frac{2}{11} =$ c) $\frac{10}{18} - \frac{7}{18} + \frac{5}{18} =$

To add fractions with different denominators:

Step 1: Find the LCM of the denominators.

$$\frac{1}{3}+\frac{2}{5}$$

Multiples of 3: 0, 3, 6, 9, 12, **15**, 18

Multiples of 5: 0, 5, 10, **15**, 20, 25, 30

LCM (3, 5) = 15

Step 2: Create equivalent fractions with that denominator.

$$\frac{1}{3}+\frac{2}{5}=\frac{5\times1}{5\times3}+\frac{2\times3}{5\times3}$$

$$=\frac{5}{15}+\frac{6}{15}$$

$$=\frac{11}{15}$$

The LCM of the denominators is called the **lowest common denominator (LCD)** of the fractions.

1. Find the LCD of each pair of fractions. Then show what numbers you would multiply the numerator and denominator of each fraction by in order to add.

   a) LCD = __6__

   $$\frac{3\times1}{3\times2}+\frac{2\times2}{3\times2}$$

   b) LCD = _____

   $$\frac{3}{4}+\frac{1}{8}$$

   c) LCD = _____

   $$\frac{1}{30}+\frac{1}{6}$$

   d) LCD = _____

   $$\frac{3}{4}+\frac{2}{3}$$

   e) LCD = _____

   $$\frac{3}{7}+\frac{1}{3}$$

   f) LCD = _____

   $$\frac{3}{4}+\frac{1}{6}$$

   g) LCD = _____

   $$\frac{4}{5}+\frac{1}{10}$$

   h) LCD = _____

   $$\frac{1}{8}+\frac{5}{7}$$

2. Add or subtract the fractions by changing them to equivalent fractions with denominator equal to the LCD of the fractions.

   a) $\dfrac{2}{5}+\dfrac{1}{4}$

   b) $\dfrac{4}{15}+\dfrac{2}{3}$

   c) $\dfrac{2}{3}-\dfrac{1}{8}$

   d) $\dfrac{2}{3}-\dfrac{1}{12}$

   =

   =

   e) $\dfrac{3}{4}+\dfrac{1}{8}$

   f) $\dfrac{1}{6}+\dfrac{13}{24}$

   g) $\dfrac{11}{28}-\dfrac{2}{7}$

   h) $\dfrac{4}{7}+\dfrac{1}{8}$

   i) $\dfrac{4}{9}-\dfrac{1}{6}$

3. Add or subtract.

   a) $\dfrac{5}{6}+\dfrac{1}{12}$

   b) $\dfrac{19}{25}-\dfrac{3}{5}$

   c) $\dfrac{5}{7}-\dfrac{1}{4}$

   d) $\dfrac{4}{9}+\dfrac{2}{5}$

   e) $\dfrac{5}{8}-\dfrac{7}{12}$

   f) $\dfrac{2}{3}+\dfrac{1}{4}+\dfrac{1}{2}$

   g) $\dfrac{3}{15}+\dfrac{2}{3}+\dfrac{1}{5}$

   h) $\dfrac{11}{15}+\dfrac{2}{3}-\dfrac{1}{5}$

   i) $\dfrac{3}{5}+\dfrac{17}{30}-\dfrac{5}{6}$

A fraction is reduced to **lowest terms** when the greatest common factor of its numerator and denominator is the number 1.

$\frac{6}{8}$ **is not** in lowest terms because the GCF of 6 and 8 is 2.

      Factors of 6: 1, **2**, 3, 6
      Factors of 8: 1, **2**, 4, 8

$\frac{3}{4}$ **is** in lowest terms because the GCF of 3 and 4 is 1.

      Factors of 3: **1**, 3
      Factors of 4: **1**, 2, 4

4. Find the GCF of the numerator and denominator. Is the fraction in lowest terms?
   Write yes or no.

a) $\frac{2}{6}$ b) $\frac{3}{5}$ c) $\frac{4}{5}$ d) $\frac{5}{10}$ e) $\frac{8}{10}$

   GCF = __2__   GCF = ____   GCF = ____   GCF = ____   GCF = ____

   ___no___

f) $\frac{7}{10}$ g) $\frac{15}{16}$ h) $\frac{14}{12}$ i) $\frac{9}{5}$ j) $\frac{5}{9}$

To reduce a fraction to lowest terms:

Step 1: Find the GCF of the numerator and denominator

Step 2: Divide both the numerator and denominator by the GCF.

---

5. Reduce the fractions below by dividing the numerator and the denominator by
   their GCF.

a) $\frac{2 \div 2}{10 \div 2} = \frac{1}{5}$ b) $\frac{2 \div}{6 \div} =$ ____   c) $\frac{2 \div}{8 \div} =$ ____   d) $\frac{2 \div}{12 \div} =$ ____

e) $\frac{6}{9} =$ ____   f) $\frac{3}{15} =$ ____   g) $\frac{4}{12} =$ ____   h) $\frac{20}{25} =$ ____

6. Add or subtract, then reduce your answer to lowest terms.

a) $\frac{5 \times 1}{5 \times 6} + \frac{1 \times 3}{10 \times 3}$ b) $\frac{13}{15} - \frac{2}{5}$ c) $\frac{5}{6} + \frac{7}{10}$ d) $\frac{22}{28} - \frac{2}{7}$

   $= \frac{5}{30} + \frac{3}{30}$

   $= \frac{8}{30} = \frac{4}{15}$

e) $\frac{1}{10} + \frac{1}{2} + \frac{1}{5}$ f) $\frac{5}{8} + \frac{1}{5} + \frac{1}{20}$ g) $\frac{1}{7} + \frac{4}{5} - \frac{8}{35}$ h) $\frac{5}{7} - \frac{8}{21} + \frac{2}{3}$

1. Add or subtract.

a) $2\frac{1}{5} \quad + \quad 3\frac{2}{5} \quad = \quad$ _____ b) $4\frac{3}{5} - 3\frac{1}{5} =$

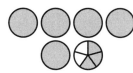   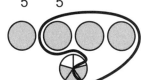

c) $2\frac{1}{5} + 2\frac{2}{5} =$ d) $3\frac{3}{7} + 2\frac{1}{7} =$ e) $5\frac{7}{8} - 3\frac{2}{8} =$ f) $7\frac{9}{15} - 4\frac{2}{15} =$

2. Add or subtract by changing the fractions to equivalent fractions.

a) $2\frac{1}{2} + 1\frac{1}{3}$

$= 2 + 1 + \frac{1}{2} + \frac{1}{3}$

$= 3 + \frac{}{6} + \frac{}{6}$

$= 3\frac{}{6}$

b) $3\frac{3}{4} - 1\frac{1}{3}$

$= 3 - 1 + \frac{3}{4} - \frac{1}{3}$

$= 2 + \frac{}{12} - \frac{}{12}$

$= 2\frac{}{12}$

c) $5\frac{2}{3} - 2\frac{3}{5}$

d) $2\frac{2}{7} + 4\frac{1}{2}$

e) $4\frac{2}{5} - 1\frac{1}{6}$

f) $2\frac{3}{8} + 4\frac{1}{3}$

3. $1\frac{1}{2} + 2\frac{2}{3} = 3\frac{7}{6}$. How can you simplify this answer?

4. $\frac{4}{5}$ is greater than $\frac{1}{3}$. How can you subtract $4\frac{1}{3} - 2\frac{4}{5}$?

5. a) Change the improper fractions to mixed numbers.

i) $\frac{7}{6} = 1\frac{1}{6}$ ii) $\frac{11}{5} =$ iii) $\frac{13}{7} =$ iv) $\frac{11}{4} =$

b) Rewrite each mixed number to make the improper fraction a proper fraction.

i) $3\frac{7}{6} = 3 + \frac{7}{6}$

$= 3 + 1\frac{1}{6}$

$= 4\frac{1}{6}$

ii) $2\frac{4}{3} =$

$=$

$=$

iii) $4\frac{8}{5} =$

$=$

$=$

c) Add by changing the fractions to equivalent fractions. Simplify your answer as in part b).

i) $2\frac{2}{5} + \frac{2}{3}$

$= 2 + \frac{2}{5} + \frac{2}{3}$

$= 2 + \frac{}{15} + \frac{}{15}$

$= 2\frac{}{15} = 3\frac{}{15}$

ii) $3\frac{2}{3} + \frac{5}{6}$

iii) $4\frac{3}{4} + 2\frac{3}{5}$

6. a) Rewrite each mixed number by regrouping 1 whole as a fraction.

Example: $4\frac{1}{3} = 3 + 1\frac{1}{3} = 3\frac{4}{3}$

i) $5\frac{3}{4}$ ii) $5\frac{1}{2}$ iii) $1\frac{1}{6}$ iv) $2\frac{3}{4}$ v) $3\frac{2}{5}$ vi) $4\frac{5}{7}$

b) Subtract by rewriting the first mixed number as in part a):

i) $3\frac{1}{5} - 1\frac{3}{4} = 3\frac{4}{20} - 1\frac{15}{20}$

$= 2\frac{24}{20} - 1\frac{15}{20} = 1\frac{9}{20}$

ii) $4\frac{1}{3} - 2\frac{3}{5}$

7. Add or subtract by first changing the mixed numbers to improper fractions.

a) $3\frac{1}{3} + 5\frac{3}{4}$

$= \frac{10}{3} + \frac{23}{4}$

$= \frac{40}{12} + \frac{69}{12}$

$= \frac{109}{12} = 9\frac{1}{12}$

b) $1\frac{1}{5} - \frac{2}{3}$

c) $4\frac{2}{3} + 2\frac{4}{5}$

d) $5\frac{1}{8} - 3\frac{1}{3}$

8. Sonjay cycled $6\frac{7}{8}$ km in the first hour, $5\frac{1}{2}$ km the second hour, and $4\frac{3}{4}$ km the third hour. How many kilometres did he cycle in the three hours?

9. A cafeteria sold $2\frac{5}{8}$ cheese pizzas, $4\frac{1}{3}$ vegetable pizzas, and $3\frac{1}{4}$ deluxe pizzas at lunchtime. How many pizzas did they sell altogether?

10. Gerome bought $5\frac{3}{4}$ metres of cloth. He used $3\frac{4}{5}$ to make a banner. How many metres of cloth were left over?

NS8-20 Mental Math

Sayaka subtracts $6 - 3\frac{2}{3}$ on a number line as follows:

She marks the number she is subtracting $\left(3\frac{2}{3}\right)$ on a number line.

She draws an arrow to show the difference between $3\frac{2}{3}$ and the nearest whole number (4).

She draws an arrow to show the difference between 4 and 6 (= 2).

She sees that:

$$6 - 3\frac{2}{3} = 2 + \frac{1}{3} = 2\frac{1}{3}$$

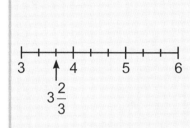

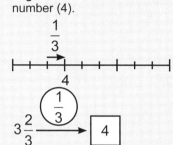

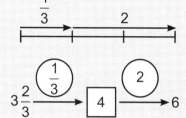

1. Follow Sayaka's steps to find the difference. The first question is started for you.

a)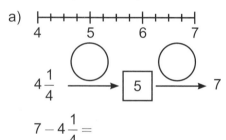

$$7 - 4\frac{1}{4} =$$

b)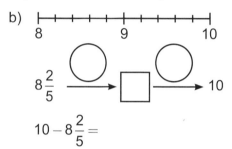

$$10 - 8\frac{2}{5} =$$

2. Find the differences.

a)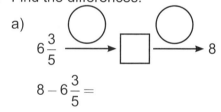

$$8 - 6\frac{3}{5} =$$

b)

$$9 - 5\frac{5}{6} =$$

c)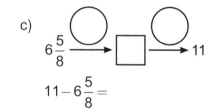

$$11 - 6\frac{5}{8} =$$

3. Find the differences mentally:

a) $4 - 1\frac{1}{7} =$ b) $9 - 6\frac{7}{9} =$ c) $12 - 7\frac{3}{10} =$ d) $23 - 20\frac{5}{8} =$

4. Find the difference by following the steps shown.

a)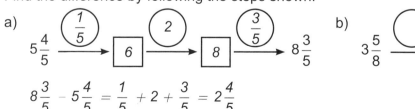

$$8\frac{3}{5} - 5\frac{4}{5} = \frac{1}{5} + 2 + \frac{3}{5} = 2\frac{4}{5}$$

b)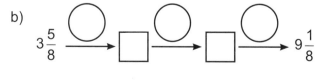

5. Find the differences mentally.

a) $6\frac{2}{5} - 5\frac{4}{5} =$ b) $9\frac{1}{7} - 3\frac{4}{7} =$ c) $17\frac{1}{8} - 13\frac{3}{8} =$ d) $13\frac{1}{6} - 6\frac{5}{6} =$

NS8-21 Investigating Fractions and Division — Advanced

1. Write each improper fraction in terms of division.

   a) $\dfrac{4}{3} = \underline{\quad 4 \div 3 \quad}$ b) $\dfrac{7}{2} = \underline{\hspace{2cm}}$ c) $\dfrac{9}{3} = \underline{\hspace{2cm}}$ d) $\dfrac{5}{4} = \underline{\hspace{2cm}}$

2. Write each mixed number in terms of addition and division.

   a) $2\dfrac{3}{4} = \underline{\quad 2 + 3 \div 4 \quad}$ b) $3\dfrac{2}{5} = \underline{\hspace{2cm}}$ c) $1\dfrac{2}{3} = \underline{\hspace{2cm}}$ d) $3\dfrac{1}{2} = \underline{\hspace{2cm}}$

3. Which improper fraction from question 1 is equivalent to a mixed number from Question 2? Verify your answer by doing the calculations directly.

To add fractions that have a common denominator, we can add the numerators.

Example 1: $\dfrac{3}{10} + \dfrac{4}{10} = \dfrac{7}{10}$ Example 2: $\dfrac{2}{9} + \dfrac{3}{9} = \dfrac{5}{9}$

---

4. Translate the examples in the box into a statement using division.

   Example 1: $\underline{\;3 \div 10\;} + \underline{\;4 \div 10\;} = \underline{\;7 \div 10\;}$ Example 2: $\underline{\hspace{1.5cm}} + \underline{\hspace{1.5cm}} = \underline{\hspace{1.5cm}}$

5. Translate each statement of addition of fractions into addition of quotients. Verify by dividing and adding.

   a) $\dfrac{9}{3} + \dfrac{6}{3} = \dfrac{9+6}{3}$ b) $\dfrac{8}{2} + \dfrac{6}{2} = \dfrac{8+6}{2}$ c) $\dfrac{20}{5} + \dfrac{35}{5} = \dfrac{20+35}{5}$

   $\quad 9 \div 3 + 6 \div 3 = (9 + 6) \div 3$

   $\quad\quad 3 \;+\; 2 \;=\; 15 \;\div 3$

   $\quad\quad\quad 5 \quad = \quad 5$

INVESTIGATION 1 ▶ To add fractions that have a common numerator, can we add the denominators?

A. Is $\dfrac{5}{8} + \dfrac{5}{14}$ more or less than $\dfrac{5}{8}$? How do you know?

B. Is $\dfrac{5}{8+14}$ more or less than $\dfrac{5}{8}$? How do you know?

C. Can $\dfrac{5}{8} + \dfrac{5}{14} = \dfrac{5}{8+14}$? Explain.

---

6. The symbol $\neq$ means "not equal to." Translate the statements using division instead of fractions. Verify by division that the two sides are not equal.

$\dfrac{6}{2} + \dfrac{6}{1} \neq \dfrac{6}{2+1}$ $\dfrac{30}{2} + \dfrac{30}{3} \neq \dfrac{30}{2+3}$ $\dfrac{24}{2} + \dfrac{24}{6} \neq \dfrac{24}{2+6}$ $\dfrac{70}{2} + \dfrac{70}{5} \neq \dfrac{70}{2+5}$

1. What fraction of a year is 3 months? $\dfrac{3}{12} = $ _____

2. What fraction of an hour is 45 minutes?

3. What fraction of a metre is 20 cm?

4. A cup is 240 mL. What fraction of a cup is 100 mL?

5. Tania cycled $5\dfrac{3}{5}$ km in the first hour, and $4\dfrac{2}{3}$ km in the second hour. How many kilometres did she cycle in two hours?

6. Monica ran $6\dfrac{3}{8}$ km in the first hour, $4\dfrac{1}{2}$ km the second hour, and $4\dfrac{1}{4}$ km the third hour. How many kilometres did she run in three hours?

7. A cafeteria sold $2\dfrac{7}{8}$ cheese pizzas, $5\dfrac{5}{6}$ vegetable pizzas, and $7\dfrac{11}{12}$ deluxe pizzas at lunchtime. How many pizzas did they sell altogether?

8. Trevor has $\dfrac{2}{3}$ of an hour to write a test. If he finishes the test in $\dfrac{1}{2}$ of an hour then how much time would remain?

9. Tegan bought $1\dfrac{1}{6}$ metres of ribbon. She needs $\dfrac{2}{5}$ metres to wrap her brother's present and $\dfrac{3}{4}$ metres to wrap her sister's present. Did she buy enough ribbon?

10. Anne just turned 19 years old. How old was she $4\dfrac{3}{4}$ years ago?

11. Tabitha ate $\dfrac{1}{4}$ of a sub and Jordan ate $\dfrac{2}{3}$ of the sub. How much of the sub was left over?

12. Sadia picked $\dfrac{2}{5}$ of a basket of berries, Tashi picked $\dfrac{1}{3}$ of a basket, Shafma picked $\dfrac{4}{7}$ of a basket, and Marzuk picked $\dfrac{4}{5}$ of a basket. Did all their berries fit into 2 baskets?

13. Soil at a beach consists of sand, clay and salt. If a sample taken is $\dfrac{3}{4}$ sand and $\dfrac{1}{6}$ salt, how much of the sample is clay?

14. Gerome has an hour and a half before he has to leave to play basketball. If it takes him $\dfrac{7}{12}$ of an hour to do his homework and $\dfrac{3}{5}$ of an hour to find his uniform, how much time will he have left?

Dan has 6 cookies. He wants to give $\frac{2}{3}$ of his cookies to his friends. To do so, he shares the cookies equally onto 3 plates:

There are 3 equal groups, so each group is $\frac{1}{3}$ of 6.

There are 2 cookies in each group, so $\frac{1}{3}$ of 6 is 2.

There are 4 cookies in two groups, so $\frac{2}{3}$ of 6 is 4.

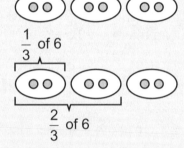

1. Write a fraction for the amount of dots shown.

a)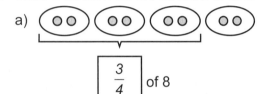

$\boxed{\frac{3}{4}}$ of 8

b)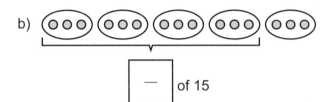

$\boxed{}$ of 15

2. Fill in the missing numbers.

a) $\boxed{\frac{1}{3}}$ of 9 = _____

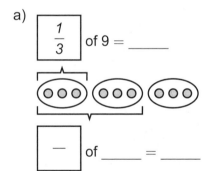

$\boxed{}$ of _____ = _____

b) $\boxed{}$ of 8 = _____

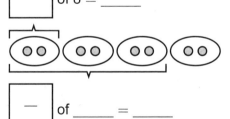

$\boxed{}$ of _____ = _____

c) $\boxed{}$ of 12 = _____

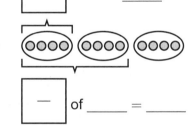

$\boxed{}$ of _____ = _____

d)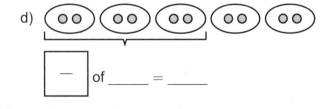

$\boxed{}$ of _____ = _____

e)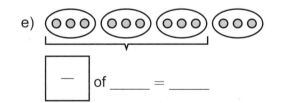

$\boxed{}$ of _____ = _____

3. Draw a circle to show the given amount.

a) $\frac{2}{3}$ of 6

b) $\frac{3}{4}$ of 8

4. Draw the correct number of dots in each circle, then draw a larger circle to show the given amount.

a) $\frac{2}{3}$ of 12

b) $\frac{1}{3}$ of 15

5. Find the fraction of the whole amount by sharing the cookies equally.

Hint: Draw the correct number of plates, place the cookies one at a time, then circle the correct amount.

a) Find $\frac{2}{3}$ of 9 cookies.

b) Find $\frac{3}{5}$ of 10 cookies.

$\frac{2}{3}$ of 9 is _____

$\frac{3}{5}$ of 10 is _____

Andy finds $\frac{2}{3}$ of 12 as follows:

Step 1: He finds $\frac{1}{3}$ of 12 by dividing 12 by 3:

12 ÷ 3 = 4 (4 is $\frac{1}{3}$ of 12)

Step 2: Then he multiplies the result by 2:

4 × 2 = 8 (8 is $\frac{2}{3}$ of 12)

---

6. Find the following amounts using Andy's method.

a) $\frac{2}{3}$ of 9 =

b) $\frac{3}{4}$ of 8 =

c) $\frac{2}{3}$ of 15 =

d) $\frac{2}{5}$ of 10 =

e) $\frac{3}{5}$ of 25 =

f) $\frac{3}{7}$ of 21 =

g) $\frac{5}{7}$ of 28 =

h) $\frac{3}{8}$ of 24 =

i) $\frac{3}{4}$ of 12 =

j) $\frac{1}{3}$ of 27 =

7. There are 24 students on a soccer team. $\frac{3}{8}$ are girls. How many girls are on the team? _____

8. A bookstore with 18 copies of a book sold $\frac{5}{6}$ of the books.

a) How many books were sold? _____

b) How many books were left? _____

9. Shade $\frac{5}{8}$ of the squares. Draw stripes in $\frac{1}{4}$ of the squares.
How many squares are blank? _____

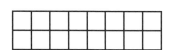

10. Una has a collection of 28 insects: $\frac{1}{4}$ are butterflies, $\frac{2}{7}$ are moths, and the rest are beetles.

How many insects are beetles? _____

11. Eldon started practising piano at 7:45. He played scales for $\frac{1}{6}$ of an hour,

popular songs for $\frac{2}{5}$ of an hour, and his solo for $\frac{1}{4}$ of an hour.

At what time did he stop playing? _____

Number Sense 8-23

REMINDER ▶ Multiplication is a short form for addition.

$$3 \times 4 = 4 + 4 + 4 \qquad\qquad 5 \times 7 = 7 + 7 + 7 + 7 + 7 \qquad\qquad 2 \times 9 = 9 + 9$$

1. Write each product as a sum.

   a) $3 \times \dfrac{1}{4} = \dfrac{1}{4} + \dfrac{1}{4} + \dfrac{1}{4}$

   b) $2 \times \dfrac{3}{7} =$

   c) $4 \times \dfrac{5}{11} =$

2. Write each sum as a product.

   a) $\dfrac{1}{2} + \dfrac{1}{2} + \dfrac{1}{2} =$

   b) $\dfrac{5}{9} + \dfrac{5}{9} =$

   c) $\dfrac{3}{4} + \dfrac{3}{4} + \dfrac{3}{4} + \dfrac{3}{4} + \dfrac{3}{4} =$

REMINDER ▶ To add fractions with the same denominator, add the numerators.

3. Find the products by first writing each product as a sum.

   a) $4 \times \dfrac{3}{5} = \dfrac{3}{5} + \dfrac{3}{5} + \dfrac{3}{5} + \dfrac{3}{5}$

   b) $2 \times \dfrac{3}{4} =$

   c) $2 \times \dfrac{4}{7} =$

   $\qquad\qquad = \dfrac{12}{5} = 2\dfrac{2}{5}$

   d) $5 \times \dfrac{4}{11} =$

   e) $6 \times \dfrac{3}{7} =$

To multiply a fraction with a whole number, multiply the numerator by the whole number and leave the denominator the same.

Example: $\dfrac{2}{9} + \dfrac{2}{9} + \dfrac{2}{9} = \dfrac{2+2+2}{9}$ so $3 \times \dfrac{2}{9} = \dfrac{3 \times 2}{9}$

4. Multiply the fractions with the whole number. Write your answer as a mixed number.

   a) $4 \times \dfrac{3}{7} = \dfrac{4 \times 3}{7} = \dfrac{12}{7} = 1\dfrac{5}{7}$

   b) $5 \times \dfrac{2}{3} = \dfrac{\quad}{3} = \dfrac{\quad}{3} = \dfrac{\quad}{3}$

   c) $3 \times \dfrac{4}{5} = \dfrac{\quad}{5} = \dfrac{\quad}{5} = \dfrac{\quad}{5}$

5. Find the products. Simplify your answer.

   a) $3 \times \dfrac{4}{6} = \dfrac{12}{6} = 2$

   b) $8 \times \dfrac{3}{4}$

   c) $5 \times \dfrac{4}{10}$

   d) $3 \times \dfrac{6}{9}$

   e) $12 \times \dfrac{2}{8}$

6. Find the products.

   a) $4 \times \dfrac{5}{4} = \dfrac{20}{4} = 5$

   b) $3 \times \dfrac{2}{3} =$

   c) $7 \times \dfrac{9}{7} =$

   d) $8 \times \dfrac{5}{8} =$

   e) $a \times \dfrac{b}{a} =$

In mathematics, the word "of" can mean multiply.

Examples: "2 groups of 3" means 2×3

"6 groups of $\frac{1}{2}$" means $6 \times \frac{1}{2} = \frac{1}{2} + \frac{1}{2} + \frac{1}{2} + \frac{1}{2} + \frac{1}{2} + \frac{1}{2}$

"$\frac{1}{2}$ of 6" means $\frac{1}{2} \times 6$ Reminder: $\frac{a}{b}$ of c is $a \times c \div b$

7. Calculate each product by finding the fraction of the whole number.

a) $\frac{1}{3}$ of 6 = _____ so $\frac{1}{3} \times 6$ = _____

b) $\frac{3}{5}$ of 10 = _____ so $\frac{3}{5} \times 10$ = _____

c) $\frac{2}{3}$ of 6 = _____ so $\frac{2}{3} \times 6$ = _____

d) $\frac{3}{4}$ of 20 = _____ so $\frac{3}{4} \times 20$ = _____

When multiplying whole numbers, the order we multiply in does not affect the answer.

Examples: $2 \times 3 = 3 \times 2 = 6$ $4 \times 5 = 5 \times 4 = 20$

INVESTIGATION 1 ▶ When multiplying a fraction and a whole number, does the order we multiply in affect the answer?

A. Calculate the products in both orders.

i) $8 \times \frac{1}{4} = \frac{1}{4} + \frac{1}{4} + \frac{1}{4} + \frac{1}{4} + \frac{1}{4} + \frac{1}{4} + \frac{1}{4} + \frac{1}{4} =$ _____

$\frac{1}{4} \times 8 = \frac{1}{4}$ of 8 = _____

ii) $6 \times \frac{2}{3} = \frac{2}{3} + \frac{2}{3} + \frac{2}{3} + \frac{2}{3} + \frac{2}{3} + \frac{2}{3} =$ _____

$\frac{2}{3} \times 6 = \frac{2}{3}$ of 6 = _____

iii) $10 \times \frac{3}{5}$ and $\frac{3}{5} \times 10$

iv) $12 \times \frac{5}{6}$ and $\frac{5}{6} \times 12$

B. Does changing the order we multiply in affect the answer? _____

INVESTIGATION 2 ▶ The fractions $\frac{1}{3}$ and $\frac{2}{6}$ are equivalent. Does multiplying by $\frac{2}{6}$ result in the same answer as multiplying by $\frac{1}{3}$?

A. Multiply these numbers by both $\frac{1}{3}$ and $\frac{2}{6}$. Reduce your answer to lowest terms.

i) $4 \times \frac{1}{3} =$ _____ $4 \times \frac{2}{6} =$ _____ = _____

ii) $11 \times \frac{1}{3} =$ _____ $11 \times \frac{2}{6} =$ _____ = _____

B. Does multiplying by $\frac{2}{6}$ result in the same answer as multiplying by $\frac{1}{3}$? _____

COPYRIGHT © 2009 JUMP MATH: NOT TO BE COPIED

Here is $\frac{1}{3}$ of a rectangle. 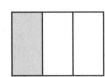	Here is $\frac{1}{4}$ of $\frac{1}{3}$ of the rectangle. 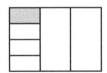	How much is $\frac{1}{4}$ of $\frac{1}{3}$? Extend the lines to find out. 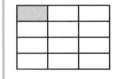 $\frac{1}{4}$ of $\frac{1}{3} = \frac{1}{12}$

1. Extend the horizontal lines in each picture, then write a fraction statement for each figure using the word "of."

   a)   b)   c)   d)   e)

   $\frac{1}{2}$ of $\frac{1}{4} = \frac{1}{8}$　　$\frac{1}{3}$ of $\frac{1}{5} =$　　$\frac{1}{5}$ of $\frac{1}{2} =$

2. Rewrite the fraction statements from Question 1 using the multiplication sign instead of the word "of."

   a) $\frac{1}{2} \times \frac{1}{4} = \frac{1}{8}$　　b)　　c)　　d)　　e)

3. Write a multiplication statement for each figure.

   a)   b) 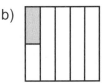   c) 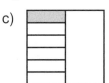   d)   e)

   $\frac{1}{3} \times \frac{1}{4} = \frac{1}{12}$　　_____　　_____　　_____　　_____

4. Write a formula for multiplying fractions that both have numerator 1.

   $\frac{1}{a} \times \frac{1}{b} =$ _____

5. Multiply.

   a) $\frac{1}{2} \times \frac{1}{5} =$　　b) $\frac{1}{2} \times \frac{1}{7} =$　　c) $\frac{1}{3} \times \frac{1}{6} =$　　d) $\frac{1}{5} \times \frac{1}{7} =$

   e) $\frac{1}{5} \times \frac{1}{2} =$　　f) $\frac{1}{7} \times \frac{1}{2} =$　　g) $\frac{1}{6} \times \frac{1}{3} =$　　h) $\frac{1}{7} \times \frac{1}{5} =$

6. Look at your answers to Question 5. Does the order you multiply in affect the answer? _____

| Here is $\frac{2}{3}$ of a rectangle. 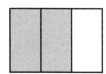 | Here is $\frac{4}{5}$ of $\frac{2}{3}$. 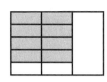 | How much is $\frac{4}{5}$ of $\frac{2}{3}$? Extend the lines to find out. 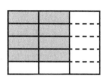 $\frac{4}{5}$ of $\frac{2}{3} = \frac{8}{15}$ | Notice: $\frac{4}{5}$ of $\frac{2}{3} = \frac{4 \times 2}{5 \times 3}$ $= \frac{8}{15}$ |

7. Write a fraction statement for each figure. Use multiplication instead of the word "of."

a)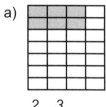

$\frac{2}{7} \times \frac{3}{4} =$

b)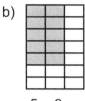

$\frac{5}{7} \times \frac{2}{3} =$

c)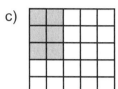

d)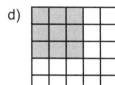

8. Find the following amounts by multiplying the numerators and denominators of the fractions.

a) $\frac{2}{3} \times \frac{4}{7} = \frac{8}{21}$

b) $\frac{1}{2} \times \frac{3}{5} =$

c) $\frac{3}{4} \times \frac{5}{7} =$

d) $\frac{2}{5} \times \frac{3}{8} =$

9. Write a formula for multiplying fractions by fractions.

$\frac{a}{b} \times \frac{c}{d} = $ _____

10. Multiply the following fractions. (Reduce your answers to lowest terms.)

a) $\frac{2}{3} \times \frac{3}{5} =$

b) $\frac{3}{4} \times \frac{5}{7} =$

c) $\frac{1}{3} \times \frac{4}{5} =$

d) $\frac{4}{6} \times \frac{8}{7} =$

e) $\frac{3}{7} \times \frac{8}{9} =$

11. Multiply the following fractions. (Reduce your answers to lowest terms.) What do you notice?

a) $\frac{3}{5} \times \frac{5}{3} =$

b) $\frac{2}{7} \times \frac{7}{2} =$

c) $\frac{3}{2} \times \frac{2}{3} =$

d) $\frac{4}{5} \times \frac{5}{4} =$

e) $\frac{7}{9} \times \frac{9}{7} =$

12. a) Circle the fractions that are more than $\frac{2}{3}$.

$\frac{5}{7}$ $\frac{5}{8}$ $\frac{3}{5}$ $\frac{7}{10}$

b) Without calculating the products, circle the products that are greater than 1 ($= \frac{2}{3} \times \frac{3}{2}$).

$\frac{5}{7} \times \frac{3}{2}$ $\frac{5}{8} \times \frac{3}{2}$ $\frac{3}{5} \times \frac{3}{2}$ $\frac{7}{10} \times \frac{3}{2}$

c) Verify your answers to part b) by calculating the products.

NS8-26 Dividing Fractions by Whole Numbers

1. In each picture, one half of the bar is shaded. What is the size of the smaller cross-shaded piece?

   Hint: How many cross-shaded pieces fit into the whole bar?

   a)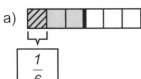
   $$\frac{1}{6}$$

   b)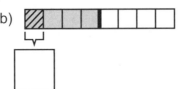

   c)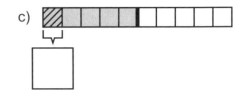

2. What is the size of the smaller cross-shaded piece?

   Hint: Cut the entire bar into smaller pieces if necessary, as in a).

   $$\frac{1}{12}$$

   a)

   b)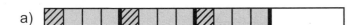

   c)

   d)

3. What fraction of the bar is cross-shaded?

   a) _____

   b) _____

   c)

4. a) Explain how the picture in Question 2 a) shows that $\frac{1}{3} \div 4 = \frac{1}{12}$.

   b) Write division statements for the other pictures in Question 2.

To divide a fraction by a whole number, use a picture. Example: $\frac{2}{3} \div 5$

Step 1: Draw a model for $\frac{2}{3}$.

Step 2: Divide each part into 5 parts.

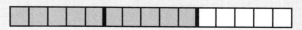

Step 3: Cross-shade 1 of every 5 shaded parts.

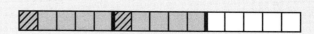

Step 4: Name the fraction shown by cross-shading. $\frac{2}{3} \div 5 = \frac{2}{15}$

5. Use the picture to find each quotient.

a) $\frac{3}{5} \div 5 =$ _____

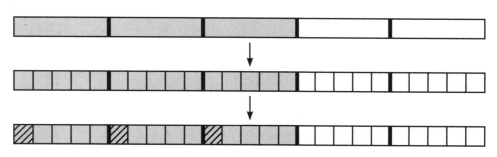

b) $\frac{2}{3} \div 4 =$ _____

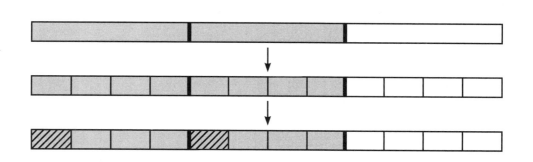

6. Draw a picture to find each quotient.

a) $\frac{4}{5} \div 2$ b) $\frac{1}{4} \div 3$ c) $\frac{3}{4} \div 2$ d) $\frac{2}{3} \div 3$ e) $\frac{2}{3} \div 2$ f) $\frac{4}{5} \div 3$

7. Look at your answers to Question 6. Finish writing the formula.

$$\frac{a}{b} \div c = \frac{a}{\underline{\hspace{3em}}}$$

8. Use your formula from Question 7 to find each quotient.

a) $\frac{2}{3} \div 5 = \frac{2}{3 \times 5} = \frac{2}{15}$ b) $\frac{3}{4} \div 7 =$ _____   c) $\frac{3}{5} \div 4 =$ _____

NS8-27 Dividing Whole Numbers by Fractions

Lina divides a string 6 m long into pieces 2 m long:

Each piece is 2 m long.

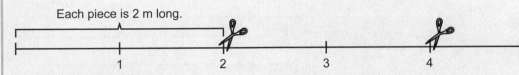

3 pieces of length 2 fit into 6, so **6 ÷ 2 = 3**

James divides a string 3 m long into pieces $\frac{1}{2}$ m long:

Each piece is $\frac{1}{2}$ m long.

2 pieces of length $\frac{1}{2}$ m fit into 1 metre, so 6 pieces fit into 3 metres ($3 \times 2 = 6$) and **$3 \div \frac{1}{2} = 6$**

1. Answer the questions and complete the division statement.

a) How many pieces of length $\frac{1}{3}$ fit into 1? _____3_____ $1 \div \frac{1}{3} =$ _____3_____

How many pieces of length $\frac{1}{3}$ fit into 2? _$2 \times 3 = 6$_ $2 \div \frac{1}{3} =$ _____6_____

How many pieces of length $\frac{1}{3}$ fit into 5? _____ $5 \div \frac{1}{3} =$ _____

b) How many pieces of length $\frac{1}{4}$ fit into 1? _____ $1 \div \frac{1}{4} =$ _____

How many pieces of length $\frac{1}{4}$ fit into 3? _____ $3 \div \frac{1}{4} =$ _____

How many pieces of length $\frac{1}{4}$ fit into 7? _____ $7 \div \frac{1}{4} =$ _____

c) How many pieces of length $\frac{1}{a}$ fit into 1? _____ $1 \div \frac{1}{a} =$ _____

How many pieces of length $\frac{1}{a}$ fit into 3? _____ $3 \div \frac{1}{a} =$ _____

How many pieces of length $\frac{1}{a}$ fit into b? _____ $b \div \frac{1}{a} =$ _____

2. Find each quotient.

a) $9 \div \frac{1}{5} =$ ___ × ___ = ___   b) $8 \div \frac{1}{4} =$ ___ × ___ = ___   c) $7 \div \frac{1}{6} =$ ___ × ___ = ___

d) $8 \div \frac{1}{3} =$ ___   e) $6 \div \frac{1}{6} =$ ___   f) $5 \div \frac{1}{7} =$ ___   g) $7 \div \frac{1}{7} =$ ___   h) $8 \div \frac{1}{9} =$ ___

How many strings of length $\frac{2}{5}$ m fit along a string of length 4 m?

Step 1: Calculate how many strings of length $\frac{1}{5}$ m fit along a string of length 4 m.

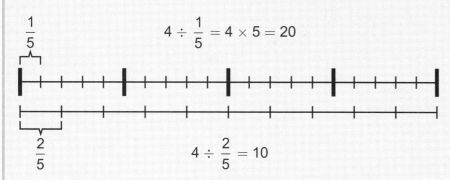

$$4 \div \frac{1}{5} = 4 \times 5 = 20$$

$$4 \div \frac{2}{5} = 10$$

Step 2: Since $\frac{2}{5}$ is twice as long as $\frac{1}{5}$, only half as many will fit.

So divide the answer from Step 1 by 2: $20 \div 2 = 10$

3. Determine how many pieces will fit.

a) How many pieces of length $\frac{2}{3}$ fit into 4?

   __12__ pieces of length $\frac{1}{3}$ fit into 4 so __12__ ÷ __2__ = __6__ pieces of length $\frac{2}{3}$ fit into 4.

b) How many pieces of length $\frac{2}{5}$ fit into 4?

   _____ pieces of length $\frac{1}{5}$ fit into 4 so _____ ÷ _____ = _____ pieces of length $\frac{2}{5}$ fit into 4.

c) How many pieces of length $\frac{3}{5}$ fit into 6?

   _____ pieces of length $\frac{1}{5}$ fit into 6 so _____ ÷ _____ = _____ pieces of length $\frac{3}{5}$ fit into 6.

d) How many pieces of length $\frac{a}{b}$ fit into c?

   _____ pieces of length $\frac{1}{b}$ fit into c so _____ ÷ _____ = _____ pieces of length $\frac{a}{b}$ fit into c.

4. Write each answer from Question 3 as a division statement.

   a) $4 \div \frac{2}{3} = 6$ b)   c)   d)

5. Find each quotient.

   a) $9 \div \frac{3}{4} =$ _____ × _____ ÷ _____ = _____   b) $8 \div \frac{4}{5} =$ _____ × _____ ÷ _____ = _____

   c) $8 \div \frac{2}{7} =$ _____   d) $6 \div \frac{3}{4} =$ _____   e) $10 \div \frac{5}{6} =$ _____   f) $12 \div \frac{4}{5} =$ _____   g) $12 \div \frac{2}{5} =$ _____

INVESTIGATION 1 ▶ The fractions $\frac{1}{3}$ and $\frac{2}{6}$ are equivalent. Does dividing by $\frac{1}{3}$ and dividing by $\frac{2}{6}$ result in the same answer?

A. Calculate each quotient.

i) $4 \div \frac{1}{3} = $ _____ $\times$ _____ $= $ _____

$4 \div \frac{2}{6} = $ _____ $\times$ _____ $\div$ _____ $= $ _____

ii) $5 \div \frac{1}{3} = $ _____ $\times$ _____ $= $ _____

$5 \div \frac{2}{6} = $ _____ $\times$ _____ $\div$ _____ $= $ _____

iii) $7 \div \frac{1}{3} = $ _____ $\times$ _____ $= $ _____

$7 \div \frac{2}{6} = $ _____ $\times$ _____ $\div$ _____ $= $ _____

iv) $8 \div \frac{1}{3} = $ _____ $\times$ _____ $= $ _____

$8 \div \frac{2}{6} = $ _____ $\times$ _____ $\div$ _____ $= $ _____

B. Does dividing by $\frac{1}{3}$ and dividing by $\frac{2}{6}$ result in the same answer? _____

INVESTIGATION 2 ▶ Does dividing by equivalent fractions always result in the same answer?

A. Write five fractions equivalent to $\frac{1}{2}$.

$$\frac{1}{2} = \frac{}{4} = \frac{}{6} = \frac{}{8} = \frac{}{10} = \frac{}{12}$$

B. Divide 3 by each fraction in your list from A.

$3 \div \frac{1}{2} = \frac{3 \times 2}{1} = 6$

$3 \div \frac{2}{4} = \frac{3 \times 4}{2} = $ _____

$3 \div \frac{}{6} = $ _____

$3 \div \frac{}{8} = $ _____

$3 \div \frac{}{10} = $ _____

$3 \div \frac{}{12} = $ _____

C. Does dividing by equivalent fractions always result in the same answer? _____

Explain why this is so. _____

_____

_____

_____

Number Sense 8-27

1. Evaluate these expressions. Do the operation in brackets first.

   a) $\dfrac{2}{3} + \left(\dfrac{1}{5} \times 4\right)$

   b) $\left(\dfrac{2}{3} + \dfrac{1}{5}\right) \times 4 =$

   c) $\dfrac{1}{5} + \left(\dfrac{4}{3} \div 2\right)$

   d) $\left(\dfrac{1}{5} + \dfrac{4}{3}\right) \div 2 =$

   e) $\dfrac{4}{3} - \left(\dfrac{2}{5} \times 2\right)$

   f) $\left(\dfrac{4}{3} - \dfrac{2}{5}\right) \times 2 =$

   g) $\dfrac{4}{3} - \left(\dfrac{2}{5} \div 2\right)$

   h) $\left(\dfrac{4}{3} - \dfrac{2}{5}\right) \div 2 =$

2. Compare the problems in Question 1 that use the same operations and numbers.

   Does the order you do the operations in affect the answer? _____

   > **REMINDER** ▶ Mathematicians have ordered the operations to avoid writing brackets all the time.
   >
   > The order is:
   >
   > 1. Operations in brackets
   > 2. Multiplication and division, from left to right
   > 3. Addition and subtraction, from left to right
   >
   > Examples: $5 - 3 \times \dfrac{2}{3} + 6 = 5 - 2 + 6$ but $(5 - 3) \times \left(\dfrac{2}{3} + 6\right) = 2 \times \dfrac{20}{3}$
   >
   > $\qquad\qquad\qquad\qquad = 3 + 6 \qquad\qquad\qquad\qquad\qquad\quad = \dfrac{40}{3}$
   >
   > $\qquad\qquad\qquad\qquad = 9 \qquad\qquad\qquad\qquad\qquad\qquad = 13\dfrac{1}{3}$

3. Evaluate.

   a) $\left(\dfrac{2}{3} + \dfrac{1}{2}\right) \times \dfrac{1}{4}$

   b) $\dfrac{2}{3} + \dfrac{1}{2} \times \dfrac{1}{4}$

   c) $\dfrac{3}{2} + \dfrac{1}{4} \times \dfrac{3}{4}$

   d) $\dfrac{3}{2} \times \left(8 \div \dfrac{3}{4}\right)$

   e) $\dfrac{5}{2} \div 5 \times \dfrac{4}{5}$

   f) $\dfrac{5}{2} \div \left(5 \times \dfrac{4}{5}\right)$

   g) $\dfrac{2}{3} + \dfrac{1}{2} - \dfrac{1}{4}$

   h) $\dfrac{2}{3} + \left(\dfrac{1}{2} - \dfrac{1}{4}\right)$

   i) $\dfrac{2}{3} - \dfrac{1}{4} + \dfrac{1}{2}$

   j) $\dfrac{2}{3} - \left(\dfrac{1}{4} + \dfrac{1}{2}\right)$

   k) $\dfrac{2}{3} - \dfrac{1}{4} \times \dfrac{1}{2}$

   l) $\left(\dfrac{2}{3} - \dfrac{1}{4}\right) \times \dfrac{1}{2}$

4. Remove any brackets that are not necessary.

   Note: In some expressions, all brackets will be necessary.

   a) $\dfrac{2}{3} + \left(\dfrac{1}{2} - \dfrac{1}{3}\right)$

   b) $\dfrac{2}{3} \times \left(\dfrac{1}{2} - \dfrac{1}{3}\right)$

   c) $\left(\dfrac{1}{2} \times \dfrac{1}{3}\right) + \left(\dfrac{1}{3} - \dfrac{1}{4}\right)$

   d) $\left[\dfrac{1}{2} - \left(\dfrac{1}{3} + \dfrac{1}{4}\right)\right] \times \dfrac{1}{5}$

NS8-29 Dividing Fractions by Fractions

1. a) Find each quotient.

    i) $(12 \times 1) \div (2 \times 1) = $ _____ $\div$ _____ $= $ _____

    ii) $(12 \times 2) \div (2 \times 2) = $ _____ $\div$ _____ $= $ _____

    iii) $(12 \times 3) \div (2 \times 3) = $ _____ $\div$ _____ $= $ _____

    iv) $(12 \times 4) \div (2 \times 4) = $ _____ $\div$ _____ $= $ _____

    v) $(12 \times 5) \div (2 \times 5) = $ _____ $\div$ _____ $= $ _____

    vi) $(12 \times 6) \div (2 \times 6) = $ _____ $\div$ _____ $= $ _____

    vii) $\dfrac{12 \times 7}{2 \times 7} = \boxed{\dfrac{}{}} = $ _____

    viii) $\dfrac{12 \times 8}{2 \times 8} = \boxed{\dfrac{}{}} = $ _____

  b)   What do you notice about your answers in part a)? _____

       Why is that so? _____

       _____

       _____

       _____

INVESTIGATION 1 ▶ In a division statement, multiplying both terms by the same whole number results in the same quotient.

Does multiplying both terms by **the same fraction** result in the same quotient?

A. Find each quotient.

  a) $\left(12 \times \dfrac{1}{2}\right) \div \left(2 \times \dfrac{1}{2}\right) = $ __6__ $\div \boxed{\dfrac{2}{2}} = $ __6__ $\times$ __2__ $\div$ __2__ $= $ __6__

  b) $\left(12 \times \dfrac{1}{3}\right) \div \left(2 \times \dfrac{1}{3}\right) = $ __4__ $\div \boxed{\dfrac{2}{3}} = $ __4__ $\times$ __3__ $\div$ __2__ $= $ _____

  c) $\left(12 \times \dfrac{1}{4}\right) \div \left(2 \times \dfrac{1}{4}\right) = $ _____ $\div \boxed{\dfrac{}{}} = $ _____ $\times$ _____ $\div$ _____ $= $ _____

  d) $\left(12 \times \dfrac{1}{6}\right) \div \left(2 \times \dfrac{1}{6}\right) = $ _____ $\div \boxed{\dfrac{}{}} = $ _____ $\times$ _____ $\div$ _____ $= $ _____

  e) $\left(12 \times \dfrac{2}{3}\right) \div \left(2 \times \dfrac{2}{3}\right) = $ _____ $\div \boxed{\dfrac{}{}} = $ _____ $\times$ _____ $\div$ _____ $= $ _____

B. What do you notice about your answers in A? _____

C. In a division statement, does multiplying both terms by the same fraction result in

     the same quotient? _____

The **reciprocal** of the fraction $\frac{a}{b}$ is the fraction $\frac{b}{a}$.

2. Write the reciprocal of each fraction.

   a) The reciprocal of $\frac{3}{4}$ is _____

   b) The reciprocal of $\frac{5}{3}$ is _____

   c) The reciprocal of $\frac{4}{7}$ is _____

   d) The reciprocal of $\frac{9}{2}$ is _____

3. If the fraction $\frac{a}{b}$ is less than 1, then its reciprocal is _____ than 1.

REMINDER ▶ $\frac{a}{b} \times \frac{b}{a} = 1$ for any a and b. Example: $\frac{3}{4} \times \frac{4}{3} = \frac{12}{12} = 1$

4. Translate the formula in the box into words:

   A fraction multiplied by its _____ is always _____.

REMINDER ▶ Dividing by 1 leaves a number unchanged.

Examples: $5 \div 1 = 5$ $\frac{2}{3} \div 1 = \frac{2}{3}$ $\frac{7}{5} \div 1 = \frac{7}{5}$

5. Multiply the reciprocals then divide by 1 to find the quotients.

   a) $\frac{5}{7} \div \left(\frac{3}{4} \times \frac{4}{3} \right)$

   $= \frac{5}{7} \div$ _____ $=$ _____

   b) $\frac{2}{3} \div \left(\frac{2}{5} \times \frac{5}{2} \right)$

   $= \frac{2}{3} \div$ _____ $=$ _____

   c) $\frac{3}{5} \div \left(\frac{2}{9} \times \frac{9}{2} \right)$

   $= \frac{3}{5} \div$ _____ $=$ _____

6. Fill in the blanks to make the quotients equal.

   a) $\frac{4}{5} \div \frac{3}{4} = \left(\frac{4}{5} \times \boxed{\frac{4}{3}} \right) \div \left(\frac{3}{4} \times \frac{4}{3} \right)$

   b) $\frac{3}{4} \div \frac{2}{5} = \left(\frac{3}{4} \times \boxed{} \right) \div \left(\frac{2}{5} \times \frac{5}{2} \right)$

   c) $\frac{2}{3} \div \frac{1}{2} = \left(\frac{2}{3} \times \boxed{} \right) \div \left(\frac{1}{2} \times \frac{2}{1} \right)$

   d) $\frac{2}{3} \div \frac{3}{5} = \left(\frac{2}{3} \times \boxed{} \right) \div \left(\frac{3}{5} \times \frac{5}{3} \right)$

7. Look at your answer to Question 6 b). Explain why $\frac{3}{4} \div \frac{2}{5} = \frac{3}{4} \times \frac{5}{2}$.

8. Fill in the blanks to make the quotient equal to the product.

a) $\dfrac{2}{5} \div \dfrac{3}{7} = \dfrac{2}{5} \times \boxed{}$

b) $\dfrac{2}{3} \div \dfrac{2}{5} = \dfrac{2}{3} \times \boxed{}$

c) $\dfrac{7}{2} \div \dfrac{3}{5} = \dfrac{7}{2} \times \boxed{}$

d) $\dfrac{3}{4} \div \dfrac{2}{7} = \dfrac{3}{4} \times \boxed{}$

e) $\dfrac{2}{5} \div \dfrac{1}{6} = \dfrac{2}{5} \times \boxed{}$

f) $\dfrac{3}{4} \div \dfrac{3}{5} = \dfrac{3}{4} \times \boxed{}$

9. Finish writing the rule: $\dfrac{a}{b} \div \dfrac{c}{d} = \dfrac{a}{b} \times \underline{}$

10. Use your rule from Question 9 to find each quotient. Express your answer in lowest terms.

a) $\dfrac{3}{5} \div \dfrac{2}{3} = \dfrac{3}{5} \times \dfrac{3}{2} = \dfrac{9}{10}$

b) $\dfrac{3}{5} \div \dfrac{2}{5} =$

c) $\dfrac{1}{3} \div \dfrac{5}{6} =$

d) $\dfrac{1}{5} \div \dfrac{3}{8} =$

e) $\dfrac{5}{8} \div \dfrac{2}{3} =$

f) $\dfrac{6}{7} \div \dfrac{2}{3} =$

g) $\dfrac{8}{5} \div \dfrac{3}{2} =$

h) $\dfrac{8}{5} \div \dfrac{2}{3} =$

i) $\dfrac{1}{5} \div \dfrac{3}{5} =$

11. Divide by first changing all mixed numbers to improper fractions.

a) $3\dfrac{1}{2} \div \dfrac{2}{3} = \dfrac{7}{2} \div \dfrac{2}{3}$

$= \dfrac{7}{2} \times \dfrac{3}{2}$

$= \dfrac{21}{4}$

$= 5\dfrac{1}{4}$

b) $4\dfrac{1}{2} \div \dfrac{1}{4}$

c) $2\dfrac{2}{3} \div \dfrac{4}{9}$

d) $3\dfrac{3}{4} \div 7\dfrac{1}{2}$

e) $5\dfrac{6}{8} \div \dfrac{1}{4}$

f) $3 \div \dfrac{1}{10}$

g) $1\dfrac{1}{9} \div 1\dfrac{2}{3}$

h) $2 \div 1\dfrac{7}{9}$

12. Divide each fraction by itself. (Reduce your answer to lower terms.)

a) $\dfrac{3}{4} \div \dfrac{3}{4} = \dfrac{3}{4} \times \dfrac{4}{3}$

$= \dfrac{12}{12} = 1$

b) $\dfrac{4}{7} \div \dfrac{4}{7} =$

c) $\dfrac{8}{3} \div \dfrac{8}{3} =$

13. What do you notice about your answers to Question 12? Why is this so?

1. Use the picture to estimate the quotient.

a) 5 ÷ 3

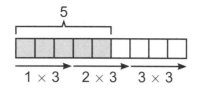

Is 5 closer to 1 × 3 or 2 × 3? _____

Is 5 ÷ 3 closer to 1 or 2? _____

b) $\frac{3}{4} \div \frac{2}{7}$

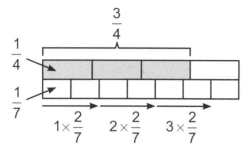

Is $\frac{3}{4}$ closer to $2 \times \frac{2}{7}$ or $3 \times \frac{2}{7}$? _____

Is $\frac{3}{4} \div \frac{2}{7}$ closer to 2 or 3? _____

c) $\frac{5}{8} \div \frac{1}{3}$

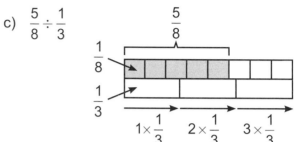

Is $\frac{5}{8}$ closer to $1 \times \frac{1}{3}$ or $2 \times \frac{1}{3}$? _____

Is $\frac{5}{8} \div \frac{1}{3}$ closer to 1 or 2? _____

How to estimate $\frac{3}{8} \div \frac{1}{5}$

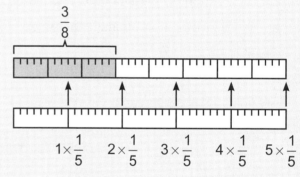

Step 1: Draw two bars **8 × 5 = 40 mm** long.

Step 2: Divide one bar into eighths (5 mm each).

Step 3: Divide the other bar into fifths (8 mm each).

Step 4: Decide how many $\frac{1}{5}$s are closest to $\frac{3}{8}$. $\frac{3}{8} \div \frac{1}{5}$ **is about 2**

---

2. Draw a picture to estimate $\frac{3}{5} \div \frac{1}{3}$.

3. Estimate each quotient to the nearest whole number.

a) $\frac{5}{12} \div \frac{1}{4}$ b) $\frac{1}{2} \div \frac{2}{5}$ c) $\frac{3}{4} \div \frac{1}{3}$ d) $\frac{5}{6} \div \frac{1}{4}$

4. a) Circle the quotients that are larger than 1.

   7 ÷ 5   5 ÷ 7 $\frac{2}{3} \div \frac{2}{5}$ $\frac{2}{5} \div \frac{2}{3}$

   b) Explain how you knew what to circle in a). _____

   c) Ahmed calculates $\frac{2}{5} \div \frac{2}{3}$ as $\frac{5}{3}$. How can you tell immediately that he's wrong?

   _____

NS8-31 Word Problems

1. A foot is 12 inches. A yard is 3 feet. What fraction of a yard is 8 inches?

   Find what fraction of a foot is 8 inches: 8 inches is $\frac{8}{12}$ of a foot.

   Find what fraction of a yard is a foot: 1 foot is $\frac{1}{3}$ of a yard.

   So 8 inches $= \frac{8}{12} \times \frac{1}{3}$ of a yard $=$ _____ of a yard.

2. A year has _____ months. A decade has _____ years.

   What fraction of a decade is 8 months?

3. What fraction of a day is 45 minutes?

4. If a year has 52 weeks, what fraction of a century is 13 weeks?

5. What fraction of a day is 40 seconds?

6. a) Bilal bought $\frac{7}{5}$ cups of flour. He used $\frac{3}{4}$ of it to bake a pie. How much flour did he use?

   b) Did Bilal use more or less than a cup of flour? How do you know?

7. Ron bought $2\frac{2}{3}$ cups of sugar. He used $\frac{1}{4}$ of it to bake a cake. He then ate $\frac{3}{10}$ of the cake. How much sugar did he eat?

8. Sam biked $\frac{2}{3}$ km in 4 minutes. How far did he bike in 1 minute?

   $\frac{2}{3} \div 4 = \boxed{-}$ km

9. A string of length $3\frac{1}{2}$ m is divided into 5 equal parts. How long is each piece?

   $3\frac{1}{2} \div 5 = \frac{7}{2} \div 5 = \boxed{-}$ m $=$ _____ cm

10. A cake recipe used $1\frac{1}{3}$ cups sugar. The cake is divided into 8 pieces. How much sugar is in each piece?

11. Rosa bought $\frac{4}{5}$ kg of dry lasagne. Each person needs $\frac{2}{35}$ kg. How many people can she feed?

12. A string of length $4\frac{4}{5}$ m long is divided into pieces of length $\frac{3}{10}$ m. How many pieces are there?

Word Problems — Advanced

1. Craig had $48 dollars. He spent $\frac{1}{4}$ of his money on a book and $\frac{3}{8}$ on a pair of gloves.

   a) How many dollars did Craig spend on the gloves?

   b) How much money does he have left over?

2. Roberto, Kendra, and Imran painted a whole wall. Roberto painted $\frac{2}{5}$ of the wall and Kendra painted $\frac{1}{3}$.

   a) What fraction of the wall did Imran paint?

   b) Each person painted a rectangular section of different length. The wall is 30 m long. How long was each person's section?

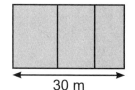

30 m

3. Sally stretches for $\frac{1}{2}$ an hour, walks for $\frac{2}{3}$ of an hour, and jogs for $\frac{2}{5}$ of an hour. Calculate how many minutes she exercised for, using both methods below.

   Method 1: Add the fractions and then convert to minutes.

   Method 2: Convert the fractions to minutes and then add.

   Do you get the same answer both ways?

4. Ron talked on the phone for $\frac{1}{5}$ of an hour. Jacob talked on the phone for $\frac{1}{100}$ of a day. Who talked longer on the phone?

5. Sara can do one jumping jack in $\frac{3}{4}$ of a second. How many jumping jacks can she do in $\frac{7}{10}$ of a minute? Circle the correct formula.

   $\frac{7}{10} \times \frac{3}{4}$ $\frac{7}{10} \div \frac{3}{4}$ $\frac{3}{4} \div \frac{7}{10}$ $42 \div \frac{3}{4}$ $\frac{7}{10} \div 45$ $45 \div \frac{7}{10}$ $42 \times \frac{3}{4}$

   Explain your choice. _____

   _____

6. Make up word problems that require finding:

   a) $\frac{4}{5} + \frac{1}{3}$ b) $\frac{4}{5} - \frac{1}{3}$ c) $\frac{1}{3} \times \frac{2}{5}$ d) $\frac{10}{3} \div \frac{2}{5}$

7. Jade spent $\frac{3}{4}$ of an hour doing math, $\frac{2}{5}$ of an hour doing geography and $\frac{5}{6}$ of an hour doing science.

a) Compare fractions to answer these questions.

   i) Did Jade spend more or less than half an hour doing geography?

   ii) Did Jade spend more time doing math or science?

b) Decide whether each problem requires addition, subtraction, multilplication, or division. Then solve the problem.

   i) Jade spent $\frac{1}{3}$ of her time doing math working on word problems.
What fraction of an hour did she spend working on word problems?

   ii) How many hours did Jade spend on homework altogether?

   iii) How many more hours did Jade spend on science than on geography?

   iv) Jade divided her time on geography evenly between reading the textbook and answering questions. What fraction of an hour did she spend reading the textbook?

c) Solve each problem below.

   i) Jade had two hours to do her homework before she had to leave to meet a friend. How many minutes before she had to leave did Jade finish her homework?

   ii) Jade spent $\frac{1}{3}$ of her time on science reading the textbook. She spent $\frac{1}{5}$ of her remaining time on science doing calculations. How many hours did she spend on calculations?

   iii) Jade's sister spent $\frac{1}{3}$ the amount of time Jade did on math, but twice the amount of time on geography and $1\frac{1}{2}$ times as much time on science. Who spent more time doing homework, Jade or her sister?

   iv) Jade's brother spent the same total amount of time on homework as Jade's sister. He spent the same amount of time on all 3 subjects. How much time did Jade's brother spend on each subject? Write your answer as a fraction of an hour.

   v) Jade's sister spent $\frac{1}{5}$ of her time on science reading the textbook. Who spent more time reading her science textbook—Jade or her sister?

Number Sense 8-32

1. Write six fractions equivalent to 1.

2. Find the sum. Hint: Group fractions that have the same denominator together.

$$\frac{1}{2} + \frac{2}{3} + \frac{1}{4} + \frac{2}{5} + \frac{5}{6} + \frac{1}{6} + \frac{3}{5} + \frac{3}{4} + \frac{1}{3} + \frac{1}{2}$$

3. Subtract.
   a) $1 - \frac{1}{2}$ b) $\frac{1}{2} - \frac{1}{3}$ c) $\frac{1}{3} - \frac{1}{4}$ d) $\frac{1}{4} - \frac{1}{5}$ e) $\frac{1}{99} - \frac{1}{100}$

4. Write each fraction as a sum of exactly three fractions, each with numerator 1.
   Example: $\frac{5}{6} = \frac{1}{2} + \frac{1}{6} + \frac{1}{6}$
   a) $\frac{7}{8}$ b) $\frac{17}{18}$ c) $\frac{13}{15}$ d) $\frac{3}{7}$ e) $\frac{7}{10}$

5. Decide whether each statement is True or False. Explain your answer.

   a) If the numerator and denominator are both even, the fraction is never in lowest terms.

   b) If the numerator and denominator are both odd, the fraction is always in lowest terms.

   c) If the numerator is prime, the fraction is always in lowest terms.

6. Olivia says the lowest common denominator for $\frac{1}{4}$ and $\frac{1}{10}$ is 40. Is this correct? Explain.

7. What mistake did Jared make when subtracting $\frac{11}{12} - \frac{2}{3} = \frac{9}{9}$?
   How can you tell by estimating that the answer is not correct?

8. Write down the prime numbers between 1 and 100, then answer these questions.

   REMINDER ▶ See Eratosthenes' Sieve for finding prime numbers on p.7.

   a) What fraction of the numbers between 1 and 20 are prime?

   b) What fraction of the numbers between 21 and 50 are prime?

   c) What fraction of the numbers between 51 and 100 are prime?

   d) Do prime numbers occur more often or less often as numbers become large? Explain.

9. 60 pieces of size $\frac{1}{10}$ fit into 6. How many pieces of size...

   a) $\frac{2}{10}$ will fit into 6?   b) $\frac{3}{10}$ will fit into 6?   c) $\frac{5}{10}$ will fit into 6?

10. Find $6 \div \dfrac{1}{2}$. Which answer from Question 9 is the same? Why is this so?

11. Which do you expect to be greater, $21\ 417\ 613 \div \dfrac{1}{2}$ or $21\ 417\ 613 \div \dfrac{3}{5}$?

Explain your answer.

12. Find the next term in each sequence by determining the number being added or multiplied.

a) $\dfrac{2}{5}$ $\dfrac{11}{15}$ $\dfrac{16}{15}$ $\dfrac{7}{5}$ _____   b) $\dfrac{1}{4}$ $\dfrac{3}{20}$ $\dfrac{9}{100}$ $\dfrac{27}{500}$ _____

13. Evaluate.

a) $\left(\dfrac{2}{3} - \dfrac{1}{3}\right) \times \dfrac{1}{2} + \dfrac{1}{4}$ b) $\dfrac{2}{3} - \dfrac{1}{3} \times \left(\dfrac{1}{2} + \dfrac{1}{4}\right)$ c) $\left(\dfrac{2}{3} - \dfrac{1}{3}\right) \times \left(\dfrac{1}{2} + \dfrac{1}{4}\right)$

d) $\dfrac{2}{3} - \left(\dfrac{1}{3} \times \dfrac{1}{2} + \dfrac{1}{4}\right)$ e) $\left(\dfrac{2}{3} - \dfrac{1}{3} \times \dfrac{1}{2}\right) + \dfrac{1}{4}$ f) $\dfrac{2}{3} - \left[\dfrac{1}{3} \times \left(\dfrac{1}{2} + \dfrac{1}{4}\right)\right]$

14. Which brackets in Question 13 can be removed without changing the answer?

15. Add brackets to make the equations true.

a) $\dfrac{3}{5} - \dfrac{2}{5} \times \dfrac{1}{2} + \dfrac{1}{5} = \dfrac{3}{10}$ b) $\dfrac{3}{5} - \dfrac{2}{5} \times \dfrac{1}{2} + \dfrac{1}{5} = \dfrac{1}{5}$ c) $\dfrac{3}{5} - \dfrac{2}{5} \times \dfrac{1}{2} + \dfrac{1}{5} = \dfrac{8}{25}$

16. Write each division statement as a fraction statement.

a) $3 \div 3 = 1$ $\dfrac{3}{3} = 1$ b) $5 \div 5 = 1$ c) $8 \div 8 = 1$ d) $a \div a = 1$

17. Multiply.

a) $\dfrac{2}{2} \times \dfrac{3}{3} \times \dfrac{4}{4} =$ ____   b) $\dfrac{3}{2} \times \dfrac{2}{3} \times \dfrac{4}{4} =$ ____   c) $\dfrac{2}{3} \times \dfrac{3}{4} \times \dfrac{4}{2} =$ ____   d) $\dfrac{2}{4} \times \dfrac{4}{3} \times \dfrac{3}{2} =$ ____

18. What do you notice about your answers to Question 17? Why is that so?

When multiplying fractions, we can **cancel** any number that occurs in both the numerator and denominator because multiplying or dividing by 1 doesn't change a number.

Example: $\dfrac{2}{3} \times \dfrac{5}{2} \times \dfrac{7}{5} = \dfrac{\cancel{2} \times \cancel{5} \times 7}{3 \times \cancel{2} \times \cancel{5}} = \dfrac{7}{3}$

---

19. Multiply by cancelling numbers that occur in both the numerator and denominator.

a) $\dfrac{\cancel{2}}{3} \times \dfrac{\cancel{3}}{\cancel{2}} \times \dfrac{4}{\cancel{3}}$ b) $\dfrac{2}{5} \times \dfrac{5}{6} \times \dfrac{7}{2}$ c) $\dfrac{2}{3} \times \dfrac{4}{7} \times \dfrac{3}{5} \times \dfrac{7}{2}$ d) $\dfrac{2}{3} \times \dfrac{3}{4} \times \dfrac{4}{5} \times \dfrac{5}{6} \times \dfrac{6}{7} \times \dfrac{7}{8} \times \dfrac{8}{9}$

= .   =   =   =

Number Sense 8-33

10, 100, 1 000, … are **powers of 10**. In a **decimal fraction**, the denominator is a power of ten.

There are 100 squares on a **hundredths grid**.

1 one 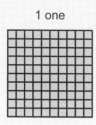   1 tenth 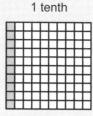   1 hundredth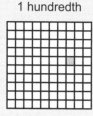

$1 \text{ column} = \dfrac{10}{100} = \dfrac{1}{10} = 1 \text{ tenth}$ $1 \text{ square} = \dfrac{1}{100} = 1 \text{ hundredth}$

1. Write two equivalent fractions for the shaded part of the grid.
   Remember: 1 column = 1 tenth.

   a) $\dfrac{2}{10} = \dfrac{}{100}$

   b) $\dfrac{}{10} = \dfrac{}{100}$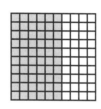

   c) $\dfrac{}{10} = \dfrac{}{100}$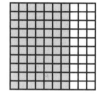

2. Write the fraction shown by the shaded part of the grid in two ways.

   a) $\dfrac{23}{100} = $
   $\dfrac{2}{10} + \dfrac{}{100}$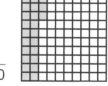

   b) $\dfrac{}{100} = $
   $\dfrac{}{10} + \dfrac{}{100}$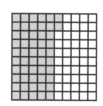

   c) $\dfrac{}{100} = $
   $\dfrac{}{10} + \dfrac{}{100}$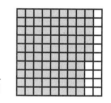

3. Shade the grid to show the fraction. Then write the fraction another way.

   a) $\dfrac{47}{100} = $
   $\dfrac{}{10} + \dfrac{}{100}$

   b) $\dfrac{92}{100} = $
   $\dfrac{}{10} + \dfrac{}{100}$

   c) $\dfrac{36}{100} = $
   $\dfrac{}{10} + \dfrac{}{100}$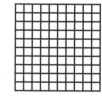

4. Determine the equivalent fraction.

   a) $\dfrac{7}{10} = \dfrac{7 \times 10}{10 \times 10} = \dfrac{}{100}$

   b) $\dfrac{36}{100} = \dfrac{36 \times \underline{}}{100 \times \underline{}} = \dfrac{}{1000}$

   c) $\dfrac{4}{100} = \dfrac{4 \times \underline{}}{100 \times \underline{}} = \dfrac{}{1000}$

5. Write the equivalent fractions.

   a) $\dfrac{5}{10} = \dfrac{}{100} = \dfrac{}{1000}$

   b) $\dfrac{}{10} = \dfrac{80}{100} = \dfrac{}{1000}$

   c) $\dfrac{73}{100} = \dfrac{}{1000}$

   d) $\dfrac{540}{1000} = \dfrac{}{100}$

NS8-35 Place Value and Decimals

Decimals are a short way to write decimal fractions.

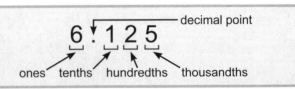

decimal point

ones tenths hundredths thousandths

1. Write the decimal fraction in the place value chart. Then write the fraction as a decimal.

a) $\dfrac{5}{10} + \dfrac{4}{100} = \underline{\ } . \underline{\ }\underline{\ }\underline{\ }$

ones	tenths	hundredths
0	5	4

b) $\dfrac{9}{10} + \dfrac{6}{100} + \dfrac{3}{1000} = \underline{\ } . \underline{\ }\underline{\ }\underline{\ }\underline{\ }$

ones	tenths	hundredths	thousandths
0			

2. Write the value of the digit **8** in each decimal in words and as a fraction.

a) 0.4**8**   8 ___*hundredths*___ or $\dfrac{8}{100}$

b) 0.34**8**   8 _____ or $\dfrac{8}{}$

c) 0.**8**76   8 _____ or $\dfrac{8}{}$

d) 0.3**8**   8 _____ or $\dfrac{8}{}$

3. Write the number shown in the place value chart as a decimal, using 0 as a placeholder.

a)

ones	tenths	hundredths
		8

$\underline{0} . \underline{0}\ \underline{8}$

b)

ones	tenths	hundredths	thousandths
			3

$\underline{\ } . \underline{\ }\underline{\ }\underline{\ }$

c)

ones	tenths	hundredths
		6

$\underline{\ } . \underline{\ }\underline{\ }$

d)

ones	tenths	hundredths	thousandths
			9

$\underline{\ } . \underline{\ }\underline{\ }\underline{\ }$

4. Write the number as a decimal. Use zeros as placeholders.

a) 6 tenths = $\underline{0} . \underline{\ }$

b) 2 tenths = $\underline{\ } . \underline{\ }$

c) 8 tenths = $\underline{\ } . \underline{\ }$

d) 6 hundredths = $\underline{0} . \underline{0}\ \underline{\ }$

e) 4 hundredths = $\underline{\ } . \underline{\ }\ \underline{\ }$

f) 3 hundredths = $\underline{\ } . \underline{\ }\ \underline{\ }$

g) 6 thousandths = $\underline{\ } . \underline{\ }\ \underline{\ }\ \underline{\ }$

h) 1 thousandth = $\underline{\ } . \underline{\ }\ \underline{\ }\ \underline{\ }$

i) 5 hundredths = $\underline{\ } . \underline{\ }\ \underline{\ }$

5. Write the number in expanded form as a decimal.

a) 3 tenths + 5 hundredths + 2 thousandths = $\underline{0} . \underline{\ }\ \underline{\ }\ \underline{\ }$

b) 7 tenths = $\underline{\ } . \underline{\ }$

c) 6 tenths + 4 hundredths = $\underline{\ } . \underline{\ }\ \underline{\ }$

d) 5 hundredths + 7 thousandths = $\underline{\ } . \underline{\ }\ \underline{\ }\ \underline{\ }$

e) 7 tenths + 5 thousandths = $\underline{\ } . \underline{\ }\ \underline{\ }\ \underline{\ }$

6. Put a decimal point in the number so the digit 3 has the value $\dfrac{3}{100}$.
Add zeros if you need to.

a)   2 3

b)   7 3 2

c)   7 6 5 3

d)   3

1. Complete the chart.

Drawing	Fraction	Decimal	Equivalent Decimal	Equivalent Fraction	Drawing
	$\dfrac{5}{10}$	0.5	0.50	$\dfrac{50}{100}$	
	$\dfrac{}{10}$	__ . __ __	__ . __ __	$\dfrac{}{100}$	

2. Fill in the missing numbers. Remember: $\dfrac{1}{10} = \dfrac{10}{100}$ and $\dfrac{1}{100} = \dfrac{10}{1000}$.

a) $0.8 = \dfrac{8}{10} = \dfrac{}{100} = 0.80$

b) $0.\underline{\ } = \dfrac{}{10} = \dfrac{40}{100} = 0.\underline{\ }\underline{\ }.$

c) $0.\underline{\ } = \dfrac{}{10} = \dfrac{}{100} = 0.30$

d) $0.03 = \dfrac{3}{100} = \dfrac{}{1000} = 0.030$

e) $0.\underline{\ }\underline{\ } = \dfrac{2}{100} = \dfrac{}{1000} = 0.020$

f) $0.\underline{\ }\underline{\ } = \dfrac{}{100} = \dfrac{70}{1000} = 0.\underline{\ }\underline{\ }\underline{\ }$

3. How many tenths and hundredths are shaded? Write a fraction and a decimal to represent them.

a)

 __47__ hundredths = _____ tenths _____ hundredths $\dfrac{47}{100} = 0.\underline{\ }\underline{\ }$

b)

 _____ hundredths = _____ tenths _____ hundredths $\dfrac{}{100} = 0.\underline{\ }\underline{\ }$

4. Write the fraction as a decimal.

a) $\dfrac{35}{100} = 0.\underline{\ }\underline{\ }$ b) $\dfrac{61}{100} = 0.\underline{\ }\underline{\ }$ c) $\dfrac{18}{100} = 0.\underline{\ }\underline{\ }$ d) $\dfrac{3}{100} = 0.\underline{\ }\underline{\ }$

5. Write the decimal in expanded form in two ways.

a) $0.52 = $ _____ tenths _____ hundredths

 $= $ _____ hundredths

b) $0.40 = $ _____ tenths _____ hundredths

 $= $ _____ hundredths

6. Write the number as a decimal.

a) 23 hundredths = $0.$ __ __   b) 61 hundredths = $0.$ __ __   c) 12 hundredths = $0.$ __ __

7. Fill in the blanks.

a) 428 thousandths = ____ tenths ____ hundredths ____ thousandths $\dfrac{428}{1000}$ = 0. __ __ __

b) 762 thousandths = ____ tenths ____ hundredths ____ thousandths $\dfrac{}{1000}$ = 0. __ __ __

8. Write the fraction as a decimal.

a) $\dfrac{268}{1000}$ = 0. __ __ __

b) $\dfrac{709}{1000}$ = 0. __ __ __

c) $\dfrac{63}{1000}$ = 0. __ __ __

9. Write the decimal in expanded form in two ways.

a) 0.678 = ____ tenths ____ hundredths ____ thousandths = ____ thousandths

b) 0.643 = ____ tenths ____ hundredths ____ thousandths = ____ thousandths

10. Write the number as a decimal.

a) 765 thousandths = _0.765_   b) 194 thousandths = _____   c) 803 thousandths = _____

d) 42 thousandths = _0.042_   e) 15 thousandths = _____   f) 75 thousandths = _____

11. Write the decimal as a fraction.

a) 0.3   b) 0.57   c) 0.654   d) 0.45   e) 0.03

f) 0.056   g) 0.002   h) 0.1   i) 0.704   j) 0.069

12. A **dime** is **one tenth** of a dollar. A **penny** is **one hundredth** of a dollar.

Express the value of each decimal in four different ways.

a) 0.64   b) 0.73

6 dimes and 4 pennies _____   _____

6 tenths and 4 hundredths _____   _____

64 pennies _____   _____

64 hundredths _____   _____

13. A **decimetre** is **one tenth** of a metre. A **centimetre** is **one hundredth** of a metre.

Express the value of each measurement in four different ways.

a) 0.28 m   b) 0.16 m

14. Keiko says 0.79 is greater than 0.9 because 79 is greater than 9. Can you explain her mistake?

15. What unit of measurement does the 5 in 0.725 m represent?

NS8-37 Decimals and Fractions Greater Than 1

The whole-number part of a decimal is the digits **to the left** of the decimal point.

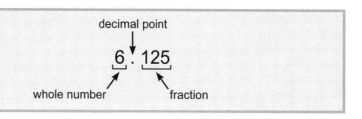

1. Underline the whole-number part of the decimal.

   a) <u>54</u>.432   b) 876.4   c) 25.23   d) 8.034   e) 0.65   f) 90.005

2. Write the decimal in expanded form.

   a) 7.5 = _____ ones + _____ tenths

   b) 4.32 = _____ ones + _____ tenths + _____ hundredths

   c) 56.426 = __5__ tens + __6__ ones + __4__ tenths + _____ hundredths + _____ thousandths

   d) 67.04 = _____ tens + _____ ones + _____ tenths + _____ hundredths

   e) 7.048 = _____ ones + _____ tenths + _____ hundredths + _____ thousandths

3. Write the number as a decimal.

   a) 4 tens + 3 ones + 8 tenths + 5 hundredths + 2 thousandths = __ __ . __ __ __

   b) 8 ones + 3 tenths + 2 hundredths + 7 thousandths = _____

   c) 3 tens + 7 ones + 6 tenths + 9 hundredths = _____

   d) 8 hundreds + 8 tens + 8 ones + 8 tenths + 8 hundredths = _____

4. Write the decimal in the place value chart.

	thousands	hundreds	tens	ones	●	tenths	hundredths	thousandths
a) 17.34			1	7	●	3	4	
b) 8.987					●			
c) 270.93					●			
d) 8 900.5					●			
e) 78.003					●			

5. Write the whole number and the hundredths or thousandths in each decimal.

   a) 6.98   _____*six*_____ and _____*ninety-eight*_____ hundredths

   b) 1.47   _____ and _____ hundredths

   c) 32.005 _____ and _____ thousandths

   d) 8.051 _____ and _____ thousandths

   e) 80.105 _____ and _____ thousandths

6. Fill in the blanks to show how to read the decimal.

    a) 6.8 is read as "_____*six and eight tenths*_____"

    b) 6.02 is read as "_____ and two _____"

    c) 27.89 is read as "twenty-seven and eighty-nine _____"

    d) 19.285 is read as "_____ and two hundred eighty-five _____"

A decimal can be written as a mixed number: $3.75 = 3\dfrac{75}{100}$

---

7. Write the number represented on the grids in three ways.

    a)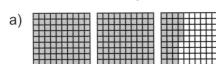

    __2__ ones __35__ hundredths   __2__ . __ __   __2__ $\dfrac{}{100}$

    b)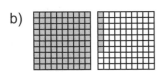

    ____ one ____ hundredths   __ . __ __   ____ $\dfrac{}{100}$

    c)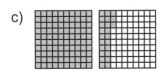

    ____ one ____ hundredths   __ . __ __   ____ $\dfrac{}{100}$

    d)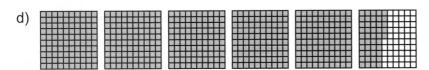

    ____ ones ____ hundredths   __ . __ __   ____ $\dfrac{}{100}$

8. Write a mixed number for the decimal.

    a) 3.51   b) 1.67   c) 8.2   d) 9.163

    e) 31.35   f) 23.956   g) 1.9   h) 24.305

9. Write a decimal for the mixed number.

    a) $2\dfrac{17}{100}$ b) $1\dfrac{67}{100}$ c) $76\dfrac{7}{10}$ d) $5\dfrac{375}{1000}$ e) $3\dfrac{9}{100}$ f) $29\dfrac{5}{1000}$

10. Which is larger, 12.056 or $12\dfrac{52}{100}$? Explain.

This number line is divided into tenths. The number represented by point **A** is $2\frac{3}{10}$ or 2.3.

1. Write a fraction or a mixed number for each point.

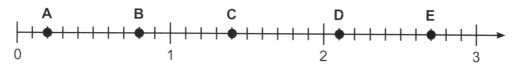

A _____   B _____   C _____   D _____   E _____

2. a) Write a decimal for each mark on the number line.

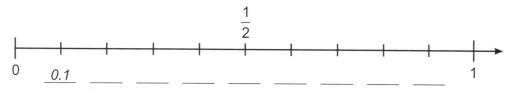

   b) Which decimal is equal to one half? $\frac{1}{2} =$ _____

3. Use the number line in Question 2 to say whether the decimal is closest to 0, $\frac{1}{2}$, or 1.

   a) 0.2 is closest to ____   b) 0.8 is closest to ____   c) 0.7 is closest to ____

   d) 0.9 is closest to ____   e) 0.3 is closest to ____   f) 0.1 is closest to ____

4. a) Mark each point with a dot and label the point with the correct letter.

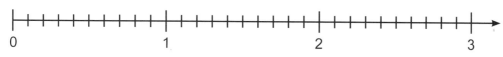

   A 1.4   **B** 2.8   **C** 0.8   **D** $\frac{12}{10}$ **E** $2\frac{1}{10}$ **F** five tenths   **G** one and nine tenths

   b) Use the number line to order the points from least to greatest.

   ___F___, ____, ____, ____, ____, ____, ____

5. a) This number line is divided into hundredths. Mark 0.50 on the number line. In your notebook, explain how you decided where to mark this point.

0.10

0   1

b) Mark and label these points on the number line above. In your notebook, explain the strategy you used to place each number on the line.

A 0.62   **B** $\frac{34}{100}$ **C** 0.04   **D** $\frac{51}{100}$

c) Use the number line to order the points from least to greatest. ____, ____, ____, ____

6. Use the number lines to compare the pairs of numbers below.
Write < (less than) or > (greater than) between each pair of numbers.

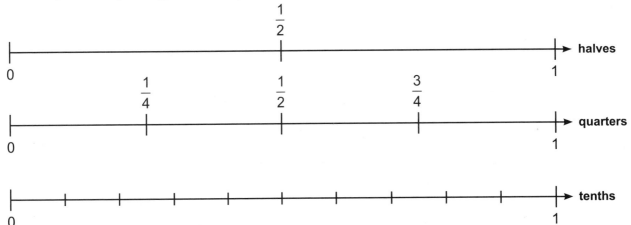

a) 0.8 ☐ $\frac{3}{4}$ b) 0.6 ☐ $\frac{7}{10}$ c) 0.7 ☐ $\frac{1}{2}$ d) 0.3 ☐ $\frac{1}{4}$

e) 0.6 ☐ $\frac{1}{2}$ f) 0.23 ☐ $\frac{1}{4}$ g) 0.08 ☐ $\frac{1}{2}$ h) $\frac{3}{4}$ ☐ 0.65

7. a) Circle the numbers that are placed on the line incorrectly. Draw the correct point(s).

0.2   0.06 $\frac{12}{10}$ $1\frac{7}{10}$ 2.4   2.8

0   1   2   3

b) Write a number between each pair of numbers.

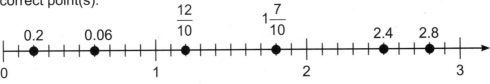

i) 0.2, _____, $\frac{12}{10}$ ii) $\frac{12}{10}$, _____, $1\frac{7}{10}$ iii) $1\frac{7}{10}$, _____, 2.5   iv) 2.5, _____, 2.8

1. Order the fractions from least to greatest. Use a common denominator.

a) $\dfrac{50}{100}$ $\dfrac{4}{10} = \dfrac{}{100}$ $\dfrac{6}{10} = \dfrac{}{100}$

b) $\dfrac{30}{100}$ $\dfrac{2}{10} =$ $\dfrac{9}{10} =$

_____ , _____ , _____   _____ , _____ , _____

2. Write the decimal as a fraction with denominator 100 by first adding a zero to the decimal.

a) $0.7 = \underline{\ 0.70\ } = \dfrac{70}{100}$

b) $0.9 = \underline{\hspace{1cm}} = \dfrac{}{100}$

c) $0.1 = \underline{\hspace{1cm}} = \dfrac{}{100}$

3. Add a zero to change decimal tenths to hundredths. Then circle the greatest decimal.

a) 0.40   0.35   0.43

b) 0.74   0.6   0.5

c) 3.6   3.55   3.7

4. Order the fractions from least to greatest. Use a common denominator.

a) $\dfrac{72}{1000}$ $\dfrac{64}{100} = \dfrac{}{1000}$ $\dfrac{68}{100} = \dfrac{}{1000}$

b) $\dfrac{54}{100} = \dfrac{}{1000}$ $\dfrac{504}{1000}$ $\dfrac{5}{10} = \dfrac{}{100} = \dfrac{}{1000}$

_____ , _____ , _____   _____ , _____ , _____

5. Write the decimal as a fraction with denominator 1 000 by first adding one or two zeros to the decimal.

a) $0.65 = \underline{\hspace{1cm}} = \dfrac{}{1000}$

b) $0.83 = \underline{\hspace{1cm}} = \dfrac{}{1000}$

c) $0.3 = \underline{\hspace{1cm}} = \dfrac{}{1000}$

6. Add zero(s) where necessary to make the decimals decimal thousandths. Then circle the greatest decimal thousandth.

a) 0.12   0.036   0.3

b) 0.2   0.69   0.082

c) 7.5   7.35   7.432

7. Write each decimal as an improper fraction with the denominator shown. Then order the decimals from greatest to least.

a) $4.6 = \dfrac{46}{10}$ $4.7 = \dfrac{}{10}$ $4.3 = \dfrac{}{10}$

$\underline{\ 4.7\ }$, _____ , _____

b) $2.97 = \dfrac{297}{100}$ $2.05 = \dfrac{}{100}$ $2.78 = \dfrac{}{100}$

_____ , _____ , _____

c) $1.3 = \dfrac{1300}{1000}$ $1.8 = \dfrac{}{1000}$ $1.6 = \dfrac{}{1000}$

_____ , _____ , _____

d) $7.2 = \dfrac{7200}{1000}$ $7.547 = \dfrac{}{1000}$ $7.85 = \dfrac{}{1000}$

_____ , _____ , _____

8. Write a decimal that matches each description.

a) between 0.83 and 0.89   0. _____

b) between 0.6 and 0.70   0. _____

c) between 0.385 and 0.39   0. _____

d) between 0.457 and 0.5   0. _____

9. Write the numbers in the place value chart. Then order the numbers
   from greatest to least.

   a) 0.242, 1.368, 1.70, 2.05

   b) 0.654, 0.555, 0.655, 0.554

ones	tenths	hundredths	thousandths
0	2	4	2

ones	tenths	hundredths	thousandths

_____, _____, _____, _____   _____, _____, _____, _____

10. Complete the number patterns.

   a) 7.5, 7.6, 7. __, 7.8, 7.9, 8. __, 8. __

   b) 10.5, 11.5, 12.5, _____, _____

   c) _____, 9.40, 9.35, _____, 9.25, 9.20

   d) 0.005, 0.010, 0.015, _____, 0.025, 0.030

   e) 25.6, _____, _____, 28.6, 29.6

   f) 50.63, 50.53, _____, 50.33, _____

11. Arrange the numbers in increasing order.

   a) 34.546, 34.456, 34.466

   b) 80.765, 80.756, 80.657

   _____, _____, _____   _____, _____, _____

12. Arrange the numbers in decreasing order.

   a) 75.240, 75.704, 77.740

   b) 0.004, 0.040, 0.041, 4.001

   _____, _____, _____   _____, _____, _____, _____

13. Write five decimals greater than 1.32 and less than 1.33.

14. Circle the greater number. Hint: First change all fractions and decimals to fractions
    with denominator 100 or 1 000. (Note: $4 \times 250 = 1\ 000$)

   a) $\dfrac{1}{2}$ 0.51

   b) $\dfrac{4}{5}$ 0.85

   c) $\dfrac{3}{4}$ 0.734

15. Write the numbers in order from least to greatest. Explain how you found your answer.

   a) 0.7   0.34 $\dfrac{3}{5}$

   b) 0.817 $\dfrac{77}{100}$ $\dfrac{4}{5}$

   c) $\dfrac{3}{5}$ 0.425 $\dfrac{1}{2}$

16. How does knowing that $\dfrac{1}{4} = 0.25$ help you find the decimal form of $\dfrac{3}{4}$?

17. Explain how you know 0.635 is greater than $\dfrac{1}{2}$.

NS8-40 Regrouping Decimals

A Base Ten Model for Decimal Tenths and Hundredths

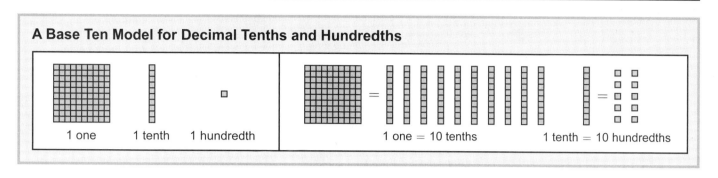

| 1 one | 1 tenth | 1 hundredth | | 1 one = 10 tenths | 1 tenth = 10 hundredths |

1. Regroup as many of the blocks as you can into bigger blocks. What decimal does each model represent?

a)

ones	tenths	hundredths

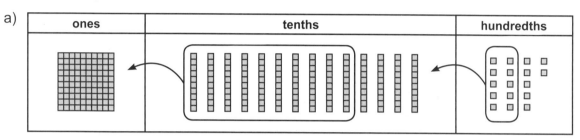

2 . __ __

b)

ones	tenths	hundredths

__ . __ __

c)

ones	tenths	hundredths

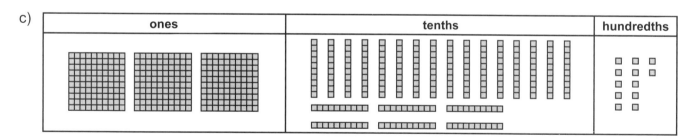

__ . __ __

2. Regroup.

a) 27 tenths = __2__ ones + _____ tenths

b) 74 hundredths = _____ tenths + _____ hundredths

c) 36 tenths = _____ ones + _____ tenths

d) 19 hundredths = _____ tenth + _____ hundredths

3. Regroup so that each place value has a single digit.

a) 3 ones + 14 tenths = __4__ ones + __4__ tenths

b) 7 tenths + 17 hundredths = _____ tenths + _____ hundredths

c) 6 hundredths + 11 thousandths = _____ hundredths + _____ thousandth

4. Exchange 1 tenth for 10 hundredths or 1 hundredth for 10 thousandths.

a) 6 tenths + 0 hundredths = __5__ tenths + __10__ hundredths

b) 8 tenths + 0 hundredths = ____ tenths + ____ hundredths

c) 9 hundredths + 0 thousandths = ____ hundredths + ____ thousandths

d) 3 tenths + 0 hundredths = ____ tenths + ____ hundredths

5. Exchange one of the larger unit for 10 of the smaller unit.

a) 3 hundredths + 6 thousandths = __2__ hundredths + __16__ thousandths

b) 6 tenths 4 hundredths = ____ tenths ____ hundredths

c) 4 ones 9 tenths = ____ ones ____ tenths

d) 8 hundredths + 1 thousandth = ____ hundredths + ____ thousandths

6. Underline the smallest place value in the decimal. Then write the decimal as an improper fraction.

a) $2.\underline{3} = \dfrac{23}{10}$ b) $9.5 =$ c) $5.6 =$ d) $3.8\underline{5} = \dfrac{}{100}$ e) $2.18 =$

f) 9.96 g) $1.63 =$ h) $1.93\underline{4} = \dfrac{}{1000}$ i) $5.735 =$ j) $3.312 =$

7. Add zeros to rewrite the whole number as decimal tenths, hundredths, and thousandths. Example: $2 = 2.0 = 2.00 = 2.000$

a) $8 =$ _____ $=$ _____ $=$ _____   b) $16 =$ _____ $=$ _____ $=$ _____

c) $240 =$ _____ $=$ _____ $=$ _____

8. Regroup the whole number as ones, tenths, hundredths, and thousandths.

a) $8 =$ _____ ones $=$ _____ tenths $=$ _____ hundredths $=$ _____ thousandths

b) $16 =$ _____ ones $=$ _____ tenths $=$ _____ hundredths $=$ _____ thousandths

9. Complete the statements.

a) $3.7 =$ _____ tenths

b) $7.2 =$ _____ tenths

c) $15.4 =$ _____ tenths

d) $78.3 =$ _____ tenths

e) $3.25 =$ _____ hundredths

f) $6.93 =$ _____ hundredths

g) $3.25 =$ _____ thousandths

h) $6.93 =$ _____ thousandths

i) $6.89 =$ _____ thousandths

j) $10.46 =$ _____ thousandths

NS8-41 Addition Strategies for Decimals

1. Write an addition statement that corresponds to the grids.

a) + =

   0. _25_ + 0. _____ = 0. _____

b) + =

   0. _____ + 0. _____ = 0. _____

2. Add by sketching a base ten model. Note: Use a hundreds block for a one and a tens block for a tenth.

a) 1.12 + 1.23

   = +

   =

b) 1.46 + 1.33

3. Use equivalent fractions to calculate the decimal sums.

a) $0.3 + 0.5 = \dfrac{3}{10} + \dfrac{}{10} = \dfrac{}{10} = 0.\underline{}$

b) $0.35 + 0.22 = \dfrac{}{100} + \dfrac{}{100} = \dfrac{}{100} = 0.\underline{}\,\underline{}$

c) $0.58 + 0.05 = \dfrac{}{100} + \dfrac{}{100} = \dfrac{}{100} = 0.\underline{}\,\underline{}$

d) $0.129 + 0.474 = \dfrac{}{1000} + \dfrac{}{1000} = \dfrac{}{1000} = 0.\underline{}\,\underline{}\,\underline{}$

4. Write the decimals as fractions with a common denominator to calculate the sums.

a) $0.27 + 0.6 = \dfrac{27}{100} + \dfrac{6}{10} = \dfrac{27}{100} + \dfrac{}{100} = \dfrac{}{100} = \underline{}\,.\,\underline{}\,\underline{}$

b) $0.57 + 0.765 = \dfrac{57}{100} + \dfrac{765}{1000} = \dfrac{}{1000} + \dfrac{765}{1000} = \dfrac{}{1000} = \underline{}\,.\,\underline{}\,\underline{}\,\underline{}$

c) $6.065 + 0.99 = \dfrac{}{1000} + \dfrac{}{100} = \dfrac{}{1000} + \dfrac{}{1000} = \dfrac{}{1000} = \underline{}\,.\,\underline{}\,\underline{}\,\underline{}$

5. Write both decimals using the smallest place value to calculate the sums.

a) 2.15 + 7.3

   = _215_ hundredths + _73_ tenths

   = _215_ hundredths + _730_ hundredths

   = _945_ hundredths

   = _9_ . _4_ _5_

b) 4.064 + 2.94

   = _____ thousandths + _____ hundredths

   = _____ thousandths + _____ thousandths

   = _____ thousandths

   = _____ . _____ _____ _____

6. Add by adding each place value.

a) $3.3 + 2.4$

$= (\underline{3}\text{ ones} + \underline{3}\text{ tenths}) + (\underline{}\text{ ones} + \underline{}\text{ tenths})$

$= (\underline{3}\text{ ones} + \underline{2}\text{ ones}) + (\underline{}\text{ tenths} + \underline{}\text{ tenths})$

$= \underline{}\text{ ones} + \underline{}\text{ tenths} = \underline{} \cdot \underline{}$

b) $5.6 + 1.3$

$= (\underline{}\text{ ones} + \underline{}\text{ tenths}) + (\underline{}\text{ ones} + \underline{}\text{ tenths})$

$= (\underline{}\text{ ones} + \underline{}\text{ ones}) + (\underline{}\text{ tenths} + \underline{}\text{ tenths})$

$= \underline{}\text{ ones} + \underline{}\text{ tenths} = \underline{} \cdot \underline{}$

7. Add by adding each place value in the chart.

a)

tens	ones	tenths	hundredths
3	2	1	
	6	7	8
		8	8

b)

ones	tenths	hundredths	thousandths
4	0	5	3
2	7	2	

8. Add by adding each place value. Regroup wherever necessary. Example:

ones	tenths
1	6
4	7
5	13

a)

ones	tenths	hundredths
	6	3
9	1	8

b)

ones	tenths	hundredths	thousandths
		5	3
	4	2	9

$\underline{13}$ tenths =

$\underline{1}$ one + $\underline{3}$ tenths,

so the sum is

6	3

$\underline{}$ hundredths =

$\underline{}$ tenths + $\underline{}$ hundredths,

so the sum is

$\underline{}$ thousandths =

$\underline{}$ hundredths + $\underline{}$ thousandths,

so the sum is

9. Use the place value chart to add the decimals. Then regroup.

a) $0.823 + 3.146 + 0.4$

tens	ones	tenths	hundredths	thousandths

Regroup:

b) $0.43 + 45.452 + 2.4$

tens	ones	tenths	hundredths	thousandths

Regroup:

BONUS ▶ Regroup twice to add: $5.412 + 11.035 + 2.357$

1. Add the decimals.

   a) 0.42 + 0.34   b) 5.71 + 4.26

   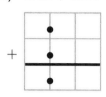   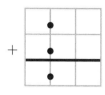

Adding Decimals

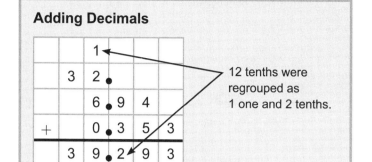

12 tenths were regrouped as 1 one and 2 tenths.

   c) 0.516 + 0.473   d) 9.317 + 0.162

   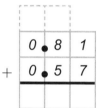   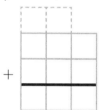

2. Add the decimals. Line up the decimal points. Put a decimal point in place ready for the answer.

   a) 0.81 + 0.57   b) 2.56 + 7.26   c) 0.583 + 1.254   d) 4.444 + 5.078

   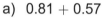   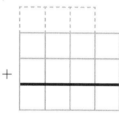   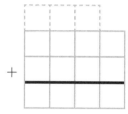

   e) 0.43 + 0.08 + 0.42   f) 5.8 + 1.42 + 0.6   g) 1.278 + 0.56 + 6.304   h) 0.9 + 0.99 + 0.999

   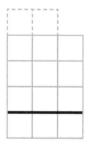   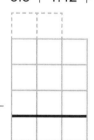   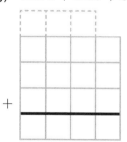   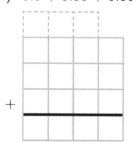

3. Add the decimals on grid paper.

   a) 4.32 + 2.88   b) 3.64 + 5.48   c) 9.493 + 3.17   d) 0.87 + 0.027

   e) 7.096 + 2.169 + 5.38   f) 0.077 + 2.84 + 0.699   g) 47.5 + 7.007 + 16.87

4. a) The mass of a nickel is 3.95 g and the mass of a penny is 2.35 g. What is the total mass of 2 nickels and 3 pennies?

   b) The mass of a dime is 1.75 g, and the mass of a quarter is 4.4 g. What is heavier, 10 dimes or 4 quarters?

5. Bill adds 43.4 + 5.65 on grid paper. He gets 99.9. Is this the right answer? If Bill's answer is incorrect, explain his mistake.

Subtracting Decimals

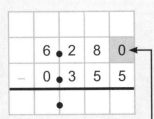

Add zeros to make each decimal
end at the same place value.

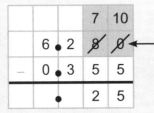

If the top digit in a column is **less than the digit below** it,
take 1 from the column to the left and add 10 to the top digit.

6. Subtract the decimals.

a) 0.43 – 0.21

b) 0.86 – 0.24

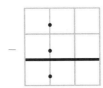

c) 3.57 – 2.2

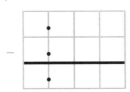

d) 6.39 – 0.35

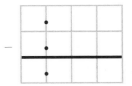

7. Subtract the decimals. Remember to line up the decimal points.

a) 0.71 – 0.58

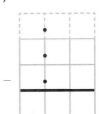

b) 5.62 – 3.56

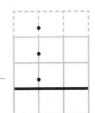

c) 7.156 – 4.25

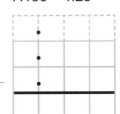

d) 2.563 – 0.271

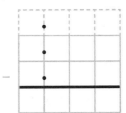

e) 4.5 – 2.67

f) 31.1 – 23.2

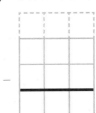

g) 7.455 – 6.78

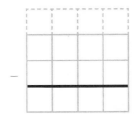

h) 5.207 – 1.239

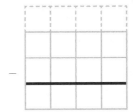

8. Subtract the decimals on grid paper.

a) 0.87 – 0.024

b) 9.435 – 3.12

c) 5.83 – 3.68

d) 4.58 – 2.72

9. What is the difference in the thickness of these coins?

a) a penny (1.45 mm) and a dime (1.22 mm)

b) a dollar (1.95 mm) and a quarter (1.58 mm)

1. Underline the digit given. Would you round **up** or **down** to round off to that digit?

a) thousands

| 2 | 4 | 3 | 2 | 5 |

round up   (round down)

b) ten thousands

| 8 | 7 | 7 | 2 | 3 |

round up   round down

c) hundreds

| 9 | 0 | 5 | 1 | 3 |

round up   round down

d) tens

| 2 | 4 | 5 | 3 | 9 | 3 |

round up   round down

e) thousands

| 1 | 9 | 6 | 7 | 9 | 2 |

round up   round down

f) thousands

| 3 | 0 | 0 | 7 | 2 | 7 |

round up   round down

To **round up**, add 1 to the digit.

To **round down**, keep the digit the same.

Example:

| 4 | 5 | 7 | 3 | 4 | 5 |
| | | 3 | | | |

round up
(round down)

The digits to the right of the rounded digit become zeros.

The digits to the left remain the same.

| 4 | 5 | 7 | 3 | 4 | 5 |
| 4 | 5 | 7 | 3 | 0 | 0 |

round up
(round down)

---

2. Round each number to the digit given. (Underline the given digit first.)

a) thousands

| 7 | 0 | 0 | 1 | 9 | 3 |
| | | | | | |

b) ten thousands

| 7 | 8 | 6 | 9 | 5 | 1 |
| | | | | | |

c) ten thousands

| 2 | 5 | 3 | 7 | 1 |
| | | | | |

d) hundred thousands

| 2 | 1 | 6 | 8 | 3 | 9 | 7 |
| | | | | | | |

e) ten thousands

| 3 | 8 | 6 | 6 | 2 | 0 | 7 |
| | | | | | | |

f) hundred thousands

| 6 | 8 | 7 | 8 | 9 | 8 | 2 |
| | | | | | | |

Sometimes in rounding, you have to regroup. Example: Round 37 952 to the nearest hundred.

| 3 | 7 | 9 | 5 | 2 |
| | | 10 | | |

900 rounds to 1 000.

| 3 | 7 | 9 | 5 | 2 |
| | | 8 | 0 | |

Regroup the 10 hundreds as 1 (thousand) and add it to the 7 (thousand).

| 3 | 7 | 9 | 5 | 2 |
| 3 | 8 | 0 | 0 | 0 |

Complete the rounding.

---

3. Round each number to the digit given (regrouping if necessary).

a) 395 721
   ten thousands

b) 987 832
   thousands

c) 39 823
   ten thousands

d) 427 296
   tens

e) 20 175
   hundreds

f) 9 729 738
   hundred thousands

g) 97 231
   ten thousands

h) 3 957 793
   hundred thousands

NS8-44 Rounding Decimals

1. What is the length of each line, to the nearest centimetre?

   a) _____ cm, to the nearest centimetre

   b) 7.7 cm is approximately _____ cm.

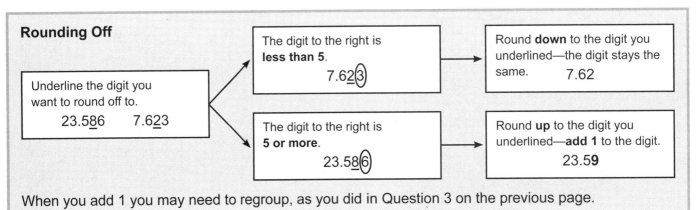

2. a) Is 3.76 closer to 3.7 or 3.8? Closer to _____

   So, 3.76 is approximately equal to _____.

   b) Is 4.256 closer to 4.25 or 4.26? Closer to _____

   So, 4.256 is approximately equal to _____.

Rounding Off

Underline the digit you want to round off to.
23.5<u>8</u>6   7.6<u>2</u>3

The digit to the right is **less than 5**.
7.6<u>2</u>③

Round **down** to the digit you underlined—the digit stays the same.   7.62

The digit to the right is **5 or more**.
23.5<u>8</u>⑥

Round **up** to the digit you underlined—**add 1** to the digit.
23.59

When you add 1 you may need to regroup, as you did in Question 3 on the previous page.

3. Follow the steps above to round the decimals. Hint: Do not forget to write the decimal point in your answer.

   a) tenths

2	.	3	7	6

   b) hundredths

3	.	1	4	3

   c) tenths

4	2	.	4	9	5

   d) ones

9	7	.	8	2

   e) tens

5	3	.	0	9

   f) ones

1	.	2

   g) tenths

3	.	4	1

   h) hundredths

4	5	.	7	3	1

   i) thousandths

3	.	2	8	0	6

   j) tenths

9	2	.	1	6	7

   k) hundredths

3	6	.	2	9	3

   l) ones

1	.	5	4	2

m) ones

7	• 7	2

n) tens

4	9	• 0	5

o) hundredths

5	• 3	9	9

The symbol ≈ means "is approximately equal to."

4. Round off the decimal to the nearest thousandth, hundredth, and tenth.

a) 0.1234 ≈ 0. __ __ __ ≈ 0. __ __ ≈ 0. __   b) 4.5678 ≈ 4. __ __ __ ≈ 4. __ __ ≈ 4. __

c) 0.6327 ≈ 0. __ __ __ ≈ 0. __ __ ≈ 0. __   d) 5.1764 ≈ 5. __ __ __ ≈ 5. __ __ ≈ 5. __

5. Round off the measurement to 1 decimal place.

a) 36.234 kg ≈ _____ kg   b) 0.593 km ≈ _____ km   c) 359.67 L ≈ _____ L

d) 300.06 m ≈ _____ m   e) 0.068 cm ≈ _____ cm   f) 931.58 g ≈ _____ g

g) 7.009 mm ≈ _____ mm   h) 5.96 mg ≈ _____ mg   i) 57.98 g ≈ _____ g

6. Round the number to either 0 or 1, whichever is closer. Examples: 0.9 ≈ 1 and 0.3 ≈ 0.

a) 0.8 ≈ ____   b) 0.2 ≈ ____   c) 0.5 ≈ ____   d) 0.97 ≈ ____   e) 0.43 ≈ ____   f) 0.55 ≈ ____

7. Calculate using a calculator. Then round off to the nearest hundredth.

a) 1 ÷ 3 ≈ 0. __ __   b) 2 ÷ 3 ≈ 0. __ __   c) 22 ÷ 7 ≈ 3. __ __   d) 45 ÷ 13 ≈ 3. __ __

8. Estimate the value by rounding off to the nearest whole number.

a) 32.8 + 4.16 ≈ _33_ + _4_   b) 25.3 − 10.657 ≈ ____ − ____   c) 2.7 + 5.4 ≈ ____ + ____

    = _37_   = ____   = ____

d) 34.926 + 7.25 ≈ ____ + ____   e) 0.64 + 0.213 ≈ ____ + ____   f) 4.39 × 2.567 ≈ ____ × ____

    = ____   = ____   = ____

g) 32.82 ÷ 2.57 ≈ ____ ÷ ____   h) 73.54 − 20.67 ≈ ____ − ____   i) 39.86 ÷ 4.974 ≈ ____ ÷ ____

    = ____   = ____   = ____

9. a) Estimate by rounding both numbers to the nearest whole number.
   Use your estimate to predict whether the answer given is reasonable.

   i)   32.7 + 4.16 = 73.8   ii)   0.7 × 8.3 = 58.1   iii) 9.2 × 10.3 = 947.6

   iv) 97.2 ÷ 0.9 = 0.8   v)   88.2 ÷ 9.8 = 9   vi) 54.3 ÷ 5.6 = 35.7

   b) Use a calculator to calculate the answers in a). Were your predictions correct?

10. The decimal hundredths that can be rounded off to 5.3 are from 5.25 to 5.34.
    Which decimal hundredths can be rounded off to 9.4? Explain.

NS8-45 Estimating Decimal Sums and Differences

1. a) Estimate the sum or difference using the whole number parts of the decimals.

    Example: For **32**.456 + **6**.71 + **0**.253, estimate **32** + **6** + **0** = 38.
    So the sum is close to 38.

    i) $2.745 + 3.75 + 20.5 \approx$ ____ + ____ + ____   ii) $13.346 - 4.97 \approx$ ____ − ____

    $=$ ____ $=$ ____

    iii) $12.77 + 10.703 + 0.27 \approx$ ____ + ____ + ____   iv) $542.403 - 140.524 \approx$ ____ − ____

    $=$ ____ $=$ ____

    b) Now calculate the sums and differences. Use your estimates to check
       your calculations.

2. a) Estimate by rounding to the nearest tenth.

    Example: For 2.877 + 3.62, you could estimate 2.9 + 3.6.
    So the sum is approximately 6.5.

    i) $0.769 - 0.35 \approx$ ____ − ____   ii) $25.08 + 0.004 + 4.53 \approx$ ____ + ____ + ____

    $=$ ____ $=$ ____

    iii) $3.25 + 2.67 + 0.48 \approx$ ____ + ____ + ____   iv) $5.467 - 2.78 \approx$ ____ − ____

    $=$ ____ $=$ ____

    b) Calculate the sums and differences in part a) using a calculator.
       Use your estimates to check your calculations.

For the problems below, estimate the solution before calculating.

3. Jade had $623.75 and spent $326.87. Would you round to the nearest tenth or the
   nearest whole number to estimate how much money she has left? Explain your choice.

4. Proxima Centauri (the nearest star to the Sun) is 4.22 light years from the Sun.
   Sirius A (the brightest star in the sky) is 8.61 light years from the Sun. How much
   farther from the Sun is Sirius A than Proxima Centauri?

5. The average temperature in Khartoum, Sudan, during the day is 37.67°C and,
   in Edmonton, Alberta, it is 8.5°C. How many degrees warmer is Khartoum than
   Edmonton, on average?

6. Each wing of a Monarch butterfly is 4.83 cm wide. Its body is 0.85 cm wide.
   How wide is the butterfly?

7. a) A slice of cheese pizza has 4.838 g of saturated fat, 2.802 g of monounsaturated
      fat, and 1.765 g of polyunsaturated fat. What is the total amount of fat?

   b) A slice of pepperoni pizza has 4.995 g of saturated fat, 3.857 g of monounsatu-
      rated fat, and 1.953 g of polyunsaturated fat. What is the total amount of fat?

   c) How much less fat does the cheese slice have than the pepperoni slice?

NS8-46 Multiplying Decimals by 10

Multiplying Decimals by 10

 = 1.0 | = 0.1 ⟶   10 × | =

If a hundreds block represents 1 whole (1.0),
then a tens block represents 1 tenth (0.1).

10 × 0.1 = 1.0
10 tenths make 1 whole.

1. Multiply the number of tens blocks by 10. Draw the number of hundreds blocks you
   would have, then complete the multiplication sentence.

   a) 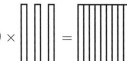10 × ||| =

   10 × 0.3 = ___3___

   b) 10 × || =

   10 × 0.2 = _____

   c) 10 × |||||| =

   10 × 0.6 = _____

2. To multiply by 10, shift the decimal one place to the right.

   a) 10 × 0.7 = ___7___   b) 10 × 0.8 = _____   c) 10 × 1.5 = _____   d) 10 × 0.9 = _____

   e) 10 × 3.4 = _____   f) 4.5 × 10 = _____   g) 15.6 × 10 = _____   h) 12.3 × 10 = _____

   i) 10 × 3.07 = ___30.7___   j) 10 × 3.78 = _____   k) 10 × 87.4 = _____   l) 62.35 × 10 = _____

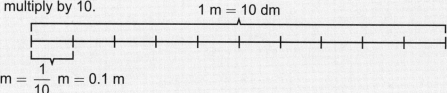

To change metres to decimetres, multiply by 10.   1 m = 10 dm

$1 \text{ dm} = \dfrac{1}{10} \text{ m} = 0.1 \text{ m}$

3. Find the answers.

   a) 0.3 m = _____ dm   b) 0.7 m = _____ dm   c) 6.5 m = _____ dm

4. 10 × 6 can be written as a sum: 6 + 6 + 6 + 6 + 6 + 6 + 6 + 6 + 6 + 6.

   Write 10 × 0.6 as a sum and skip count by 0.6 to find the answer.

5. A dime is a tenth of a dollar (10¢ = $0.10). Draw a picture or use money to show that
   10 × $0.70 = $7.00.

Number Sense 8-46

= 1.0   □ = 0.01 ───────────────▶ 100 × □ =

If a hundreds block represents 1 whole (1.0),
then a ones block represents 1 hundredth (0.01).

100 × 0.01 = 1.0
100 hundredths make 1 whole.

1. Write a multiplication sentence for each picture.

a)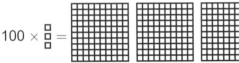

100 × □ =

_____100 × 0.03_____ = _____

b)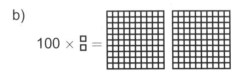

100 × □ =

_____ = _____

The picture shows why the decimal shifts two places to the right when you multiply by 100.

100 ×  = 100 × | + 100 × □ = 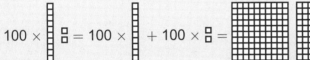   +

100 × 0.12   =   100 × 0.1 (= 10)   +   100 × 0.02 (= 2) = 12

2. To multiply by 100, shift the decimal two places to the right.

a) 100 × 0.6 = _____60_____
b) 4.5 × 100 = _____
c) 100 × 8.2 = _____

d) 100 × 7.3 = _____
e) 3.1 × 100 = _____
f) 100 × 7.0 = _____

g) 0.24 × 100 = _____
h) 100 × 0.86 = _____
i) 0.03 × 100 = _____

3. Multiply.

a) 100 × 0.02 = _____
b) 100 × 0.03 = _____
c) 0.73 × 100 = _____
d) 0.48 × 100 = _____

e) 100 × 3.72 = _____
f) 4.08 × 100 = _____
g) 100 × 0.34 = _____
h) 100 × 0.8 = _____

i) 2.4 × 100 = _____
j) 100 × 0.05 = _____
k) 1.24 × 100 = _____
l) 3.5 × 100 = _____

4. a) What do 1 000 thousandths add up to? _____   b) What is 1 000 × 0.001? _____

5. Look at your answer to Question 4 b).

How many places right does the decimal shift when you multiply by 1 000? _____

6. Multiply the numbers by shifting the decimal.

a) 1 000 × 0.83 = _____
b) 0.836 × 1 000 = _____
c) 1 000 × 7.436 = _____

d) 0.36 × 1 000 = _____
e) 1 000 × 3.45 = _____
f) 2.7 × 1 000 = _____

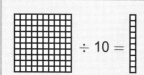

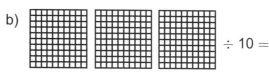

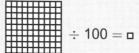

÷ 10 =	÷ 10 = ▫	÷ 100 = ▫
Divide 1 whole into 10 equal parts; each part is 1 tenth:	Divide 1 tenth into 10 equal parts; each part is 1 hundredth:	Divide 1 whole into 100 equal parts; each part is 1 hundredth:
$1.0 \div 10 = 0.1$	$0.1 \div 10 = 0.01$	$1.0 \div 100 = 0.01$

1. Complete each picture and write a division statement for it.

   a) 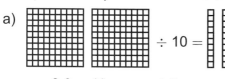 ÷ 10 =

   $$\underline{\quad 2.0 \div 10 \quad} = \underline{\; 0.2 \;}$$

   b) 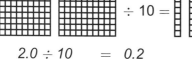 ÷ 10 =

   $$\underline{\qquad\qquad} = \underline{\qquad}$$

   c) 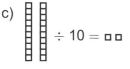 ÷ 10 = ▫ ▫

   $$\underline{\quad 0.2 \div 10 \quad} = \underline{\qquad}$$

   d)  ÷ 10 =

   $$\underline{\qquad\qquad} = \underline{\qquad}$$

   e) 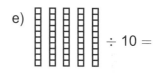 ÷ 10 =

   $$\underline{\qquad\qquad} = \underline{\qquad}$$

   f) 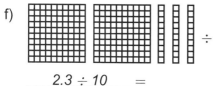 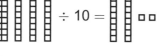 ÷ 10 = ▫ ▫ ▫

   $$\underline{\quad 2.3 \div 10 \quad} = \underline{\qquad}$$

   g) 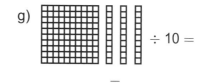 ÷ 10 =

   $$\underline{\qquad\qquad} = \underline{\qquad}$$

2. Division undoes multiplication. How do you undo multiplying by 10 or 100?

   a) To multiply by 10, I move the decimal point _____ place(s) to the _____,

   so to divide by 10, I move the decimal point _____ place(s) to the _____.

   b) To multiply by 100, I move the decimal point _____ place(s) to the _____,

   so to divide by 100, I move the decimal point _____ place(s) to the _____.

3. Shift the decimal one or two places to the left by drawing an arrow, then write the answer in the blank. Hint: If there is no decimal, add one to the right of the number first.

   a) $0.5 \div 10 =$ _____   b) $0.8 \div 10 =$ _____   c) $0.7 \div 10 =$ _____   d) $4.1 \div 10 =$ _____

   e) $36 \div 10 =$ _____   f) $71 \div 10 =$ _____   g) $0.6 \div 10 =$ _____   h) $23.4 \div 10 =$ _____

   i) $3.0 \div 100 =$ _____   j) $8.1 \div 100 =$ _____   k) $0.8 \div 100 =$ _____   l) $51.3 \div 100 =$ _____

4. Explain why $1.00 \div 100 = 0.01$, using a dollar coin as a whole.

5. A wall 3.5 m wide is painted with 100 stripes of equal width. How wide is each stripe?

6. $6 \times 3 = 18$ and $18 \div 6 = 3$ are in the same fact family. Write a division statement in the same fact family as $10 \times 0.1 = 1.0$.

1. a) To multiply by 10, I move the decimal ___1___ place(s) to the _____right_____.

    b) To multiply by 1 000, I move the decimal _____ place(s) to the _____.

    c) To divide by 100, I move the decimal _____ place(s) to the _____.

    d) To divide by 10, I move the decimal _____ place(s) to the _____.

    e) To _____ by 1 000, I move the decimal _____ places to the left.

    f) To _____ by 10, I move the decimal _____ place to the left.

    g) To _____ by 100, I move the decimal _____ places to the right.

    h) To divide by 10 000 000, I move the decimal _____ places to the _____.

    i) To multiply by 100 000, I move the decimal _____ places to the _____.

2. Fill in the blanks. Next, draw arrows to show how you would shift the decimal. Then write your final answer in the grid.

    a) 6.345×100

    I move the decimal ___2___ places _____right_____.

    | | 6. | 3 | 4 | 5 | | rough work
    |---|---|---|---|---|---|

    | | 6 | 3 | 4. | 5 | | final answer
    |---|---|---|---|---|---|

    b) $7.8 \div 1\ 000$

    I move the decimal ___3___ places _____left_____.

    | | | | 7. | 8 | | rough work
    |---|---|---|---|---|---|

    | | .0 | 0 | 7 | 8 | | final answer
    |---|---|---|---|---|---|

    c) $238.567 \times 1\ 000$

    I move the decimal _____ places _____.

    | | 2 | 3 | 8. | 5 | 6 | 7 | | rough work
    |---|---|---|---|---|---|---|---|

    | | | | | | | | | final answer
    |---|---|---|---|---|---|---|---|

    d) $200.75 \div 100$

    I move the decimal _____ places _____.

    | | 2 | 0 | 0. | 7 | 5 | | rough work
    |---|---|---|---|---|---|---|

    | | | | | | | | final answer
    |---|---|---|---|---|---|

    e) $0.401 \times 100\ 000$

    I move the decimal _____ places _____.

    | | | | 0. | 4 | 0 | 1 | | rough work
    |---|---|---|---|---|---|---|

    | | | | | | | | | final answer
    |---|---|---|---|---|---|---|

    f) $23.683 \div 10\ 000$

    I move the decimal _____ places _____.

    | | | 2 | 3. | 6 | 8 | 3 | | rough work
    |---|---|---|---|---|---|---|

    | | | | | | | | | final answer
    |---|---|---|---|---|---|---|

3. Copy the numbers onto grid paper. Show how you would shift the decimal in each case.

    a) $2.78 \times 1\ 000$ b) 48.002×100 c) 0.054×10 d) $60.07 \times 1\ 000$ e) $0.08 \times 10\ 000$

    f) $0.845 \div 10$ g) $180.67 \div 100$ h) $89.07 \div 1\ 000$ i) $19.34 \div 10\ 000$ j) $0.06 \div 1\ 000$

The picture shows how to multiply a decimal by a whole number.

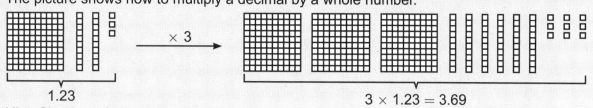

$\xrightarrow{\times 3}$

1.23

$3 \times 1.23 = 3.69$

Hint: Simply multiply each digit separately.

1. Multiply mentally.

   a) $3 \times 1.23 =$ _____   b) $2 \times 3.4 =$ _____   c) $6 \times 2.01 =$ _____   d) $3 \times 4.2 =$ _____

   e) $4 \times 1.21 =$ _____   f) $5 \times 4.1 =$ _____   g) $2 \times 7.13 =$ _____   h) $7 \times 8.01 =$ _____

2. Multiply by exchanging tenths for ones.

   a) $7 \times 1.4 =$ __7__ ones + __28__ tenths = __9__ ones + __8__ tenths = __9.8__

   b) $3 \times 4.6 =$ _____ ones + _____ tenths = _____ ones + _____ tenths = _____

   c) $4 \times 5.7 =$ _____ ones + _____ tenths = _____ ones + _____ tenths = _____

   d) $3 \times 6.9 =$ _____

3. Multiply by exchanging tenths for ones or hundredths for tenths.

   a) $3 \times 3.61 =$ __9__ ones + __18__ tenths + __3__ hundredths

   = _____ ones + _____ tenths + _____ hundredths = _____

   b) $4 \times 2.15 =$ _____ ones + _____ tenths + _____ hundredths

   = _____ ones + _____ tenths + _____ hundredths = _____

4. Multiply. In some questions you will have to regroup twice.

   a) 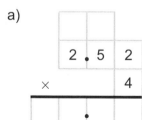   b) 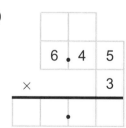   c) 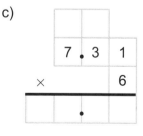   d)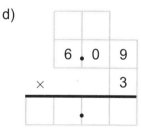

5. Find the products.

   a) 6×4.6 b) 7×0.5 c) 8×5.2 d) 2×2.37 e) 3×35.6 f) 6×4.7

   g) 5×2.8 h) 6×9.62 i) 4×5.96 j) 9×6.27 k) 4×46.82 l) 5×38.75

6. You can rewrite the product 70×3.6 as $10 \times 7 \times 3.6$. Use this method to find these products.

   a) 50×3.1 b) 70×0.6 c) 40×9.67 d) 300×7.4 e) 600×0.3

1. To multiply a number by 10, move the decimal point ___1___ place to the _____*right*_____.

To multiply a number by 100, move the decimal point _____ places to the _____.

To multiply a number by 1 000, move the decimal point _____ places to the _____.

2. a) Multiply by 10, 100, or 1 000. Use the rules in Question 1.

$10 \times 0.1 =$ ___1.0___ $100 \times 0.1 =$ _____ $1\,000 \times 0.1 =$ _____

b) Rule: To multiply a number by 0.1, move the decimal point _____ place to the _____.

c) Use your rule from part b) to find these products.

    i) $0.1 \times 0.1 =$ _____   ii) $0.01 \times 0.1 =$ _____   iii) $0.001 \times 0.1 =$ _____

    iv) $5 \times 0.1 =$ _____   v) $0.2 \times 0.1 =$ _____   vi) $0.07 \times 0.1 =$ _____

3. a) Multiply by moving the decimal point. Use the rules in Question 1.

$10 \times 0.01 =$ _____ $100 \times 0.01 =$ _____ $1\,000 \times 0.01 =$ _____

b) Rule: To multiply a number by 0.01, move the decimal point _____ places to the _____.

c) Predict: To multiply a number by 0.001, move the decimal point _____ places to the _____.

d) Use your rule from part b) and your prediction from part c) to determine these products. Use a calculator to check your answers.

    i) $0.1 \times 0.01 =$ _____   ii) $0.01 \times 0.01 =$ _____   iii) $0.3 \times 0.001 =$ _____

    iv) $2.5 \times 0.01 =$ _____   v) $13.9 \times 0.001 =$ _____   vi) $810.6 \times 0.001 =$ _____

4. Multiply.

    a) 0.05×0.01 b) 0.32×0.001 c) 50×0.01 d) 0.001×23.7

    e) 0.1×72.35 f) 0.01×853.2 g) $90\,014 \times 0.001$ **BONUS ▶** $17.03 \times 0.000\,01$

5. When you multiply a number n by a number less than 1, the product is _____ than n.

6. Convert the measurements. Use 1 mm = 0.1 cm, 1 cm = 0.01 m, 1 m = 0.001 km.

    a) 36 mm = (36 × ___0.1___) cm   b) 470 cm = (470 × _____) m   c) 85 m = (85 × _____) km

       = _____ cm   = _____ m   = _____ km

7. a) Rewrite each decimal as a product with one factor that is 0.1, 0.01, or 0.001.

    i) $0.2 = 2 \times$ ___0.1___   ii) $0.7 = 7 \times$ _____   iii) $0.03 =$ _____ $\times 0.01$ iv) $0.005 = 5 \times$ _____

b) Rewrite the decimal as you did in part a). Then multiply.

    i) $16 \times 0.2 = 16 \times 2 \times 0.1$ ii) $75 \times 0.04 = 75 \times$ _____ $\times 0.01$ iii) $18 \times 0.005 = 18 \times$ _____ $\times 0.001$

       = _____ $\times 0.1$ = _____ $\times 0.01$ = _____ $\times 0.001$

       = _____   = _____   = _____

NS8-52 Multiplying Decimals by Decimals

> A place value after the decimal point is called a **decimal place**.

1. How many decimal places does each number have?

   a) 201.4 has _____   b) 72.03 has _____   c) 214.126 has _____   d) 80.023 007 has _____

2. a) Change each decimal to a fraction with denominator 10, 100, or 1 000.

   i) $0.2 =$ _____   ii) $0.02 =$ _____   iii) $0.12 =$ _____   iv) $5.1 =$ _____   v) $8.247 =$ _____

   b) Compare the number of zeros in the denominator of the fraction to the number of decimal places in the decimal. What do you notice?

3. Shade squares to show each amount. Find the product.

   a)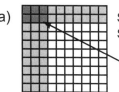
   Shade 2 rows to show 2 tenths.
   Shade 3 columns to show 3 tenths.

   $\dfrac{6}{100}$

   $\dfrac{2}{10}$ of $\dfrac{3}{10}$ is $\dfrac{6}{100}$ so $\dfrac{2}{10} \times \dfrac{3}{10} = \dfrac{6}{100}$

   b)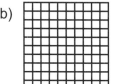

   $\dfrac{2}{10} \times \dfrac{5}{10} =$

   c)

   $\dfrac{7}{10} \times \dfrac{4}{10} =$

4. Write a multiplication sentence for each figure.

   a)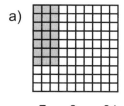

   $\dfrac{7}{10} \times \dfrac{3}{10} = \dfrac{21}{100}$

   b)

   _____

   c)

   _____

   d)

   _____

5. Multiply the fractions (see p. 39).

   a) $\dfrac{3}{100} \times \dfrac{5}{10}$ b) $\dfrac{3}{10} \times \dfrac{5}{10}$ c) $\dfrac{3}{100} \times \dfrac{5}{100}$ d) $\dfrac{3}{1000} \times \dfrac{5}{10}$

6. Look at your answers to Question 5. When multiplying fractions with denominator 10, 100, 1 000, etc., how can you find the number of zeros in the denominator of the product?

7. a) To find each product, first change each decimal to a fraction and multiply using the rule for multiplying fractions. Then change your answer back into a decimal.

   i) $0.3 \times 0.7 = \dfrac{3}{10} \times \dfrac{7}{10} = \dfrac{21}{100} = 0.21$ ii) 0.5×0.4

   iii) 0.2×0.8 iv) 0.05×0.4 v) 0.05×0.03 vi) 0.02×0.007

   b) How can you find the number of decimal places in the product without multiplying?

Example:	**Step 1:** Multiply the decimals	**Step 2:** 0.28 has 2 decimal places and 0.4
0.28×0.4	as if they were whole numbers.	has 1 decimal place. So the product should have
	$28 \times 4 = 112$	$2 + 1 = 3$ decimal places.
		$0.28 \times 0.4 = 0.112$

8. Using the rule given above, multiply the decimals in your notebook.

a) 0.5×0.8 b) 0.7×0.9 c) 0.2×0.6 d) 0.15×0.8 e) 0.26×0.3

f) 0.4×0.67 g) 0.32×0.9 h) 0.04×0.7 i) 0.2×0.7 j) 0.8×0.46

BONUS ▶ $0.4 \times 0.3 \times 0.02 \times 0.02 \times 0.003$

9. Round each decimal number to the first digit from the left that is not 0—this is called the **leading digit**.

a) $0.023\,7 \approx$ _0.02_   b) $0.003\,89 \approx$ _____   c) $92.156 \approx$ _____   d) $0.007\,777\,77 \approx$ _____

10. Estimate the products.

a) $2.1 \times 6.8 \approx$ _____ $\times$ _____ $=$ _____   b) $6.54 \times 3.417 \approx$ _____ $\times$ _____ $=$ _____

c) 3.25×5.498 d) 15.125×2.064 e) 9.678×44.7 f) 35.78×46.72

11. Estimate the product, then place the decimal point correctly in each answer.

a) $7.8 \times 4 = 3\ 1\ 2$ b) $35.60 \times 4.8 = 1\ 7\ 0\ 8\ 8$

c) $5.25 \times 1.78 = 9\ 3\ 4\ 5$ d) $47.35 \times 3.187 = 1\ 5\ 0\ 9\ 0\ 4\ 4\ 5$

12. Estimate each product, then correct the answers that are wrong.

a) $3.4 \times 2.01 = 6\ .\ 8\ 3\ 4$ b) $3.4 \times 2.05 = 0\ .\ 6\ 9\ 7$

c) $3.4 \times 2.056 = 6\ .\ 9\ 9\ 0\ 4$ d) $76.35 \times 11.23 = 8\ 5\ 7\ .\ 4\ 1\ 0\ 5$

13. Multiply as if the numbers were whole numbers. Then estimate to place the decimal point.

a) 2.7×3.6 b) 6.8×0.73 c) 4.5×3.9

14. $a \times b = 0.24$. Write as many possible values for a and b as you can find.

15. Gus asks Katie and Anna to place the decimal point in the answer. $2.74 \times 32.5 = 8\ 9\ 0\ 5$

Katie estimates $2.74 \times 32.5 \approx 3 \times 30 = 90$ and writes $8\ 9.0\ 5$

Anna counts decimal places: $2 + 1 = 3$ and writes $8\ .\ 9\ 0\ 5$

a) Check on a calculator to see who is right.

$2.74 \times 32.5 =$ _____ so _____ is right.

b) Calculate 274×325. What answer did you get? How does it compare to 8 905? Explain why it is important to multiply the decimals as if they were whole numbers before counting decimal places.

1. Multiply the place values separately and finish the charts.

   a) $6.5 \times 2.3 = $ 6.5×2 $+$ 6.5×0.3

   $= (6 \times 2) + (0.5 \times 2) + (6 \times 0.3) + (0.5 \times 0.3)$

   $= \underline{\ 12\ } + \underline{\ 1.0\ } + \underline{\ 1.8\ } + \underline{\ 0.15\ }$

   $= \underline{\quad 13.0 \quad} + \underline{\quad 1.95 \quad}$

   $= \underline{\quad 14.95 \quad}$

×	2	0.3
6	12	1.8
0.5	1	0.15

   b) $7.4 \times 3.5 = 7.4 \times \underline{\quad} + 7.4 \times \underline{\quad}$

   $= (7 \times \underline{\quad}) + (0.4 \times \underline{\quad}) + (7 \times \underline{\quad}) + (0.4 \times \underline{\quad})$

   $= \underline{\quad} + \underline{\quad} + \underline{\quad} + \underline{\quad}$

   $= \underline{\qquad\quad} + \underline{\qquad\quad}$

   $= \underline{\qquad\quad}$

×	3	0.5
7		
0.4		

   c) 9.3×2.8 Find the products of the parts.

×	____	____
____		
____		

   Add the products of the parts.

   $9.3 \times 2.8 = \underline{\quad} + \underline{\quad} + \underline{\quad} + \underline{\quad}$

   $= \underline{\quad} + \underline{\quad}$

   $= \underline{\quad}$

   d) 9.3×10.4 e) 20.5×10.2 f) 6.6×6.6 g) 100.7×2.3

2. Multiply. Estimate or count decimal places to place the decimal point.

   a)
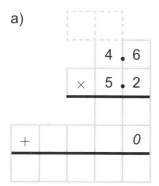

   b)
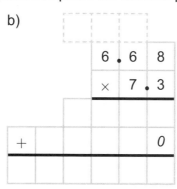

   c)
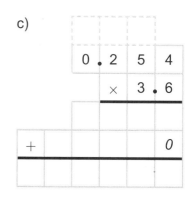

3. Multiply. Use long multiplication. Estimate or count decimal places to place the decimal point.

   a) 2.8×3.6 b) 16.7×0.73 c) 5.205×1.4 d) 432.74×0.32 e) 9.452×4.6

4. Calculate using a calculator. Estimate to check your answer. Round answers to 2 decimal places.

   a) 6.235×5.88 b) 78.401×31.72 c) 457.13×0.786 d) 2.222×2.222

Problem: Divide 95 objects into 4 groups (95 ÷ 4).

Here is a base ten model of the problem.

 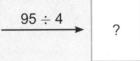

$95 = 9$ tens $+ 5$ ones

Solve the problem using **long division**.

Step 1: Write the numbers like this: $4\overline{)95}$

the number of groups ↗   ↖ the number you are dividing

Step 2: How can you divide 9 tens blocks equally into the 4 groups?

You can divide 8 of the 9 tens blocks into 4 equal groups of size 2:

There are 2 tens blocks in each group. ⟶ $\begin{array}{r} 2 \\ 4\overline{)95} \end{array}$ $\begin{array}{r} 2 \\ 4\overline{)95} \\ 8 \end{array}$ ← $2 \times 4 = 8$ tens blocks placed

There are 4 groups.

1. How many groups are you going to make? How many tens blocks can you put in each group?

    a) $4\overline{)91}$

    groups _____

    number of tens in
    each group _____

    b) $3\overline{)74}$

    groups _____

    number of tens in
    each group _____

    c) $6\overline{)85}$

    groups _____

    number of tens in
    each group _____

    d) $2\overline{)73}$

    groups _____

    number of tens in
    each group _____

2. Decide how many tens can be placed in each group. Then multiply to find out how many tens have been placed.

    a)   b)   c)   d)   e)

Step 3: How many tens blocks are left?
Subtract to find out.   ← There are $9 - 8 = 1$ left over.

3. For each question, carry out the first **three** steps of long division.

    a) $5\overline{)6\ 2}$ b) $4\overline{)4\ 8}$ c) $2\overline{)8\ 7}$ d) $3\overline{)6\ 4}$ e) $5\overline{)8\ 5}$ f) $7\overline{)8\ 3}$

Step 4: There is 1 tens block left over, and there are 5 ones in 95.

So there are 15 ones left in total. Write the 5 beside the 1 to show this.

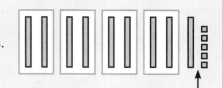

```
      2                        2
   ┌──┬──┐                  ┌──┬──┐
4 )│ 9│ 5│    ──────►    4 )│ 9│ 5│
 - │ 8│  │               - │ 8│↓ │
   ├──┼──┤                  ├──┼──┤
   │ 1│  │                  │ 1│ 5│
```

There are still 15 ones to place in 4 groups.

There are still this many ones to place.

4. Carry out the first **four** steps of long division.

a)
```
   ┌──┬──┐
6 )│ 8│ 5│
 - │  │  │
   ├──┼──┤
```

b)
```
   ┌──┬──┐
8 )│ 9│ 7│
 - │  │  │
   ├──┼──┤
```

c)
```
   ┌──┬──┐
5 )│ 9│ 2│
 - │  │  │
   ├──┼──┤
```

d)
```
   ┌──┬──┐
3 )│ 7│ 5│
 - │  │  │
   ├──┼──┤
```

e)
```
   ┌──┬──┐
3 )│ 7│ 3│
 - │  │  │
   ├──┼──┤
```

Step 5: How many ones can you put in each group?

Divide to find out:
```
      2  3        ◄── 15 ÷ 4 = 3 R ____
4 )│ 9│ 5│
 - │ 8│  │
   ├──┼──┤
   │ 1│ 5│
```

    ?

How many ones are left over?

5. Carry out the first **five** steps of long division.

a)
```
   ┌──┬──┐
5 )│ 7│ 1│
 - │  │  │
   ├──┼──┤
```

b)
```
   ┌──┬──┐
4 )│ 5│ 7│
 - │  │  │
   ├──┼──┤
```

c)
```
   ┌──┬──┐
2 )│ 9│ 6│
 - │  │  │
   ├──┼──┤
```

d)
```
   ┌──┬──┐
3 )│ 9│ 3│
 - │  │  │
   ├──┼──┤
```

e)
```
   ┌──┬──┐
5 )│ 8│ 2│
 - │  │  │
   ├──┼──┤
```

Steps 6 and 7: Find the number of ones left over.

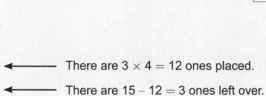

```
      2  3
4 )│ 9│ 5│
 - │ 8│  │
   ├──┼──┤
   │ 1│ 5│
 - │ 1│ 2│    ◄────── There are 3 × 4 = 12 ones placed.
   ├──┼──┤
   │  │ 3│    ◄────── There are 15 − 12 = 3 ones left over.
```

Long division and the model both show that **95 ÷ 4 = 23 with 3 left over**.

6. Carry out all the steps of long division on grid paper.

a) 6)83   b) 4)55   c) 3)95   d) 3)82   e) 4)69   f) 7)87

How to divide 334 objects into 2 groups using a base ten model and long division.

Base ten model of 334: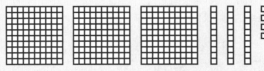

Step 1: Divide the hundreds into 2 groups.

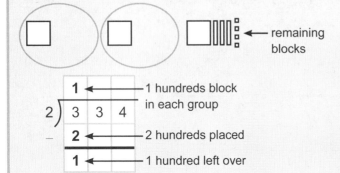

```
    1  ←—————— 1 hundreds block
  ┌─────────     in each group
2 │ 3  3  4
  │ 2  ←—————— 2 hundreds placed
  └─────────
    1  ←—————— 1 hundred left over
```

Step 2: Regroup the remaining hundreds as tens.

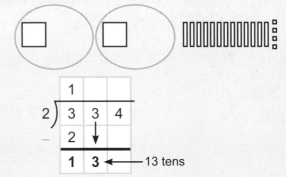

```
    1
  ┌─────────
2 │ 3  3  4
  │ 2  ↓
  └─────────
    1  3  ←—————— 13 tens
```

Step 3: Divide the tens into 2 groups.

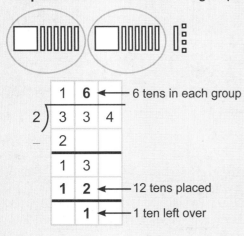

```
    1  6  ←—————— 6 tens in each group
  ┌─────────
2 │ 3  3  4
  │ 2
  └─────────
    1  3
    1  2  ←—————— 12 tens placed
  ─────────
       1  ←—————— 1 ten left over
```

Step 4: Regroup and divide the remaining ones.

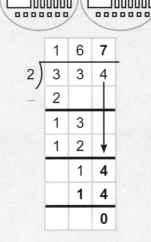

```
    1  6  7
  ┌─────────
2 │ 3  3  4
  │ 2
  └─────────
    1  3
    1  2  ↓
  ─────────
       1  4
       1  4
  ─────────
          0
```

7. Divide.

a)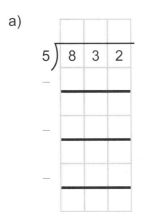

```
5 ) 8 3 2
```

b)

```
3 ) 6 4 5
```

c)

```
6 ) 8 4 1
```

d)

```
8 ) 9 7 8
```

Number Sense 8-54

8. In each question below, there are fewer hundreds than the number of groups.

Write a zero in the hundreds position to show that no hundreds can be placed in equal groups.
Then perform the division as if the hundreds had automatically been exchanged for tens.

a)
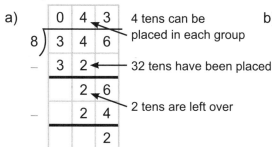
4 tens can be placed in each group

32 tens have been placed

2 tens are left over

b)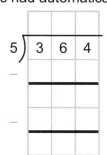

c)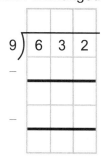

d)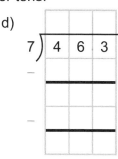

9. In each question below say how many tens or hundreds can be placed in 5 groups.
Underline the place values you will divide by 5.

a) $5\overline{)315}$

31 tens

b) $5\overline{)726}$

7 hundreds

c) $5\overline{)623}$

_____

d) $5\overline{)321}$

_____

e) $5\overline{)892}$

_____

f) $5\overline{)240}$

_____

g) $5\overline{)987}$

_____

h) $5\overline{)412}$

_____

10. Divide.

a)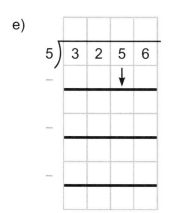

b) $4\overline{)373}$

c) $8\overline{)410}$

d) $6\overline{)304}$

e)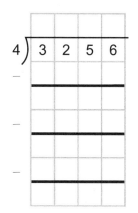

f) $4\overline{)3256}$

g) $4\overline{)5213}$

h) $6\overline{)9431}$

i) $9\overline{)784}$

j) $7\overline{)3\,512}$

k) $8\overline{)312}$

l) $8\overline{)65\,135}$

m) $2\overline{)7\,463}$

n) $3\overline{)7\,913}$

o) $5\overline{)6\,417}$

p) $8\overline{)6\,417}$

q) $6\overline{)6\,417}$

r) $7\overline{)6\,417}$

Number Sense 8-54

You can divide a decimal by a whole number by making a base ten model. Here is what the blocks represent:

= **1 one** or **1 unit**   = **1 tenth**   □ = **1 hundredth**

Keep track of your work using long division.

1. Find **3.14 ÷ 2** by making a base ten model and by long division.

    Step 1: Draw a base ten model for 3.14.

    Draw your model here.

    Step 2: Divide the largest (unit) blocks into 2 equal groups.

    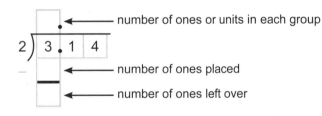

    ← number of ones or units in each group

    ← number of ones placed

    ← number of ones left over

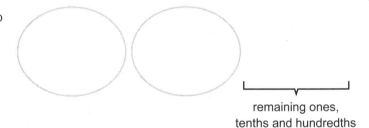

remaining ones,
tenths and hundredths

    Step 3: Exchange the leftover unit blocks for 10 tenths.

    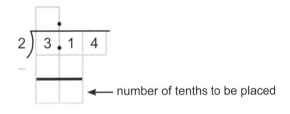

    ← number of tenths to be placed

regroup a one
as 10 tenths

    Step 4: Divide the tenths blocks into 2 equal groups.

    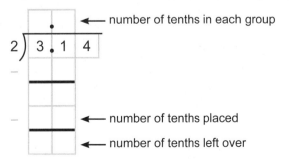

    ← number of tenths in each group

    ← number of tenths placed

    ← number of tenths left over

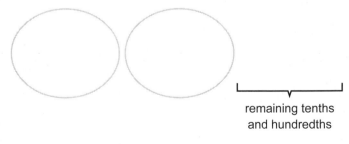

remaining tenths
and hundredths

Step 5: Exchange the leftover tenth block for 10 hundredths.

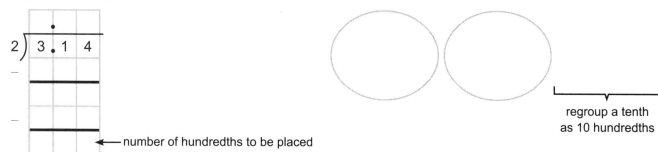

←—— number of hundredths to be placed

regroup a tenth
as 10 hundredths

Steps 6 and 7: Divide the hundredths into 2 equal groups.

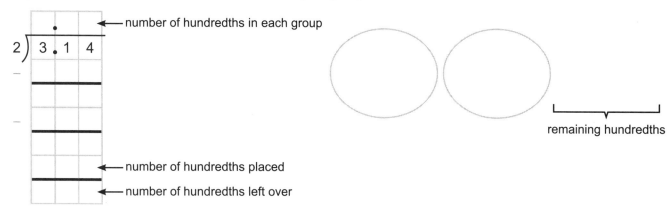

←—— number of hundredths in each group

remaining hundredths

←—— number of hundredths placed

←—— number of hundredths left over

2. Divide.

a)

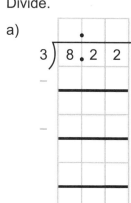

b)

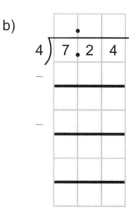

c)

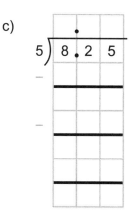

d)

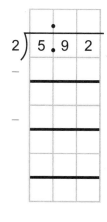

---

3. Divide.

a) $8\overline{)6.48}$ b) $9\overline{)8.1}$ c) $8\overline{)3.44}$ d) $9\overline{)6.21}$ e) $5\overline{)36.45}$

4. Five oranges cost $3.65. How much does each orange cost?

5. A regular octagon has a perimeter of 3.12 m. How long is each side?

6. Philip cycled 58.4 km in 4 hours. How many kilometres did he cycle in an hour?

7. Louise earned $95.36 in 8 hours. How much did she earn each hour?

8. Which is a better deal, 8 markers for $4.96 or 7 markers for $4.55.

Number Sense 8-55

NS8-56 Dividing Decimals by Decimals

1. a) How many strings of length 2 mm fit into a string of length 18 mm? _____

   b) Convert the measurements to centimetres.

   2 mm = _____ cm and 18 mm = _____ cm

   c) How many strings of length 0.2 cm fit into a string of length 1.8 cm? _____

   d) Explain why 18 ÷ 2 and 1.8 ÷ 0.2 have the same answer.

   e) Why is the quotient easier to find when the measurements are written in millimetres than in centimetres?

2. These decimal numbers represent the length of strings in centimetres. Convert the measurements to millimetres, then find the quotient.

   a) 2.4 ÷ 0.6

   2.4 cm = _____ mm and 0.6 cm = _____ mm

   so 2.4 ÷ 0.6 = _____ ÷ _____ = _____

   b) 4.9 ÷ 0.7

   4.9 cm = _____ mm and 0.7 cm = _____ mm

   so 4.9 ÷ 0.7 = _____ ÷ _____ = _____

   c) 7.2 ÷ 0.9   d) 12 ÷ 0.4   e) 20 ÷ 0.5   f) 5.6 ÷ 0.4   g) 9.8 ÷ 0.7

3. Multiply both terms by 10 to find the quotient.

   a) 8.4 ÷ 0.6

   = _____ ÷ _____

   = _____

   b) 78 ÷ 0.6

   = _____ ÷ _____

   = _____

   c) 42 ÷ 0.7

   = _____ ÷ _____

   = _____

4. These decimal numbers represent the length of strings in metres. Convert the measurements to centimetres, then find the quotient.

   a) 2.84 ÷ 0.02

   = _____ ÷ _____

   = _____

   b) 16.5 ÷ 0.05

   = _____ ÷ _____

   = _____

   c) 7.32 ÷ 0.03

   = _____ ÷ _____

   = _____

5. These decimal numbers represent the length of strings in metres. Convert the measurements to millimetres, then find the quotient.

   a) 1.112 ÷ 0.008   b) 1.778 ÷ 0.007   c) 6.3 ÷ 0.009   d) 5.28 ÷ 0.006

6. Multiply both the dividend and divisor by 10, 100, or 1000 to change them to whole numbers. (Be sure to multiply both by the same number!) Then divide.

   a) 24 ÷ 0.4 = _____ ÷ _____

   = _____

   b) 51 ÷ 0.03 = _____ ÷ _____

   = _____

   c) 16 ÷ 0.2   d) 63 ÷ 0.07   e) 680 ÷ 0.4   f) 60 ÷ 0.005   g) 12 ÷ 0.003

   h) 4.5 ÷ 0.5   i) 0.08 ÷ 0.4   j) 0.48 ÷ 0.2   k) 62.8 ÷ 0.2   l) 8.8 ÷ 1.1

1. Write a decimal for each description. Some questions have more than one answer.

   a) Between 5.63 and 5.68: ☐.☐☐

   b) Between 2.70 and 2.80: ☐.☐☐

   c) Between 21.75 and 21.8: ☐☐.☐☐

   d) Between 0.6 and 0.7: ☐.☐☐

   e) One tenth greater than 4.54: ☐.☐☐

   f) One hundredth less than 6.00: ☐.☐☐

2. Put a decimal in each number so that the digit **4** has the value $\frac{4}{10}$.

   a) 3 4 8

   b) 5 0 4

   c) 1 5 4 7 9

   d) 4

3. Under which deal do you pay less per pen, 3 pens for $2.88 or 5 pens for $4.65?

4. The chart shows the greatest lengths ever recorded for certain sea creatures.

   a) Order the lengths from least to greatest.

   b) How much longer than the great white shark is the blue whale?

   c) About how many times longer than the turtle is the great white shark?

   d) About how long would 3 blue whales be if they swam head to tail?

Animal	Length (m)
Blue Whale	33.58
Great White Shark	7.92
Pacific Leatherback Turtle	2.13
Ocean Sunfish	2.95

5. The wind speed in Vancouver was 26.7 km/h on Monday, 16.0 km/h on Tuesday, and 2.4 km/h on Wednesday. What was the average wind speed over the 3 days?

6. Jacob walks 0.05 kilometres per minute. At that speed, how long would it take him to walk 15 km?

7. Encke's Comet appears in our sky every 3.3 years. It was first seen in 1786. When was the last time the comet was seen in the 1700s (that is, before 1800)? Show your work.

8. Our **ecological footprint** is the area of land required to provide us with food, clothing, and other resources, and to absorb our waste (for example, pollution).

   a) In Canada, the average ecological footprint is 7.25 hectares of land per person. In Sudbury, the ecological footprint is 6.87 hectares per person. How much less is this than the Canadian average?

   b) The world average is 2.7 hectares per person. How much bigger is a Canadian's ecological footprint than the world average?

   c) There are 33.2 million Canadians. How big is our total footprint, in millions of hectares?

PA8-1 Extending Patterns

1. These sequences were made by adding the same number to each term. Find the number, then extend the pattern.

a) 1 , 4 , 7 ,_____,_____,_____

b) 2 , 8 , 14 ,_____,_____,_____

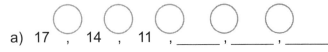

c) 4 , 9 , 14 ,_____,_____,_____

d) 1 , 11 , 21 ,_____,_____,_____

2. These sequences were made by subtracting the same number from each term. Find the number, then extend the pattern.

a) 17 , 14 , 11 ,_____,_____,_____

b) 85 , 81 , 77 ,_____,_____,_____

c) 51 , 46 , 41 ,_____,_____,_____

d) 99 , 91 , 83 ,_____,_____,_____

3. Find the numbers that are added or subtracted, then extend the pattern.

Write a plus sign (+) if you add the number and a minus sign (−) if you subtract the number.

a) 2 , 3 , 6 , 11 , 18 ,_____

b) 21 , 16 , 12 , 9 , 7 ,_____

c) 3 , 6 , 12 , 24 , 48 ,_____

d) 57 , 37 , 22 , 12 , 7 ,_____

e) 1 , 1 , 2 , 3 , 5 , 8 , 13 , 21 , 34 ,_____,_____,_____

4. The sequence in Question 3 e) is called the **Fibonacci sequence**. How can you get each term from the previous two terms? _____

_____.

5. Find the gaps between the gaps and extend the patterns.

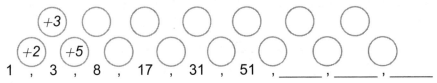

1 , 3 , 8 , 17 , 31 , 51 ,_____,_____,_____

PA8-2 Describing Patterns

1. Write the amount by which each term in the sequence increases (goes up) or decreases (goes down). Use a plus sign (+) if the sequence increases and a minus sign (−) if it decreases.

a) 3 $\overset{+4}{,}$ 7 $\overset{-2}{,}$ 5 $\overset{+7}{,}$ 12 $\overset{-4}{,}$ 8

b) 4 ◯ 9 ◯ 5 ◯ 14 ◯ 19

c) 2 ◯ 9 ◯ 10 ◯ 20 ◯ 29

d) 4 ◯ 6 ◯ 8 ◯ 7 ◯ 12

e) 56 ◯ 47 ◯ 45 ◯ 39 ◯ 31

f) 45 ◯ 54 ◯ 59 ◯ 63 ◯ 55

2. Match each sequence with the correct description.

a) **A** increases by 5 each time
   B increases by different amounts

   _____ 11 , 16 , 21 , 26 , 31

   _____ 9 , 15 , 17 , 34 , 37

b) **A** increases by different amounts
   B increases by 7 each time

   _____ 12 , 19 , 26 , 33 , 40

   _____ 6 , 13 , 18 , 26 , 33

c) **A** decreases by the same amount
   B decreases by different amounts

   _____ 21 , 20 , 18 , 15 , 11

   _____ 13 , 10 , 7 , 4 , 1

d) **A** decreases by 13 each time
   B decreases by different amounts

   _____ 72 , 59 , 46 , 33 , 20

   _____ 48 , 35 , 22 , 15 , 3

BONUS ▶

A increases by 5 each time
B decreases by different amounts
C increases by different amounts

_____ 23 , 28 , 29 , 35 , 43

_____ 27 , 24 , 20 , 19 , 16

_____ 34 , 39 , 44 , 49 , 54

A increases and decreases
B increases by the same amount
C decreases by different amounts
D decreases by the same amount

_____ 41 , 39 , 35 , 23 , 7

_____ 10 , 14 , 23 , 19 , 11

_____ 38 , 36 , 34 , 32 , 30

_____ 28 , 31 , 34 , 37 , 40

3. Make 3 sequences that match the descriptions. Ask a partner to match each sequence with the correct description. (Write the sequences out of order!)

A increases by 6 each time   _____ _____

B decreases by different amounts _____ _____

C increases and decreases   _____ _____

4. These sequences were made by multiplying each term by the same number. Find the number, then extend the pattern.

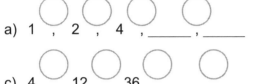

a) 1 , 2 , 4 , _____ , _____

b) 50 , 100 , 200 , _____ , _____

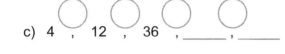

c) 4 , 12 , 36 , _____ , _____

d) 3 , 30 , 300 , _____ , _____

5. These sequences were made by dividing each term by the same number. Find the number, then extend the pattern.

a) 400 , 200 , 100 , _____ , _____

b) 96 , 48 , 24 , _____ , _____

c) 500 , 100 , 20 , _____

d) 1600 , 400 , 100 , _____

6. Write a rule for each pattern. Use the words **add**, **subtract**, **multiply**, or **divide**.

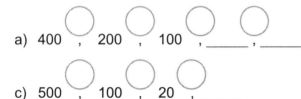

a) 3 , 6 , 12 , 24   *start at 3 and multiply by 2* _____

b) 5 , 8 , 11 , 14   _____

c) 31 , 28 , 25 , 22   _____

d) 81 , 27 , 9 , 3   _____

e) 2, 10, 50, 250   f) 32, 16, 8, 4   g) 30 000, 3 000, 300, 30   h) 10, 200, 4 000, 80 000

7. Describe each pattern as **increasing**, **decreasing**, or **repeating**.

a) 2 , 4 , 8 , 16 , 32 , 64 _____

b) 4 , 8 , 0 , 4 , 8 , 0 _____

c) 30 , 28 , 26 , 24 , 23 _____

d) 2 , 6 , 10 , 14 , 17 _____

e) 11 , 9 , 6 , 11 , 9 , 6 _____

f) 63 , 58 , 53 , 48 , 43 _____

Patterns and Algebra 8-2

PA8-3 T-tables

Claude makes an **increasing pattern** with squares. He records the number of squares in each figure in a chart or T-table. He also records the number of squares he adds each time he makes a new figure.

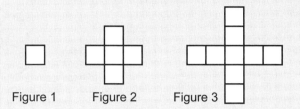

Figure 1   Figure 2   Figure 3

Figure	Number of Squares
1	1
2	5
3	9

④

④

Number of squares added each time

The number of squares in the figures are 1, 5, 9, … Claude writes a rule for this number pattern:
Rule: Start at 1 and add 4 each time.

1. Claude makes other increasing patterns with squares.

   How many squares does he add to make each new figure? Write your answers in the circles. Then write a rule for the pattern.

a)
Figure	Number of Squares
1	2
2	7
3	12

◯ ◯

Rule: Start at _____ and add _____.

b)
Figure	Number of Squares
1	2
2	9
3	16

◯ ◯

Rule:

c)
Figure	Number of Squares
1	1
2	4
3	7

◯ ◯

Rule:

2. Extend the number pattern. How many squares would be used in Figure 6?

a)
Figure	Number of Squares
1	6
2	11
3	16
4	
5	
6	

◯ ◯ ◯ ◯ ◯

b)
Figure	Number of Squares
1	2
2	6
3	10
4	
5	
6	

◯ ◯ ◯ ◯ ◯

c)
Figure	Number of Squares
1	3
2	9
3	15
4	
5	
6	

◯ ◯ ◯ ◯ ◯

3. At the end of Week 1, Ryan has $150 in his savings account. He spends $15 each week.

   a) How much money will he have left at the end of Week 5?

   _____

   b) At the end of which week will he have no money left?

   _____

Week	Savings
1	$150
2	
3	
4	
5	

4. The water in a rain barrel is 18 cm deep at 5 p.m. If 3 cm of rain fall each hour, how deep is the water at 9 p.m.?

5. A marina rents kayaks for $8 for the first hour and $6 for every hour after that. How much would it cost to rent a kayak for 6 hours?

6. a) Copy and complete the chart for these figures: 1 2 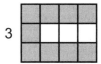 3

Figure	Number of light squares	Number of dark squares	Total number of squares
1	1	5	6
2			
3			

   b) How many dark squares will be needed for a figure with 7 light squares?
   c) How many squares will be needed for a figure with 15 dark squares?

7. The chart shows how much fuel an airplane burns as it travels.

Time (minutes)	Fuel (kL)	Distance from Airport (km)
0	150	3 600
30	143	3 150
60	136	2 700

   a) How much fuel will be left in the airplane after $2\frac{1}{2}$ hours?
   b) How far from the airport will the plane be after 3 hours?
   c) How much fuel will be left in the airplane when it reaches the airport?

8. Halley's Comet returns to Earth every 76 years. It was last seen in 1986.

   a) List the next three dates it will return to Earth.
   b) When was the first time Halley's comet was seen in the 1900s?

PA8-4 Patterns (Advanced)

1. Here are some number pyramids: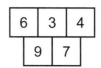

   Can you find the rule used to make the patterns in the pyramids? Describe it here:

   _____

2. Using the rule you described in Question 1, find the missing numbers:

   a)

   b)

   c)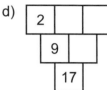

   d)

   e)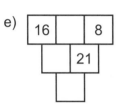

   f)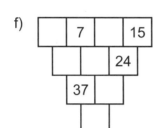

   g)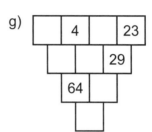

   h)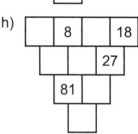

3. **Pascal's Triangle** is made using the rule above, but with all 1s on the outer part of the pyramid.

   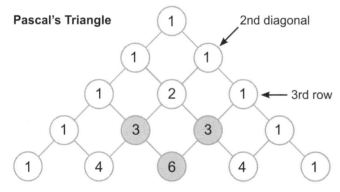

   Pascal's Triangle
   2nd diagonal
   3rd row

   a) Create Pascal's Triangle in your notebook, up to 7 rows.

   b) What is the 3rd number in the 9th row of Pascal's Triangle? Hint: Extend the pattern in the 3rd diagonal.

   c) Add the numbers in each of the first five rows of Pascal's Triangle. What pattern do you see in the sums?

   d) Using the pattern you found in part c), predict the sum of the numbers in the 8th row.

4. a) How many shaded squares will be on the perimeter of the 10th figure? How do you know?

b) How many white squares will there be in a figure that has 32 shaded squares?

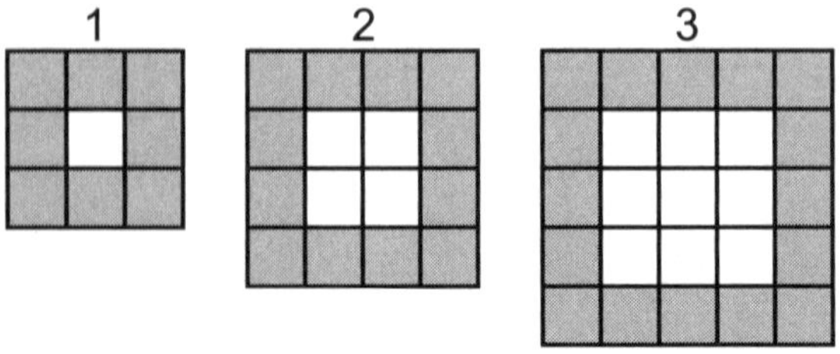

INVESTIGATION ▶ How many hidden rectangles?

Figure 1

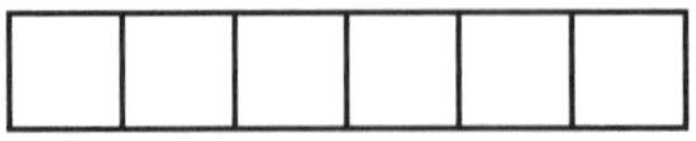

Figure 2

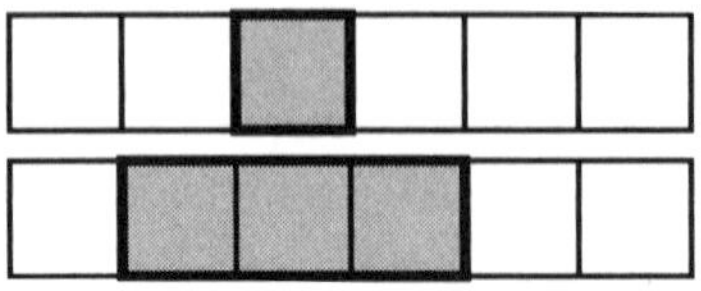

Figure 1 is made of 6 squares. How many rectangles are hidden in Figure 1? Remember: A square is also a rectangle.

Figure 2 shows **two** of the hidden rectangles, but there are many others.

Starting with a figure made of a smaller number of squares, can you discover a pattern that will tell you how many hidden rectangles there are in **any** array of squares?

If you need help, you can follow these steps:

A. A square (☐) has only one hidden rectangle: the square itself.

1 square: ___1___ hidden rectangle

B. Find all the hidden rectangles in a figure with two squares. Shade one rectangle in each figure. Note: There may be more figures than you need.

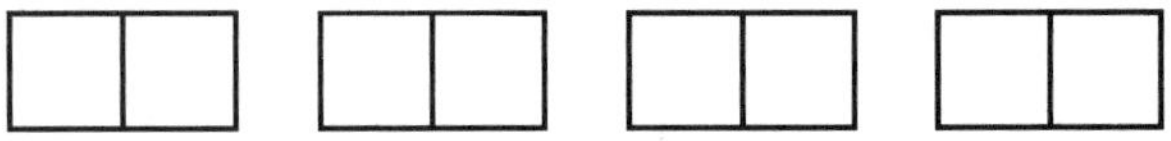

2 squares: _____ hidden rectangles

C. Draw copies of a figure with three squares and find all the hidden rectangles.

3 squares: _____ hidden rectangles

D. Draw copies of a figure with four squares and find all the hidden rectangles. Hint: Start by finding all the hidden rectangles made of 1 square, then 2 squares, then 3 squares and, finally, 4 squares. Show your work in your notebook.

4 squares: _____ hidden rectangles

E. Write the numbers you found in parts A , B , C, and D below. Find the gap between the numbers and use the pattern in the gap to extend the sequence and find the number of hidden rectangles in Figure 2.

A	B	C	D		
1 square	2 squares	3 squares	4 squares	5 squares	6 squares

F. Predict the number of hidden rectangles in an array of 10 squares: _____

PA8-5 Variables

A **numeric expression** is a combination of numbers, operation signs, and sometimes brackets, that represents a quantity. For example, these expressions all represent 10:

$$7 + 3 \qquad\qquad 12 - 2 \qquad\qquad 100 \div 10 \qquad\qquad (4 + 1) \times 2$$

1. Calculate each expression.

   a) $1 + 3 + 4 =$ _____   b) $3 \times 4 =$ _____   c) $2 \times 2 \times 2 =$ _____   d) $5 + 2 =$ _____

An **equation** is a mathematical statement that has two expressions representing the same quantity separated by an equal sign. Example: $12 - 2 = 100 \div 10$

2. Circle two expressions from Question 1 that represent the same quantity.

   Write an equation using those two expressions. _____

A **variable** is a letter or symbol (such as x, n, or h) that represents a number. An **algebraic expression** is a combination of one or more variables that may include numbers, operation signs, and brackets.

Examples of algebraic expressions: $\qquad 5 \times (t + 7) \qquad n \div 5 \qquad (3 + z) \div 5 - y$

3. Make your own example of an algebraic expression. _____

In the product of a number and a variable, the multiplication sign is usually dropped.

Example: $3 \times t = t \times 3$ are both written as **3t**.

4. Rewrite these expressions without multiplication signs.

   a) $3 \times s = \underline{\quad 3s \quad}$ b) $n \times 5 + 2 = \underline{\quad 5n + 2 \quad}$ c) $12 - 4 \times r = \underline{\qquad\quad}$

   d) $7 \times a - 3 = \underline{\qquad\quad}$ e) $b \times 4 - 3 = \underline{\qquad\quad}$ f) $5 + 6 \times w = \underline{\qquad\quad}$

5. Rewrite these expressions with multiplication signs.

   a) $3h = \underline{\quad 3 \times h \quad}$ b) $2 - 3g = \underline{\qquad\quad}$ c) $3f + 4 = \underline{\qquad\quad}$

6. It costs $5 per hour to rent a pair of skis. Write an algebraic expression for the cost of renting skis for…

   a) h hours: $\underline{\ 5 \times h\ }$ or $\underline{\ 5h\ }$ b) t hours: _____ or _____   c) x hours: _____ or _____

7. A **flat fee** is a fixed charge that doesn't depend on how long you rent an item. Example: A company charges a flat fee of $7 to rent a boat, plus $3 for each hour the boat is used.

   Write an expression for the amount you would pay to rent a boat for…

   a) h hours
      Hourly rate: $4
      Flat fee: $5

      $\underline{\quad 4h + 5 \quad}$

   b) t hours
      Hourly rate: $3
      Flat fee: $8

      $\underline{\qquad\qquad}$

   c) w hours
      Hourly rate: $5
      Flat fee: $6

      $\underline{\qquad\qquad}$

When replacing a variable with a number in a product, we use brackets.

Example: To substitute 7 for n in $3n = 3 \times n$, we write $3(7) = 3 \times 7$.

8. Write the number 2 in each bracket and evaluate.

a) $5(\underline{\ 2\ }) = \underline{\ 5 \times 2\ } = \underline{\ 10\ }$ b) $3(\underline{\ 2\ }) = \underline{\ 3 \times 2\ } = \underline{\qquad}$ c) $4(\underline{\qquad}) = \underline{\qquad} = \underline{\qquad}$

d) $2(\underline{\qquad}) + 5$ e) $4(\underline{\qquad}) - 2$ f) $6(\underline{\qquad}) + 3$

$= \underline{\qquad} = \underline{\qquad}$ $= \underline{\qquad} = \underline{\qquad}$ $= \underline{\qquad} = \underline{\qquad}$

9. Replace n with 2 in each expression.

a) $4n + 3$
$= 4(2) + 3$
$= 8 + 3$
$= 11$

b) $5n + 1$

c) $3n - 2$

d) $2n + 3$

10. A company charges a flat fee of \$6 to rent a pair of skis plus \$3 for each hour you use the skis. The total cost is given by the expression $3h + 6$. Find the cost of renting a pair of skis for…

a) 4 hours

b) 2 hours

c) 5 hours

d) 7 hours

$3(4) + 6$
$= 12 + 6$
$= 18$

11. Replace the variable with the given value and evaluate. This is called **substitution**.

a) $5h + 2, h = 3$

b) $2n + 3, n = \dfrac{1}{2}$

c) $5t - 2, t = 0.8$

$5(3) + 2$
$= 15 + 2$
$= 17$

d) $3m + 9, m = \dfrac{2}{3}$

e) $9 - 2z, z = 4$

f) $3n + 2, n = 0.6$

12. Evaluate each expression.

a) $2n + 3, n = 5$

b) $2t + 3, t = 5$

c) $3 + 2n, n = 5$

$2(5) + 3$
$= 10 + 3 = 13$

13. a) What do you notice about your answers in Question 12? _____

b) Why is that so? _____

PA8-6 Substituting Fractions and Decimals for Variables

1. Replace the variables with the given fraction and evaluate. Write your answer as a mixed or proper fraction.

a) $2x$, $x = \dfrac{1}{3}$

$2x = 2(\dfrac{1}{3}) = \dfrac{2}{3}$

b) $u + 5$, $u = \dfrac{5}{7}$

c) $3r$, $r = \dfrac{2}{5}$

d) $s + 6$, $s = \dfrac{3}{5}$

e) $3x + 2$, $x = \dfrac{5}{8}$

f) $z - 2$, $z = \dfrac{13}{5}$

g) $5z - 1$, $z = \dfrac{3}{5}$

h) $3v - 2$, $v = \dfrac{4}{5}$

i) $2h - 1$, $h = \dfrac{2}{3}$

j) $4t + 1$, $t = \dfrac{3}{8}$

k) $5t - 6$, $t = \dfrac{7}{4}$

l) $3w - 8$, $w = 2\dfrac{3}{4}$

2. Replace the variables with the given decimal and evaluate. Write your answer as a decimal.

a) $6x$, $x = 0.5$

$6x = 6(0.5)$
$= 3.0$

b) $9p$, $p = 4.2$

c) $w - 2$, $w = 3.7$

d) $z + 4$, $z = 5.83$

e) $4x + 3$, $x = 1.3$

f) $3m - 5$, $m = 4.75$

g) $3t - 2$, $t = 0.8$

h) $4z - 5$, $z = 2.31$

3. a) Which parts from Questions 1 and 2 have the same answer? _____ and _____

   b) Why are these parts the same?

4. Sandwiches cost $3 and drinks cost $2. The cost of s sandwiches and d drinks is $3s + 2d$.

   Find the cost of the following amounts:

   a) 5 sandwiches and 4 drinks

   $3s + 2d = 3(5) + 2(4)$
   $= 15 + 8$
   $= 23$

   The cost is __$23__

   b) 6 sandwiches and 6 drinks

   The cost is _____

   c) 2 sandwiches and 7 drinks

   The cost is _____

5. Replace the variables with the given values and evaluate.

a) $3x + 5y$, $x = 6$ and $y = 2$

$3(6) + 5(2)$
$= 18 + 10$
$= 28$

b) $4x - y$, $x = 5$ and $y = 3$

c) $4x - y$, $x = 0.5$ and $y = 1$

d) $7x + 2y$, $x = \dfrac{1}{3}$ and $y = \dfrac{2}{3}$

e) $3x + 4y - 2z$, $x = 5$, $y = 2$, $z = 7$

f) $2x - 3y + 5z$, $x = 5$, $y = \dfrac{1}{3}$, $z = 3$

g) $2x + y - 3z$, $x = \dfrac{2}{5}$, $y = \dfrac{2}{3}$, $z = \dfrac{1}{6}$

h) $5x - 3y + 2z$, $x = 3$, $y = \dfrac{1}{3}$, $z = 5$

6. Which two parts of Question 5 have the same answer? _____ and _____

BONUS ▶ Why are these two parts the same? _____

7. Write an expression for the total value, v, in cents, of these coins:

a) n nickels $5n$ _____

b) w nickels   _____

c) n nickels and d dimes   _____

d) a quarters and b pennies   _____

e) a quarters, b dimes, c nickels, and d pennies   _____

8. Use your expression from Question 7 e). How much money, in cents, is 3 quarters, 4 dimes, 7 nickels and 8 pennies? Show your work.

9. Write an expression for the maximum number of points to be scored on a 10-question test if Questions 1, 2, and 3 are each worth m points, Questions 4 and 5 are each worth p points, and Questions 6 to 10 are each worth r points.

10. Natalia needs to buy 14 sandwiches, 12 pizzas, and 40 drinks for a party.

a) If sandwiches cost \$$s$, pizzas cost \$$p$, and drinks cost \$$d$, write an expression for the total cost of the food.

b) Company A charges \$2 for each sandwich, \$7 for each pizza, and \$1 for each drink. How much would Natalia pay if she bought the food at Company A?

c) Company B charges \$2.50 for each sandwich, \$6.80 for each pizza, and \$0.95 for each drink. How much would Natalia pay if she bought the food at Company B?

d) Where should Natalia buy the food for the party—Company A or Company B? Why?

> Only one value of x will make the equation $x + 3 = 7$ true.
>
> Finding the value of a variable that makes an equation true is called **solving for the variable**.

1. a) Calculate $3n$ ($= 3 \times n$) and $3n - 5$ for each value of n given in the chart.

n	2	3	4	5	6	7	8	9	10	11	12
$3n$	6	9	12								
$3n - 5$	1	4	7								

b) Use the chart to solve for n.

i) $3n - 5 = 16$ ii) $3n - 5 = 25$ iii) $3n - 5 = 10$ iv) $3n - 5 = 31$

     $n = $ _____ $n = $ _____ $n = $ _____ $n = $ _____

> **REMINDER ▶** Division is often written in fractional form:
>
> $$12 \div 4 = \frac{12}{4} \qquad 15 \div 5 = \frac{15}{5} \qquad x \div 3 = \frac{x}{3} \qquad w \div 7 = \frac{w}{7}$$

2. a) Calculate $x \div 4$ ($= \frac{x}{4}$) and then $\frac{x}{4} + 5$ for each value of x given in the chart.

x	0	4	8	12	16	20	24	28	32	36	40	44
$\frac{x}{4}$	0	1	2	3	4							
$\frac{x}{4} + 5$	5	6	7	8								

b) Use the chart to solve for x.

i) $\frac{x}{4} + 5 = 7$ ii) $\frac{x}{4} + 5 = 15$ iii) $\frac{x}{4} + 5 = 13$ iv) $\frac{x}{4} + 5 = 9$

     $x = $ _____ $x = $ _____ $x = $ _____ $x = $ _____

3. Substitute $n = 8$ into the expression on the left side of the equation. Then decide if n needs to be greater than 8, less than 8, or equal to 8 to make the equation true.

a) $3n + 2 = 29$

     $3(8) + 2 = $ ___26___ is ___less than___ 29.

     So n should be ___greater than___ 8.

b) $2n + 3 = 19$

     $2(8) + 3 = $ _____ is _____ 19.

     So n should be _____ 8.

c) $\frac{n}{2} + 6 = 9$

     $\frac{8}{2} + 6 = $ _____ is _____ 9.

     So n should be _____ 8.

d) $\frac{n}{4} + 7 = 10$

     $\frac{8}{4} + 7 = $ _____ is _____ 10.

     So n should be _____ 8.

4. Solve for n by guessing small values for n, checking, and revising.

a) $3n + 2 = 8$

$n = $ _____

b) $5n - 2 = 13$

$n = $ _____

c) $\dfrac{n}{3} + 5 = 7$

$n = $ _____

d) $\dfrac{n}{2} - 5 = 3$

$n = $ _____

5. Sara solves $7x + 11 = 67$ and gets $x = 8$.

a) Verify Sara's answer.

b) What value for t solves $7t + 11 = 67$? _____

c) What value for x solves $11 + 7x = 67$? _____

How do you know? _____

d) What value for x solves $67 = 7x + 11$? _____

How do you know? _____

6. Circle the equations that are just another way of writing $8x + 3 = 51$.

$3 + 8x = 51$ $8t + 3 = 51$ $3w + 8 = 51$ $8 + 3x = 51$

$51 = 3 + 8x$ $51 = 8w + 3$ $r \times 8 + 3 = 51$ $51 = 3 + 8t$

$3 + 8r = 51$ $51 + 8r = 3$ $8z + 3 = 51$ $8z + 51 = 3$

7. Solve these equations by guessing, checking, and revising.

a) $2 + 7x = 23$

$x = $ _____

b) $3 + 5x = 38$

$x = $ _____

c) $8 + 2x = 26$

$x = $ _____

d) $5 + 3n = 20$

$n = $ _____

e) $3 + 5x = 18$

$x = $ _____

f) $23 = 7u + 2$

$u = $ _____

g) $7u + 5 = 40$

$u = $ _____

h) $30 = 3 + 9n$

$n = $ _____

8. Circle the two equations from Question 7 that are the same, but just written differently.

9. **BONUS** ▶ Solve this equation for x and y: $2x + 1 = 7 = 4y - 1$.

EXTRA CHALLENGE ▶ Both x and y are whole numbers. How many solutions can you find for $2x + 1 = 4y - 1$?

10. a) Solve each equation by guessing, checking, and revising.

$2x = 8$ $\qquad$ $2x + 1 = 9$ $\qquad$ $2x + 2 = 10$ $\qquad$ $2x + 3 = 11$

$x = \underline{\hphantom{xxxx}}$ $\qquad$ $x = \underline{\hphantom{xxxx}}$ $\qquad$ $x = \underline{\hphantom{xxxx}}$ $\qquad$ $x = \underline{\hphantom{xxxx}}$

b) What do you notice about your answers in part a)? $\underline{\hphantom{xxxxxxxxxxxxxxxxxxxxxxxxxx}}$

Why is this the case? $\underline{\hphantom{xxxxxxxxxxxxxxxxxxxxxxxxxxxxxxxxxxxx}}$

$\underline{\hphantom{xxxxxxxxxxxxxxxxxxxxxxxxxxxxxxxxxxxxxxxxxxxxxxxxxxxxxxxx}}$

c) Which problem from part a) was easiest to solve? $\underline{\hphantom{xxxx}}$

Why? $\underline{\hphantom{xxxxxxxxxxxxxxxxxxxxxxxxxxxxxxxxxxxxxxxxxxxxxxxxxx}}$

d) Write another equation that has the same answer as the equations in part a).

$\underline{\hphantom{xxxxxxxxxxxxxxxxxxxxxxxxxxxxxxxxxxxxxxxxxxxxxxxxxxxxxxxxxx}}$

e) Fill in the box so that the equation has the same answer as the equations in part a).

$2x - \square = 5$

11. Do $3x = 15$ and $3x - 2 = 13$ have the same answer? How do you know?

12. a) Solve each equation by guessing, checking, and revising.

i) $2x + 1 = 5$ $\qquad$ ii) $4x + 2 = 10$ $\qquad$ iii) $6x + 3 = 15$ $\qquad$ iv) $8x + 4 = 20$

$x = \underline{\hphantom{xxxx}}$ $\qquad$ $x = \underline{\hphantom{xxxx}}$ $\qquad$ $x = \underline{\hphantom{xxxx}}$ $\qquad$ $x = \underline{\hphantom{xxxx}}$

b) What do you notice about your answers in part a)? $\underline{\hphantom{xxxxxxxxxxxxxxxxxxxxxxx}}$

Why is this the case? $\underline{\hphantom{xxxxxxxxxxxxxxxxxxxxxxxxxxxxxxxxxxxx}}$

$\underline{\hphantom{xxxxxxxxxxxxxxxxxxxxxxxxxxxxxxxxxxxxxxxxxxxxxxxxxxxxxxxx}}$

13. Do $3x - 1 = 11$ and $15x - 5 = 55$ have the same answer? How do you know?

14. The same value of x solves all the equations. Write the missing numbers.

$3x = 15$ $\qquad$ $3x + \square = 16$ $\qquad$ $3x + 4 = \square$

$3x - \square = 11$ $\qquad$ $6x + \square = 32$ $\qquad$ $\square\, x = 150$

PA8-8 Solving Equations — Preserving Equality

1. Write the number that makes each equation true.

   a) $8 + 4 - \boxed{} = 8$
   b) $8 \times 3 \div \boxed{} = 8$
   c) $8 \div 2 \times \boxed{} = 8$
   d) $8 - 5 + \boxed{} = 8$

2. Write the operation that makes each equation true.

   a) $7 + 2 \bigcirc 2 = 7$
   b) $8 \times 3 \bigcirc 3 = 8$
   c) $12 \div 2 \bigcirc 2 = 12$
   d) $15 - 4 \bigcirc 4 = 15$

3. Write the operation and number that make each equation true.

   a) $17 + 3 \underline{\quad -3 \quad} = 17$
   b) $20 \div 4 \underline{\qquad} = 20$
   c) $18 + 2 \underline{\qquad} = 18$

   d) $6 \div 2 \underline{\qquad} = 6$
   e) $6 \times 2 \underline{\qquad} = 6$
   f) $6 - 2 \underline{\qquad} = 6$

4. How could you undo each action to get back to the number you started with?

   a) add 4 _____ *subtract 4* _____
   b) multiply by 3 _____

   c) divide by 2 _____
   d) subtract 7 _____

5. Start with the number 3. Do the operations in order and then undo them in
   backwards order.

   Add 7 _____10_____   Subtract 7 _____
   Multiply by 2 _____20_____   Divide by 2 _____
   Subtract 5 _____   Add 5 _____
   Divide by 3 _____ ⟶ Multiply by 3 _____

   Did you finish with the number you started with? _____

6. Start with the number 11. Do the operations in order and then undo them in
   backwards order.

   Add 4 _____15_____   _____ _____
   Divide by 3 _____   _____ _____
   Subtract 1 _____   _____ _____
   Multiply by 4 _____ ⟶ *Divide by 4* _____

   Did you finish with the number you started with? _____

7. Start with 3. Multiply by 2. Then add 4.

   Circle the sequence of operations that will get you back where you started
   (that is, back to 3).

   Divide your answer by 2, then subtract 4.   *Subtract 4 from your answer, then divide by 2.*

Patterns and Algebra 8-8

Remember: The variable x represents a number, so you can treat it like a number.

Operation	Result	Operation	Result
Add 3 to x	$x + 3$	Multiply 3 by x	$3 \times x = 3x$
Add x to 3	$3 + x$	Multiply x by 3	$x \times 3 = 3x$
Subtract 3 from x	$x - 3$	Divide x by 3	$x \div 3 = \dfrac{x}{3}$
Subtract x from 3	$3 - x$	Divide 3 by x	$3 \div x = \dfrac{3}{x}$

8. Show the result of each operation.

   a) Multiply x by 7 ___7x___

   b) Add 4 to x ___$x + 4$___

   c) Subtract 5 from x _____

   d) Subtract x from 5 _____

   e) Divide x by 10 _____

   f) Divide 9 by x _____

   g) Multiply 8 by x _____

   h) Add x to 9 _____

   BONUS ▶ Add x to y _____

9. What happens to the variable x?

   a) $2x$ ___Multiply by 2___

   b) $3x$ _____

   c) $x + 4$ _____

   d) $x - 5$ _____

   e) $\dfrac{x}{3}$ _____

   f) $\dfrac{6}{x}$ _____

   g) $4 - x$ _____

   BONUS ▶ $x + x$ _____

10. Write the correct operation and number to get back to the variable.

   a) $n + 3$ ___-3___ $= n$

   b) $n \times 3$ _____ $= n$

   c) $5m$ _____ $= m$

   d) $x - 5$ _____ $= x$

   e) $x + 7$ _____ $= x$

   f) $\dfrac{x}{14}$ _____ $= x$

   g) $\dfrac{z}{5}$ _____ $= z$

   h) $7y$ _____ $= y$

   i) $r + 8$ _____ $= r$

11. Circle the expressions that always equal m, for any number m. Check your answers for m = 5.

   $7m - 7$ $7m \div 7$ $m \div 7 \times 7$ $7 \div m \times 7$ $7 + m - 7$ $7 - m + 7$

12. Solve for x by doing the same thing to both sides of the equation. Check your answer.

   a) $3x = 12$ ◀——— Check by replacing x with your answer:
      $3x \div 3 = 12 \div 3$
      $x = 4$
      $3(4) = 12$

   b) $x - 4 = 11$

   c) $4x = 20$

   d) $x + 5 = 8$

   e) $3 + x = 9$

   f) $\dfrac{x}{6} = 3$

   g) $5x = 15$

   h) $x - 7 = 10$

   i) $2x = 18$

   j) $\dfrac{x}{2} = 3$

   k) $x + 1 = 20$

   l) $10x = 90$

   m) $9x = 54$

   n) $x + 26 = 53$

PA8-9 Solving Equations — Two Operations

1. Jason does some operations to the secret number x. He gets 37 every time.
   Write an equation and then work backwards to find x.

   a) **Perform Jason's operations**   **Work backwards to find x**

Start with x x	Write the equation again $5x + 7 = 37$
Multiply by 5 $5x$	Undo adding 7 by subtracting 7 $5x + 7 - 7 = 37 - 7$
Add 7 $5x + 7$	Write the new equation $5x = 30$
Get 37 $5x + 7 = 37$	Undo multiplying by 5 by dividing by 5 $5x \div 5 = 30 \div 5$
	Write the new equation $x = 6$
	You solved for x!

   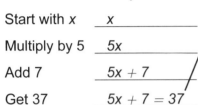

   Check your answer by doing the operations in order:

   Start with your answer: __6__ Multiply by 5: __30__ Add 7: __37__ Do you get 37? __Yes__

   b) **Perform Jason's operations**   **Work backwards to find x**

Start with x x	Write the equation again _____
Multiply by 8 _____	Undo adding 5 by subtracting 5 _____
Add 5 _____	Write the new equation _____
Get 37 _____	Undo multiplying by 8 by dividing by 8 _____
	Write the new equation _____
	You solved for x!

   Check your answer by doing the operations in order:

   Start with your answer: _____ Multiply by 8: _____ Add 5: _____ Do you get 37? _____

   c) **Perform Jason's operations**   **Work backwards to find x**

Start with x x	Write the equation again _____
Multiply by 4 _____	Undo subtracting 3 by adding 3 _____
Subtract 3 _____	Write the new equation _____
Get 37 _____	Undo multiplying by 4 by dividing by 4 _____
	Write the new equation _____
	You solved for x!

   Check your answer by doing the operations in order:

   Start with your answer: _____ Multiply by 4: _____ Subtract 3: _____ Do you get 37? _____

          Patterns and Algebra 8-9

2. Jason does some operations to the secret number x. He gets 10. Write an equation and then work backwards to find x.

a) **Perform Jason's operations**   **Work backwards to find x**

Start with x x

Divide by 6 $\dfrac{x}{6}$

Add 3 $\dfrac{x}{6} + 3$

Get 10 $\dfrac{x}{6} + 3 = 10$

Write the equation again $\dfrac{x}{6} + 3 = 10$

Undo adding 3 by subtracting 3 $\dfrac{x}{6} + 3 - 3 = 10 - 3$

Write the new equation $\dfrac{x}{6} = 7$

Undo dividing by 6 by multiplying by 6 $\dfrac{x}{6}(6) = 7(6)$

Write the new equation $x = 42$

You solved for x!

Check your answer by doing the operations in order:

Start with your answer: ___42___ Divide by 6: ___7___ Add 3: ___10___ Do you get 10? ___Yes___

b) **Perform Jason's operations**   **Work backwards to find x**

Start with x x

Divide by 4   _____

Subtract 1   _____

Get 10   _____

Write the equation again   _____

Undo subtracting 1 by adding 1   _____

Write the new equation   _____

Undo dividing by 4 by multiplying by 4   _____

Write the new equation   _____

You solved for x!

Check your answer by doing the operations in order:

Start with your answer: _____ Divide by 4: _____ Subtract 1: _____ Do you get 10? _____

c) **Perform Jason's operations**   **Work backwards to find x**

Start with x x

Divide by 5   _____

Add 2   _____

Get 10   _____

Write the equation again   _____

Undo adding 2 by subtracting 2   _____

Write the new equation   _____

Undo dividing by 5 by multiplying by 5   _____

Write the new equation   _____

You solved for x!

Check your answer by doing the operations in order:

Start with your answer: _____ Divide by 5: _____ Add 2: _____ Do you get 10? _____

Patterns and Algebra 8-9

3. Solve for the variable by undoing each operation in the equation.

a) $8x + 3 = 27$

$8x + 3 - 3 =$ ___27___ $-$ ___3___

$8x =$ _____

$8x \div 8 =$ _____ $\div$ _____

$x =$ _____

b) $4h - 3 = 37$

$4h - 3 + 3 = 37 +$ _____

$4h =$ _____

$4h \div 4 =$ _____ $\div$ _____

$h =$ _____

c) $\dfrac{x}{3} + 2 = 9$

$\dfrac{x}{3} + 2 - 2 =$ ___9___ $-$ ___2___

$\dfrac{x}{3} =$ ___7___

$\dfrac{x}{3}(3) =$ ___7___ (___3___)

$x =$ ___21___

d) $\dfrac{x}{2} + 3 = 9$

$\dfrac{x}{2} + 3 - 3 =$ _____ $-$ _____

$\dfrac{x}{2} =$ _____

$\dfrac{x}{2}(2) =$ _____ (_____)

$x =$ _____

e) $3s - 4 = 29$

f) $2t + 3 = 11$

g) $\dfrac{x}{3} + 5 = 7$

h) $\dfrac{x}{2} - 4 = 7$

4. Write an expression for the amount of money (in dollars) that each person earns.

a) Katie earns $1 for every 3 phone calls she makes and she makes x calls. _____ $\dfrac{x}{3}$ _____

b) Ru earns $3 for every call he makes and he makes m calls. _____

c) Tim earns $1 for every 5 people he serves and he serves p people. _____

d) Sylvia earns $5 for every person she serves and she serves p people. _____

5. a) A store charges $3 each hour to rent a pair of roller blades. Write an expression (using h for hours) for the cost of renting the roller blades. _____

b) Mary rented the roller blades for 4 hours. How much did she pay? _____

c) Sue paid $15 to rent the roller blades. How many hours did she rent the roller blades for? _____

6. Kim has $35 in savings. She earns $1 for every 5 clients she serves.

a) Write an expression for the total amount she will have saved after serving x clients. _____

b) How much will she have saved after serving 100 clients? _____

c) How many clients does she have to serve to be able to buy a shirt for $90? _____

7. a) For which part of Question 6 did you **substitute** for x? _____

b) For which part of Question 6 did you **solve** for x? _____

PA8-10 Solving Equations — Advanced

> The expression 3×2 is short for $2 + 2 + 2$. Similarly, the expression $3x$ is short for $x + x + x$.

1. Write $6x$ in three ways.

   a) $6x = \underbrace{x + x + x}_{} + \underbrace{x + x + x}_{}$ b) $6x = \underbrace{x + x}_{} + \underbrace{x + x + x + x}_{}$ c) $6x = \underbrace{x}_{} + \underbrace{x + x + x + x + x}_{}$

        $6x = \quad 3x \quad + \quad 3x$ $6x = \qquad + $ $6x = \qquad + $

2. Add.

   a) $3x + 5x = \underline{\quad 8x \quad}$ b) $4x + 3x = \underline{\qquad}$ c) $7x + x = \underline{\qquad}$ d) $4x + 2x + 3x = \underline{\qquad}$

3. Group the x's together, then solve the equation for x.

   a) $2x + 5x = 21$ b) $5x + 4x + 2 = 20$ c) $6x + x - 4 = 31$ d) $3x + 2x - 2 = 23$

4. Fill in the blanks.

   a) $3 - 3 = \underline{\qquad}$ b) $8 - 8 = \underline{\qquad}$ c) $132 - 132 = \underline{\qquad}$ d) $x - x = \underline{\qquad}$

   e) $3 + 3 - 3 = \underline{\qquad}$ f) $7 + 7 - 7 = \underline{\qquad}$ g) $5 + 5 - 5 = \underline{\qquad}$ h) $x + x - x = \underline{\qquad}$

> Every time you see a number or variable subtracted by itself in an equation (Examples: $3 - 3$, $5 - 5$, $8 - 8$, $x - x$), you can cross out both numbers or variables because they will add to 0. Crossing out parts of an equation that make 0 is called **cancelling**.

5. Fill in the blanks by crossing out numbers or variables that add 0 to the equation.

   a) $4 + \cancel{3} - \cancel{3} = \underline{\quad 4 \quad}$ b) $5 + 2 - 2 = \underline{\qquad}$ c) $7 + 1 - 1 = \underline{\qquad}$ d) $8 + 6 - 6 = \underline{\qquad}$

   e) $3 + 7 - 3 = \underline{\qquad}$ f) $2 + 9 - 2 = \underline{\qquad}$ g) $4 + 3 - 3 + 7 - 7 + 6 - 6 = \underline{\qquad}$

   h) $5 + 2 - 2 + 4 - 5 = \underline{\qquad}$ i) $7 + x - x = \underline{\qquad}$ j) $x + 12 - x = \underline{\qquad}$

   k) $x + x - x = \underline{\qquad}$ l) $x + x + x - x = \underline{\qquad}$ m) $x + x - x + x + x + x - x - x = \underline{\qquad}$

6. Rewrite these expressions as sums of individual variables and then cancel. Write what's left.

   a) $5x - 2x = \underline{\quad 3x \quad}$ b) $4x - x = \underline{\qquad}$ c) $5x - x + 2x = \underline{\qquad}$

       $x + x + x + \cancel{x} + \cancel{x} - \cancel{x} - \cancel{x}$

7. Solve these expressions without writing them as sums of individual x's.

   a) $7x - 5x = \underline{\qquad}$ b) $8x - 4x = \underline{\qquad}$ c) $4x - 2x + 3x = \underline{\qquad}$ d) $9x - 3x + 4x = \underline{\qquad}$

8. Group the x's together, then solve for x.

   a) $8x - 3x + x - 2 = 28$ b) $5x + x - x - 2x + 4 = 19$ c) $7x + 4 - 2x - 3 = 26$

PA8-11 Modelling Equations

A triangle has a mass of x kg and a circle has a mass of 1 kg.

1. Draw triangles and circles to show each mass (given in kg).

   a) $x + 2$

   b) $3(x + 2)$

   c) $2x + 3$

   d) $2(x + 3)$

   e) $4(x + 1)$

2. Draw a picture for each expression and write a new expression without brackets.

   a) $2(x + 3)$

   <u> $2x + 6$ </u>

   b) $3(x + 1)$

   _____

   c) $2(x + 5)$

   _____

   d) $3(x + 4)$

   _____

   e) $4(x + 2)$

   _____

   f) $4(x + 4)$

   g) $3(x + 5)$

   h) $5(x + 3)$

   i) $2(x + 4)$

   j) $6(x + 1)$

   _____   _____   _____   _____   _____

3. Finish the equation.

   a) $3(x + 1) = 3x +$ _____

   b) $3(x + 2) = 3x +$ _____

   c) $3(x + 3) = 3x +$ _____

   d) $3(x + 4) = 3x +$ _____

   e) $3(x + 5) = 3x +$ _____

   f) $3(x + b) = 3x +$ _____

   g) $2(x + 3) = 2x +$ _____

   h) $4(x + 1) = 4x +$ _____

   i) $6(x + 2) = 6x +$ _____

   j) $4(x + 5) =$ _____ $+$ _____

   k) $5(x + 3) =$ _____ $+$ _____

   l) $a(x + b) =$ _____ $+$ _____

4. Write the expression on the left without brackets. Then solve the equation.

   a) $3(x + 2) = 18$
          $3x + 6 = 18$
       $3x + 6 - 6 = 18 - 6$
             $3x = 12$
              $x = 4$

   b) $2(x + 5) = 14$

   c) $5(x + 2) = 35$

   BONUS ▶ $2(x + 2) + 3(x + 1) = 27$

A triangle has a mass of x kg and a circle has a mass of 1 kg.

5. Scale A is balanced. Write the equation for each scale.

a)

$2x + 3 = 9$

b)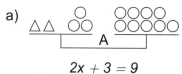

c)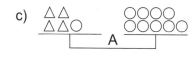

6. Write the equation that Scale A shows. Draw Scale B so that it balances only the triangles from Scale A, and write the new equation.

a)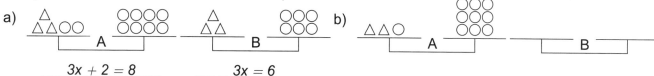

$3x + 2 = 8$ $3x = 6$

b)

7. Scale B is balanced and has only triangles on one side and only circles on the other. Divide the circles into the number of groups given by the number of triangles. Show on Scale C what balances 1 triangle.

a)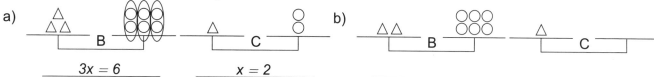

$3x = 6$ $x = 2$

b)

c)

d)

8. Scale A is balanced. Draw scales B and C as in Questions 6 and 7. Write the new equations.

a)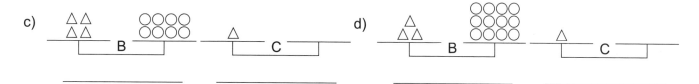

b)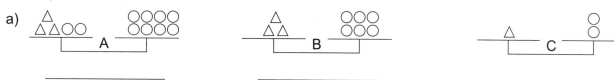

9. Draw Scales A, B, and C to model the process of solving the equation $3x + 5 = 11$.

PA8-12 Counter-examples

To prove that a statement is false, all you need is one **counter-example**. Example: To prove that the statement "All girls wear glasses" is false, you just need to find one girl who does **not** wear glasses.

1. For each statement, circle the counter-example.

   a) All circles in the set are shaded.

   b) All triangles in the set are white.

   c) All striped shapes in the set are circles.

   d) All white shapes in the set are circles.

2. Circle all the counter-examples. (Some questions will have more than one.)

   a) All balls are spheres.

   b) All vehicles have four wheels.

   c) All words have an "e."

   person   place   thing   object   bcjxp   bcjxe

   d) All English sentences end in a period.

   Who's there?   No way!   ¿Cual es tu nombre?   My name is Ahmed.

3. In Question 2 b), why isn't the banana a counter-example? _____

   _____

   _____

4. Ms. K gives each student a card with both a number and a letter. She says that all cards with an even number (0, 2, 4, 6, ...) should have a vowel (A, E, I, O, or U).

a) The number 3 is not even. Can the card | 3 | J | be a counter-example? _____

Why or why not? _____

b) Find all the cards that are wrong.

| 3 | J | | 6 | A | | 5 | E | | 12 | R | | 24 | U | | 7 | O |

| 19 | X | | E | 19 | | J | 16 | | H | 13 | | A | 14 | | C | 28 |

> To prove a statement false, you need to **find only one counter-example**.
>
> To prove a statement true, you need to **make sure it is true for all examples**.

5. Each card below has a letter and a number. Decide whether each statement is true (T) or false (F) for all the cards shown. A statement will be true if it is true for all the cards and false if you can find a counter-example. For the statements that are false, write the first counter-example you find.

| r | 15 | | E | 13 | | U | 3 | | B | 4 | | D | 7 |

| M | 6 | | j | 3 | | e | 5 | | F | 8 | | H | 10 |

a) All cards with capital letters have even numbers.   T   F

b) All cards with vowels have odd numbers.   T   F

c) All cards with capital vowels have odd numbers.   T   F

d) All cards with odd numbers have capital letters.   T   F

e) All cards with even numbers have capital letters.   T   F

f) All cards with odd numbers have vowels.   T   F

g) All cards with even numbers have a consonant.   T   F

h) All cards with lower case letters have odd numbers.   T   F

i) All cards with odd numbers have lower case letters.   T   F

j) All cards with lower case consonants have odd numbers.   T   F

6. Was it easier to prove a statement true or false? Explain.

The two false statements below are **the reverse** of each other.

"All girls are teenagers."   "All teenagers are girls."

7. A counter-example for a statement will be different from a counter-example for
   its reverse. Find a counter-example for each statement and for its reverse.

   A. ☐   **B.** ◯   **C.** ▪   **D.** ◦   **E.** ☐   **F.** ◯

   a) All dark shapes are circles.   Counter-example: ___C___

       All circles are dark.   Counter-example: _____

   b) All white shapes are big.   Counter-example: _____

       All big shapes are white.   Counter-example: _____

   c) All circles are big.   Counter-example: _____

       All big shapes are circles.   Counter-example: _____

8. Sometimes a statement is true but its reverse isn't. Find the reverse of each
   statement and then find a counter-example for the reverse.

   a) All **boys** are **people**.

       Reverse: All _____ are _____.

       Counter-example: _____.

   b) All **bananas** are **fruit**.

       Reverse: All _____ are _____.

       Counter-example: _____.

   c) All **fish** are **animals that live in water**.

       Reverse: All _____ are _____.

       Counter-example: _____.

   d) Any sequence of words that **forms a sentence** must **start with a capital letter**.

       Reverse: Any sequence of words that _____ must _____.

       Counter-example: _____.

9. Write the reverse of each statement and whether the statements are true or false.

   a) All vehicles with wheels are cars.   ___False___

       Reverse: ___All cars are vehicles with wheels.___   ___True___

   b) All apples are red fruits.   _____

       Reverse: _____   _____

   c) All girls are soccer players.   d) All circles are shapes.   e) All Canadian coins worth $2 are toonies.

PA8-13 Exploring Preservation of Equality

1. Describe what happens to x in each expression.

   a) $3x + 5$ _Multiply by 3. Then add 5._

   b) $3(x + 5)$ _Add 5. Then multiply by 3._

   c) $5(x - 4)$ _____

   d) $5x - 4$ _____

   e) $\dfrac{x}{2} + 1$ _____

   f) $\dfrac{x + 1}{2}$ _____

   g) $3(x + 5) - 2$ _____

   h) $3(x + 5) \div 3$ _____

   i) $2(x + 3) - 2$ _____

   j) $2x + 3 - 3$ _____

   k) $2(x + 3) - 3$ _____

2. Write an expression that shows the operations done to x in order.

   a) Add 2. Multiply by 3.   _$3(x + 2)$_   b) Multiply by 3. Add 2. _____

   c) Subtract 3. Multiply by 2. _____   d) Multiply by 2. Subtract 3. _____

   e) Divide by 2. Add 3. _____   f) Add 3. Divide by 2. _____

   g) Add 2. Multiply by 3. Subtract 2. _____

   h) Add 2. Multiply by 3. Divide by 3. _____

   i) Multiply by 3. Add 2. Subtract 2. _____

   j) Multiply by 3. Add 2. Divide by 3. _____

3. Which expression from Question 2 is the same as just adding 2? _____

4. Which expression from Question 2 is the same as just multiplying by 3? _____

5. a) Do these operations to x: Multiply by 3. Then add 6. Then divide by 3. _____

   b) Sara thinks that since dividing by 3 undoes multiplying by 3, she will end up with the result of adding 6, for any x:

   $$(3x + 6) \div 3 = x + 6 \text{ for all } x.$$

   Show that $x = 0$ is a counter-example.

   c) Explain why Sara's thinking is wrong.

6. a) Circle the two expressions that are equal for all x.

$4x - 4$ $\qquad$ $4x \div 4$ $\qquad$ $4x + 4$ $\qquad$ x $\qquad$ $4x$ $\qquad$ $4 + x$ $\qquad$ $4 - x$

b) Substitute $x = 3$ into each expression from part a).

$4x - 4$ $\qquad$ $4x \div 4$ $\qquad$ $4x + 4$ $\qquad$ x $\qquad$ $4x$ $\qquad$ $4 + x$ $\qquad$ $4 - x$
$= 4(3) - 4$
$= 12 - 4$
$= 8$

c) Which two expressions are equal for $x = 3$? _____ and _____

d) Does this agree with your answer to part a)? _____

7. Sara notices that $3x + 5$ and $3 + 5x$ have the same value when $x = 1$:

$$3x + 5 = 3(1) + 5 \qquad \text{and} \qquad 3 + 5x = 3 + 5(1)$$
$$= 3 + 5 \qquad\qquad\qquad\qquad\qquad = 3 + 5$$
$$= 8 \qquad\qquad\qquad\qquad\qquad\quad = 8$$

She thinks that $3x + 5 = 3 + 5x$ for **all values** of x. Find a counter-example to show that she's wrong.

8. Solve for x by working backwards.

a) $\quad 3(x + 2) = 18$
$\quad 3(x + 2) \div 3 = 18 \div 3$
$\quad\quad\quad x + 2 = 6$
$\quad x + 2 - 2 = 6 - 2$
$\quad\quad\quad\quad x = 4$

b) $\quad 5(x - 3) = 30$
$\quad 5(x - 3) \div 5 =$

c) $\quad 2(x + 1) = 18$

9. Solve the same equations a different way: first change the expression on the left to an expression without brackets.

a) $\quad 3(x + 2) = 18$
$\quad\quad 3x + 6 = 18$
$\quad 3x + 6 - 6 = 18 - 6$
$\quad\quad\quad 3x = 12$
$\quad\quad 3x \div 3 = 12 \div 3$
$\quad\quad\quad x = 4$

b) $\quad 5(x - 3) = 30$
$\quad\quad 5x - 15 =$

c) $\quad 2(x + 1) = 18$

10. Compare your answers to Questions 8 and 9. Do you get the same answers both ways? Why should you look for a mistake if you **don't** get the same answer both ways?

Patterns and Algebra 8-13

PA8-14 Correcting Mistakes

1. Here are three ways to solve $2x + 6 = 14$:

Method 1

$2x + 6 = 14$	
$2x + 6 - 6 = 14 - 6$	Subtract 6 from both sides
$2x = 8$	Rewrite both sides
$2x \div 2 = 8 \div 2$	Divide both sides by 2
$x = 4$	Rewrite both sides

Method 2

$2x + 6 = 14$
$2(x + 3) = 14$
$x + 3 = 7$
$x + 3 - 3 = 7 - 3$
$x = 4$

Method 3

$2x + 6 = 14$
$2(x + 6) = 14$
$x + 6 = 7$
$x + 6 - 6 = 7 - 6$
$x = 1$

a) Do the three ways give the same answer? _____

b) Substitute $x = 4$ into the expression $2x + 6$. Do you get 14? _____

   Substitute $x = 1$ into the expression $2x + 6$. Do you get 14? _____

   What is the correct answer? _____

c) Describe in words each step in Methods 2 and 3. Where is the mistake in Method 3?

2. Decide whether each solution is correct by substituting the answer into the original expression. For each incorrect solution, describe the mistake. If the solution is correct, write "correct."

a) $3x + 6 = 21$
$3(x + 6) = 21$
$x + 6 = 7$
$x + 6 - 6 = 7 - 6$
$x = 1$

b) $3x + 6 = 21$
$3(x + 2) = 21$
$x + 2 = 21$
$x + 2 - 2 = 21 - 2$
$x = 19$

c) $3x + 6 = 21$
$3(x + 2) = 21$
$x + 2 = 7$
$x + 2 - 2 = 7 - 2$
$x = 5$

d) $3x + 6 = 21$
$3x + 6 - 6 = 21 + 6$
$3x = 27$
$3x \div 3 = 27 \div 3$
$x = 9$

e) $\dfrac{x}{2} - 5 = 15$
$2\left(\dfrac{x}{2}\right) - 5 = 30$
$x - 5 = 30$
$x - 5 + 5 = 30 + 5$
$x = 35$

f) $\dfrac{x}{2} - 5 = 15$
$\dfrac{x}{2} - 5 + 5 = 15 + 5$
$\dfrac{x}{2} = 20$
$\dfrac{x}{2}(2) = 20(2)$
$x = 40$

g) $5(x + 2) = 30$
$5(x + 2) \div 5 = 30 \div 5$
$x + 2 = 4$
$x + 2 - 2 = 4 - 2$
$x = 2$

h) $5(x + 2) = 30$
$5x + 10 = 30$
$5x + 10 - 10 = 30 - 10$
$5x = 20$
$x = 4$

PA8-15 Word Problems

To solve word problems, you turn the words into algebraic expressions. The words give clues to the operations you need to use. Here are some of the clues for different operations:

Add	Subtract	Multiply	Divide
increased by	less than	product	divided by
sum	difference	times	divided into
more than	decreased by	twice as many	quotient
	reduced by		

1. Match each algebraic expression with the correct phrase.

2 more than a number	$4x$	2 divided into a number	$3x$
a number divided by 3	$x - 2$	a number reduced by 4	$x \div 2$
2 less than a number	$x + 2$	a number times 3	$x + 3$
the product of a number and 4	$x - 3$	twice as many as a number	$x - 4$
a number decreased by 3	$x \div 3$	a number increased by 3	$2x$

2. Write an algebraic expression for each description.

a) Four more than a number.   b) A number decreased by 10.   c) The product of 7 and a number.

d) A number divided by 8.   e) Two less than a number.   f) The sum of a number and 7.

g) Five times a number.   h) Six divided into a number.   i) The product of a number and 3.

j) Five more than a number, then three times the answer.   k) A number reduced by 4, then multiplied by 2.   l) Twice as many as 3 less than a number.

When solving word problems, the word "is" translates to the equal sign ($=$).

Example: "Two more than a number is seven" can be written $x + 2 = 7$.

3. Solve the following problems by first writing an equation.

a) Four more than a number is thirty-two.   b) Five less than a number is 19.

c) Five times a number is thirty.   d) A number divided by four is seven.

e) Six divided into a number is four.   f) The product of a number and 5 is forty.

g) A number multiplied by two then decreased by five is thirty-five.   h) A number divided by three then increased by four is seventeen.

i) 3 divided into a number is 2 less than 8.   j) 3 less than a number is 5 times smaller than 20.

k) Three times two more than a number is seventeen.   l) Three times a number is 14 more than 5.

Two numbers are **consecutive** if one is the next number after the other.

Examples: 6 and 7 are consecutive numbers because 7 is the next number after 6
6 and 8 are consecutive even numbers because 8 is the next even number after 6

4. Fill in the blanks.

a) 36, 37, 38, and _____ are consecutive numbers.

b) 4, 6, 8, and _____ are consecutive even numbers.

c) 7 and _____ are consecutive odd numbers.

d) 7 and _____ are consecutive prime numbers.

e) x, $x + 1$, and _____ are consecutive numbers.

f) x is even. x, _____, and _____ are consecutive even numbers.

g) x is odd. x, _____, and _____ are consecutive odd numbers.

5. The sum of three consecutive numbers is 48. What are the numbers?

Solve this problem in two ways.

a) Use a T-table to list all possible pairs of consecutive numbers, in order, and find the sums. Stop when you reach 48.

3 consecutive numbers	their sum
1, 2, 3	$1 + 2 + 3 = 6$
2, 3, 4	$2 + 3 + 4 = 9$
3, 4, 5	$3 + 4 + 5 = 12$
4, 5, 6	
5, 6, 7	

b) Use algebra.

i) If the smallest of the consecutive numbers is x, write a formula for the other numbers.

Smallest number $= x$

Middle number $=$ _____ Largest number $=$ _____

ii) Write an equation using the given information:

The sum of the three consecutive numbers is 48. _____ $= 48$

iii) Solve your equation. What is the smallest number? What are the three numbers?

6. The sum of three consecutive even numbers is 42. What are the three numbers?

   a) Let the smallest number be *x* and solve the problem.
   b) Let the middle number be *x* and solve the problem.
   c) Let the largest number be *x* and solve the problem.
   d) Did you get the same answer all three ways?

7. a) Do Question 6 by using T-tables.
   b) Did you get the same answer using T-tables as you did using algebra?
   c) Which method do you like better: T-tables or algebra? Explain.

8. a) The area (*A*) of a rectangle is given by $A = l \times w$ (also written $A = lw$), where l = length and w = width. Evaluate the expression for the area of a rectangle with:

   i) $l = 2$ $w = 7$ ii) $l = 8$ $w = 9$ iii) $l = 3.7$ $w = 10$

   b) A rectangle has area 72 and length 8. Write an equation for the width *w* and solve your equation.

REMINDER ▶ The perimeter of a shape is the distance around the shape.

---

9. a) Write an expression for the perimeter of each shape (*x* stands for the length of one or more unknown sides).

   i) 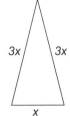   ii) 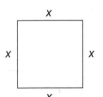   iii) 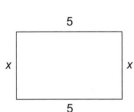   iv)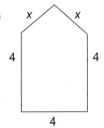

   b) The perimeter of each shape in part a) is 28. Find the unknown side lengths.

10. Mark's dad is three times older than Mark. Mark's sister is 2 years younger than Mark.

    The sum of their ages is 48. How old is Mark?

BONUS ▶

   Amal's sister is half as old as Amal.
   Amal's mother is 3 times Amal's age.
   Amal's father is 4 years older than Amal's mother.
   The sum of all 4 ages is 94.
   How old was Amal's mother when Amal was born?

NS8-58 Perfect Squares

1. Find the factors of each number below by drawing all the different rectangles (with whole number side lengths) that have an area equal to the number.

Example:

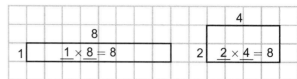

So the factors of 8 are: 1, 2, 4, and 8.

a) 4   b) 5   c) 6

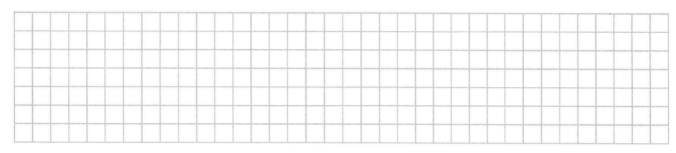

d) 7   e) 8   f) 9

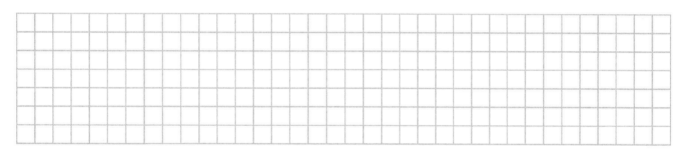

2. For which numbers in Question 1 could you draw a square? _____

> A number larger than 0 is called a **perfect square** if you can draw a square with whole number side lengths having that area.

3. a) Draw squares with side lengths 1, 2, 3, 4, and 5 on the grid.

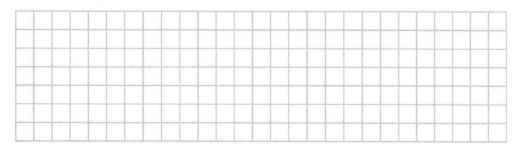

   b) Write the first five perfect squares larger than 0.

   _____ _____ _____ _____ _____

4. Explain why a square with an area of 20 cm² does not have a whole number side length.

5. Can a prime number be a perfect square? Explain.

6. Show that 36 is a perfect square by drawing a square with area 36.

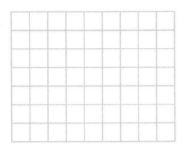

7. Show that 10 is not a perfect square by drawing all non-congruent rectangles with area 10.

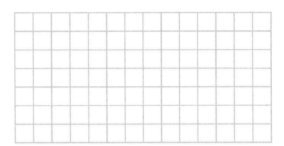

Any perfect square can be written as a product of a whole number with itself.

Example: $25 = 5 \times 5$.

 Area = $5 \times 5 = 25$ squares

NOTE: Since $0 = 0 \times 0$, we say that 0 is a perfect square even though you cannot draw a square with area 0.

8. Write the first ten perfect squares larger than 0.

$1 \times 1 =$ _____ $2 \times 2 =$ _____ $3 \times 3 =$ _____ $4 \times 4 =$ _____ $5 \times 5 =$ _____

$6 \times 6 =$ _____ $7 \times 7 =$ _____ $8 \times 8 =$ _____ $9 \times 9 =$ _____ $10 \times 10 =$ _____

When we multiply a number by itself, we get a perfect square. This process is called **squaring the number**. Example: 6 squared is $6 \times 6 = 36$. We write $6^2 = 36$. (The 2 is because we multiplied two 6s.)

9. Write each perfect square as a product and evaluate it.

a) $5^2 = 5 \times 5 = 25$ b) $3^2 =$ c) $8^2 =$ d) $0^2 =$ e) $7^2 =$

10. Write the numbers from smallest to largest.

a) 3^2 5^2 4^2

  $\underline{\ 9\ }$ $\underline{\ 25\ }$ $\underline{\ 16\ }$

  $\underline{\ 9\ }$ $\underline{\ 16\ }$ $\underline{\ 25\ }$

b) 10^2 8^2 9^2

  _____   _____   _____

  _____   _____   _____

c) 5^2 12^2 7^2

  _____   _____   _____

  _____   _____   _____

d) 3^2 5 10 4^2 2^2

  _____   _____   _____   _____   _____

  _____   _____   _____   _____   _____

e) 50 7^2 9^2 8^2 85

  _____   _____   _____   _____   _____

  _____   _____   _____   _____   _____

NS8-59 Factors of Perfect Squares

To list all the factors of a given number (the pairs of numbers that multiply to give that number), stop when you get a number that is already part of a pair.

1. Make a chart to find all the pairs of numbers that multiply to give each number.

a) 20

1st	2nd
1	20
2	10
3	
4	5
5	Done!

b) 12

1st	2nd

c) 15   d) 14   e) 25

f) 5   g) 26   h) 30

i) 42   j) 72   k) 63

l) 100   m) 64   n) 91

A **factor rainbow** for a number pairs the factors that multiply to give that number.

Factor rainbow for 9

Factor rainbow for 10

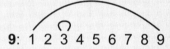

9: 1 2 3 4 5 6 7 8 9

10: 1 2 3 4 5 6 7 8 9 10

---

2. Finish the factor rainbow for each number.

6: 1 2 3 4 5 6   8: 1 2 3 4 5 6 7 8   12: 1 2 3 4 5 6 7 8 9 10 11 12

As a shortcut to making a factor rainbow, we can leave out all numbers that are not factors.

Example:

6: 1 2 3 6

---

3. Using the shortcut, make a factor rainbow for each number from 1 to 20.
   For the numbers from 11 to 20, you will need to list the factors first.

1: 1

2: 1 2

3: 1 3

4: 1 2 4

5: 1 5

6: 1 2 3 6

7: 1 7

8: 1 2 4 8

9: 1 3 9

10: 1 2 5 10

11:

12:

13:

14:

15:

16:

17:

18:

19:

20:

4. a) Look at your answers to Question 3. Which numbers have an odd number of factors?

_____ , _____ , _____ , and _____ .

b) Extend the sequence of numbers you found in part a) by using the gaps between the numbers.

◯　　　◯　　　◯　　　◯　　　◯

_____ , _____ , _____ , _____ , _____ , _____

Do you recognize the numbers in the sequence? What are they called? _____

c) All perfect squares have an odd number of factors. Why?

Hint: Look at the factor rainbows from Question 3. When is there a factor that is paired up with itself?

d) Write the reverse (see p. 116) of the statement from part c). Is it also true?

INVESTIGATION ▶ Which numbers have exactly 3 factors?

A. Explain why any number with exactly 3 factors is a perfect square.

B. List all the factors of the first 10 perfect squares greater than 0.

Perfect Square	Factors
$1=1^2$	1
$4=2^2$	1, 2, 4
$9=3^2$	1, 3, 9
$16=4^2$	1, 2, 4, 8, 16
$25=5^2$	
$36=6^2$	
$49=7^2$	
$64=8^2$	
$81=9^2$	
$100=10^2$	

C. Which perfect squares between 1 and 100 have exactly 3 factors?

_____^{2} , _____^{2} , _____^{2} , and _____^{2}

D. What are the prime numbers between 1 and 10?

_____ , _____ , _____ , and _____

E. Compare your answers to parts C. and D. What do you notice?

F. Make a conjecture about which numbers have exactly 3 factors.

G. Use your conjecture to find the first 3 numbers greater than 100 that have exactly 3 factors.

　　　　　　　　　　　　　　　　　　　　Number Sense 8-59

NS8-60 Square Roots of Perfect Squares

> The number 5 is called the **square root** of 25 because 25 is the **square** of 5.
>
> We write $\sqrt{25} = 5$ because $25 = 5^2 = 5 \times 5$.
>
> Square roots are numbers, so you can add, subtract, multiply, and divide them.

1. Find the square root by writing the same number in each box.

   a) $9 = \boxed{} \times \boxed{}$ b) $49 = \boxed{} \times \boxed{}$ c) $0 = \boxed{} \times \boxed{}$ d) $25 = \boxed{} \times \boxed{}$

2. Evaluate.

   a) $\sqrt{49} = \underline{\quad 7 \quad}$ b) $\sqrt{16} = \underline{\quad\quad}$ c) $\sqrt{9} = \underline{\quad\quad}$ d) $\sqrt{36} = \underline{\quad\quad}$

   e) $\sqrt{1} = \underline{\quad\quad}$ f) $\sqrt{100} = \underline{\quad\quad}$ g) $\sqrt{81} = \underline{\quad\quad}$ h) $\sqrt{64} = \underline{\quad\quad}$

3. Evaluate.

   a) $\sqrt{25} + \sqrt{4}$ b) $\sqrt{36} \times \sqrt{25}$ c) $\sqrt{64} - \sqrt{9}$ d) $\sqrt{100} \div \sqrt{4}$ e) $\sqrt{49} + \sqrt{64}$
   $= 5 + 2 = 7$

   f) $\sqrt{36} - \sqrt{25}$ g) $\sqrt{36} \div \sqrt{4}$ h) $\sqrt{36} + \sqrt{25} - \sqrt{1}$ **BONUS** ▶ $\sqrt{25} + \sqrt{16} \times \sqrt{9}$

4. Order these numbers from smallest to largest.

   a) $\sqrt{49} \quad \sqrt{64} \quad \sqrt{25} \quad \sqrt{9} \quad \sqrt{16}$ b) $\sqrt{100} \quad 3^2 \quad 5 \quad 4^2 \quad \sqrt{4} \quad \sqrt{8^2}$

5. Evaluate the two expressions. Then write = (equal) or ≠ (not equal) in the box.

   a) $\sqrt{4 \times 9}$ $\boxed{=}$ $\sqrt{4} \times \sqrt{9}$

   $= \sqrt{36}$ $= \underline{\ 2\ } \times \underline{\ 3\ }$

   $= \underline{\ 6\ }$ $= \underline{\ 6\ }$

   b) $\sqrt{9 + 16}$ $\boxed{}$ $\sqrt{9} + \sqrt{16}$

   $= \sqrt{\underline{\quad}}$ $= \underline{\quad} + \underline{\quad}$

   $= \underline{\quad}$ $= \underline{\quad}$

   c) $\sqrt{169 - 25}$ $\boxed{}$ $\sqrt{169} - \sqrt{25}$

   $= \sqrt{\underline{\quad}}$ $= \underline{\quad} - \underline{\quad}$

   $= \underline{\quad}$ $= \underline{\quad}$

   d) $\sqrt{100 \div 4}$ $\boxed{}$ $\sqrt{100} \div \sqrt{4}$

   $= \sqrt{\underline{\quad}}$ $= \underline{\quad} \div \underline{\quad}$

   $= \underline{\quad}$ $= \underline{\quad}$

6. The factor rainbow for each perfect square is shown. Find the square root.

   a)

   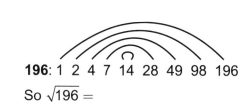

   144: 1 2 3 4 6 8 9 12 16 18 24 36 48 72 144

   So $\sqrt{144} =$

   b)

   196: 1 2 4 7 14 28 49 98 196

   So $\sqrt{196} =$

7. a) How can you find the square root of a perfect square by looking at its factor rainbow?

   b) Draw a factor rainbow for 225 and find $\sqrt{225}$.

1. Find the prime factorization of each perfect square by first finding the prime factorization of its square root. Circle the prime numbers.

a)   144

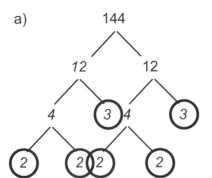

b)   196

c)   64

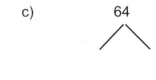

d)   225

e)   256

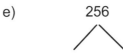

f)   400

2. How many times does the prime number 2 occur in the prime factorization of each number and its square root in Question 1?

a) $144 = 2 \times 2 \times 3 \times 2 \times 2 \times 3$ and $12 = 2 \times 2 \times 3$ So 2 occurs __4__ times in 144 and __2__ times in 12.

b) $196 =$ and $14 =$ So 2 occurs _____ times in 196 and _____ times in 14.

c) $64 =$ and _____ =   So 2 occurs _____ times in 64 and _____ times in _____.

d) $256 =$ and _____ =   So 2 occurs _____ times in 256 and _____ times in _____.

e) $225 =$ and _____ =   So 2 occurs _____ times in 225 and _____ times in _____.

f) $400 =$ and _____ =   So 2 occurs _____ times in 400 and _____ times in _____.

3. The prime number 2 occurs three times in the prime factorization of 56.

How many times will 2 occur in the prime factorization of $56 \times 56 = 56^2$? _____

How do you know? _____

_____

4. Can the prime number 2 occur an **odd** number of times in the prime factorization of a perfect square? Explain. _____

_____

INVESTIGATION ▶ Can any prime number occur an odd number of times in the prime factorization of a perfect square?

A. $18 = 2 \times 3 \times 3$ so $18^2 = 18 \times 18 = $ _____

The prime number 3 occurs two times in the prime factorization of 18.

How many times does it occur in the prime factorization of $18^2 = 18 \times 18$? _____

B. $250 = 2 \times 5 \times 5 \times 5$ so $250^2 = 250 \times 250 = $ _____

The prime number 5 occurs three times in the prime factorization of 250.

How many times does it occur in the prime factorization of $250^2 = 250 \times 250$? _____

C. a) **Double** the number of times each prime factor occurs. Then use a calculator to find the **square root** of the result. In parts iii)–vii) you have to find the factors first.

   i) $45 = 3 \times 3 \times 5$ <u>$3 \times 3 \times 3 \times 3 \times 5 \times 5$</u> $=$ <u>2025</u> and $\sqrt{2025} = $ <u>45</u>

   ii) $28 = 2 \times 2 \times 7$ _____ $=$ _____ and $\sqrt{} = $ _____

   iii) 48   iv) 35   v) 91   vi) 27   vii) 63

   b) What do you notice? _____

D. a) **Halve** the number of times each prime factor occurs, then find the **square** of the result. In parts iii)–vii) you have to find the factors first.

   i) $144 = 2 \times 2 \times 2 \times 2 \times 3 \times 3$ <u>$2 \times 2 \times 3$</u> $=$ <u>12</u> and <u>12</u> $^2 = $ <u>144</u>

   ii) $324 = 2 \times 2 \times 3 \times 3 \times 3 \times 3$ _____ $=$ _____ and _____ $^2 = $ _____

   iii) 5625   iv) 576   v) 1936   vi) 11 025   vii) 27 225

   b) What do you notice? _____

E. Explain why a number is a perfect square if all its prime factors occur an even number of times in its prime factorization.

***

5. Which numbers are perfect squares? Find their prime factorizations to decide.

   a) 6 300   b) 6 400   c) 2 268   d) 243   e) 729   f) 1 296

6. a) Extend the pattern.

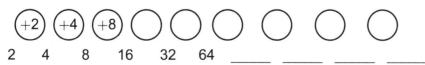

   b) Find the prime factorization of all 10 terms in the pattern.

   c) Circle the perfect squares in the pattern in part a).

   d) Will the 100th term be a perfect square? How do you know?

We can find the square of non-whole numbers, too. Example: $1.3^2 = 1.3 \times 1.3 = 1.69$

1. Evaluate each square.

a) $1.4^2 = \underline{1.4 \times 1.4}$
= _____

b) $0.8^2 = \underline{0.8 \times 0.8}$
= _____

c) $2.5^2 = \underline{\quad} \times \underline{\quad}$
= _____

The number 19 is not a perfect square because there is no whole number whose square is 19.

$4^2 = 16$ is **less** than 19   and $5^2 = 25$ is **more** than 19.

But we can still try to find its square root! The number $\sqrt{19}$ is the decimal number that, multiplied by itself, gives 19.

2. a) Explain why $\sqrt{19}$ is more than 4 and less than 5.

b) Calculate $4.5 \times 4.5 = \underline{\quad}\,\underline{\quad}.\underline{\quad}\,\underline{\quad}$. Is $\sqrt{19}$ more or less than 4.5? _____

c) Guess $\sqrt{19}$ to one decimal place. $\sqrt{19} \approx 4.\underline{\quad}$

d) Check your guess by multiplying. $4.\underline{\quad} \times 4.\underline{\quad} = \underline{\quad}$

e) Was your guess too low or too high? _____

f) Increase your estimate by one tenth if your estimate was too low and decrease it by one tenth if your estimate was too high. Square your new estimate. $4.\underline{\quad} \times 4.\underline{\quad} = \underline{\quad}$

g) Is your new answer closer to 19 or farther away?

h) Continue guessing and revising until your answer is as close to 19 as you can make it.

i) Estimate $\sqrt{19}$ to one decimal place. $\sqrt{19} \approx 4.\underline{\quad}$

To calculate $\sqrt{19}$ on a calculator, one of these three sequences will work:

Step 1: Key in 19.   OR **Step 1:** Key in 19.   OR **Step 1:** Press the $\boxed{\sqrt{}}$ key.
Step 2: Press the $\boxed{2^{nd}}$ or $\boxed{INV}$ key.   **Step 2:** Press the $\boxed{\sqrt{}}$ key.   **Step 2:** Key in 19.
Step 3: Press the $\boxed{x^2}$ key.

3. Calculate $\sqrt{19}$ on a calculator. Round your answer to two decimal places, then one decimal place.

$\sqrt{19} \approx 4.\underline{\quad}\,\underline{\quad} \approx 4.\underline{\quad}$ Does your answer agree with your answer to Question 2 i)? Explain.

4. Shade as many full layers as you can until you have shaded the given number of squares.

Which two perfect squares is the number between? Do parts c)–i) on grid paper.

a)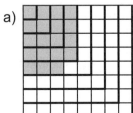
19 is between
$\underline{\quad}^2$ and $\underline{\quad}^2$

b)
11 is between
$\underline{\quad}^2$ and $\underline{\quad}^2$

c) 44   d) 21   e) 35   f) 50   g) 72   h) 65   i) 42

5. Which perfect squares is each whole number between? Which consecutive whole numbers is each square root between?

a) 7 is between _____4_____ and _____9_____

So 7 is between ____2^2____ and ____3^2____

So $\sqrt{7}$ is between ____2____ and ____3____

b) 15 is between _____ and _____

So 15 is between _____^{2} and _____^{2}

So $\sqrt{15}$ is between _____ and _____

c) 85 is between _____ and _____

So 85 is between _____^{2} and _____^{2}

So $\sqrt{85}$ is between _____ and _____

d) 52 is between _____ and _____

So 52 is between _____^{2} and _____^{2}

So $\sqrt{52}$ is between _____ and _____

e) $\sqrt{45}$ f) $\sqrt{91}$ g) $\sqrt{13}$ h) $\sqrt{55}$ i) $\sqrt{6}$ j) $\sqrt{72}$

6. Estimate each square root to one decimal place by guessing, checking, and revising. Show your work.

a) $\sqrt{12}$ b) $\sqrt{22}$ c) $\sqrt{15}$ d) $\sqrt{30}$

7. Calculate each square root on a calculator and round your answer to one decimal place.

a) $\sqrt{12} \approx$ _____   b) $\sqrt{22} \approx$ _____   c) $\sqrt{15} \approx$ _____   d) $\sqrt{30} \approx$ _____

8. Do your answers to Questions 6 and 7 agree? Explain.

9. Guled took the square root of a number and his calculator showed 6.324 555 3.

a) Multiply this number by itself. What number did Guled take the square root of?

b) Was the calculator's answer an approximation? How do you know?

10. Find the closest perfect square to each number and the closest whole number to its square root.

a) closest perfect square to **19** is __16__ = __4__^{2}

closest whole number to $\sqrt{19} \approx$ __4.36__ is __4__.

b) closest perfect square to **27** is ____ = ____^{2}

closest whole number to $\sqrt{27} \approx$ ____ is ____

c) closest perfect square to **21** is ____ = ____^{2}

closest whole number to $\sqrt{21} \approx$ ____ is ____

d) closest perfect square to **44** is ____ = ____^{2}

closest whole number to $\sqrt{44} \approx$ ____ is ____

11. Look at your answers to Question 10 and complete this statement.

If n^2 is the closest perfect square to x, then ____ is the closest whole number to $\sqrt{x}$.

12. Estimate each square root to its nearest whole number by finding the nearest perfect square to the number you are taking the square root of.

a) $\sqrt{24}$ b) $\sqrt{32}$ c) $\sqrt{20}$ d) $\sqrt{75}$ e) $\sqrt{68}$

NS8-63 Estimating Square Roots

Estimate $\sqrt{11}$ as follows.

11 is between $9 = 3^2$ and $16 = 4^2$.

11 is $\dfrac{2}{7}$ of the way from 9 to 16.

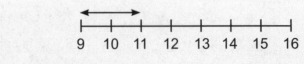

So $\sqrt{11}$ is approximately $\dfrac{2}{7}$ of the way from 3 to 4.

So $\sqrt{11} \approx 3\dfrac{2}{7} = 3 + (2 \div 7) \approx 3.285\,7 \approx 3.3$. On a calculator, $\sqrt{11} \approx 3.316\,6 \approx 3.3$.

1. Use a number line to estimate each square root.
   Write your answer rounded to one decimal place.

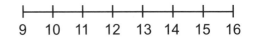

   a) 12 is _____ of the way from 9 to 16.

   So $\sqrt{12}$ is approximately _____ of the way from 3 to 4.

   So $\sqrt{12}$ is approximately _____ $= 3 +$ _____ $\div$ _____ $\approx$ _____

   b) $\sqrt{15} \approx$ _____
   c) $\sqrt{10} \approx$ _____
   d) $\sqrt{14} \approx$ _____
   e) $\sqrt{13} \approx$ _____

2. Estimate each square root using the number line.

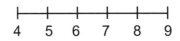

   Write your answer as a mixed number.

   a) $\sqrt{5} \approx$ _____
   b) $\sqrt{6} \approx$ _____
   c) $\sqrt{7} \approx$ _____
   d) $\sqrt{8} \approx$ _____

3. Calculate each square root from Question 2 to one decimal place using a calculator.
   Were your estimates correct?

   a) $\sqrt{5} \approx$ _____
   b) $\sqrt{6} \approx$ _____
   c) $\sqrt{7} \approx$ _____
   d) $\sqrt{8} \approx$ _____

4. Estimate each square root to two decimal places and then to one decimal place.
   Use a number line.

   a) $\sqrt{32} \approx 5.$___ ___ $\approx 5.$___
   b) $\sqrt{50} \approx 7.$___ ___ $\approx 7.$___
   c) $\sqrt{85} \approx$ ___.___ ___ $\approx$ ___.___

5. Calculate each square root from Question 4 on your calculator.

   a) $\sqrt{32} \approx 5.$___ ___ $\approx 5.$___
   b) $\sqrt{50} \approx 7.$___ ___ $\approx 7.$___
   c) $\sqrt{85} \approx$ ___.___ ___ $\approx$ ___.___

6. For how many decimal places did your estimates and calculations in Questions 4 and 5 agree? _____

7. Estimate and then calculate each square root. To how many decimal places is your
   estimate accurate?

   a) $\sqrt{21}$
   b) $\sqrt{13}$
   c) $\sqrt{39}$
   d) $\sqrt{69}$
   e) $\sqrt{45}$
   f) $\sqrt{2}$

PDM8-1 Bar Graphs

A **bar graph** has four parts: vertical and horizontal **axes**, a **scale**, **labels** (including a title), and **data** (given by the bars).

▶ The bars in a bar graph can be vertical or horizontal.

▶ The scale tells how much each interval on the axis represents.

▶ The labels indicate what the data in the bars is.

1. frequency table   bar graph

Mode of Transportation	Number of Students
bike	51
subway	45
walking	144
bus	120
car	27

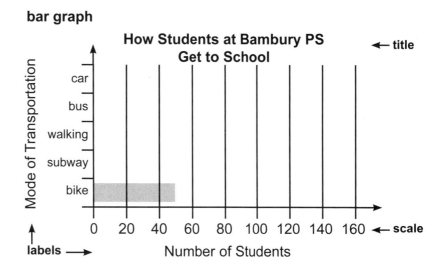

a) Complete the bar graph.

b) What scale was used in the bar graph? Do you think it was a good choice? Why or why not?

_____

_____

c) Dana wants to make another bar graph for the same data. All the numbers in the frequency table are divisible by 3. Dana thinks she could use intervals of 3 for the scale. What do you think of her choice? Explain.

_____

_____

d) Think of the students at your school. How do they get to school? Would you predict similar or different results from those found at Bambury PS? Explain.

2. Bobby made a tally chart and bar graph of all the wildlife he saw at his cottage.

a) Based on the information in the bar graph, recreate Bobby's original tally chart.

b) Which bars were the most difficult to read? What strategy did you use to read them?

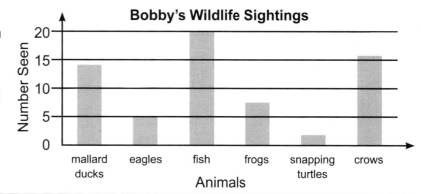

3. A teacher tallied the marks on a science test and then made a bar graph (Figure 1) to show the distribution of marks.

a) Fill in the frequency table for the test.

Mark	Tally	Frequency
A		
B		
C		
D		
E		

b) How many students received an A on the test? _____

c) How many students received a C? _____

d) How many students took the test? _____

e) Circle the most common mark:

   A   B   C   D   E

f) Use the axes in Figure 2 to show the same data, but make the bars horizontal.

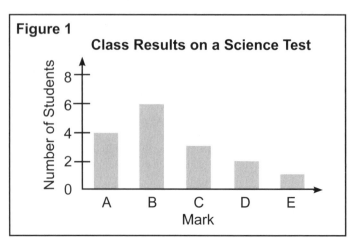

Figure 1

Class Results on a Science Test

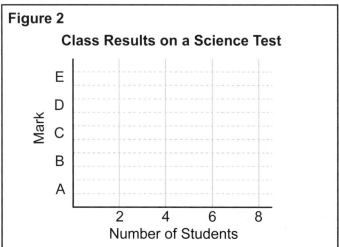

Figure 2

Class Results on a Science Test

4. Draw a bar graph for each frequency table (use the grids at the bottom of the page). For each graph, you will first need to decide the scale. Example: In part b), you might use the scale 5, 10, 15, 20, 25.

a)

Mark	A	B	C	D	E
Frequency	2	9	6	1	0

_____ students should be represented by each division in the scale

b)

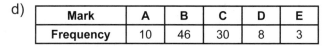

Mark	A	B	C	D	E
Frequency	16	23	17	5	2

_____ students should be represented by each division in the scale

c)

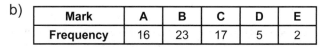

Mark	A	B	C	D	E
Frequency	19	24	13	3	2

_____ students should be represented by each division in the scale

d)

Mark	A	B	C	D	E
Frequency	10	46	30	8	3

_____ students should be represented by each division in the scale

a)
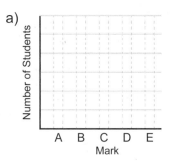

b)
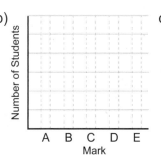

c)
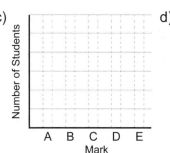

d)
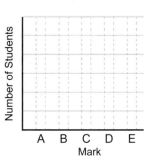

Probability and Data Management 8-1

PDM8-2 Double Bar Graphs

1. Two sporting goods companies graph their sales for January through June.

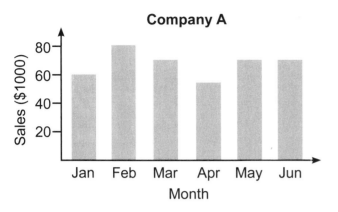

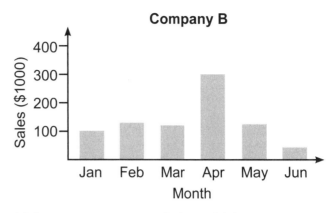

a) When you glance quickly at the two graphs, which company appears to have higher monthly sales?_____ Why? _____

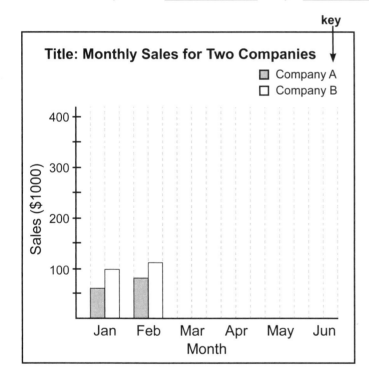

key

Title: Monthly Sales for Two Companies

☐ Company A
☐ Company B

b) When you look closely at the scales, which company actually has higher sales? _____

c) Why are most of the bars on the graph for Company B so short? _____

_____

_____

_____

d) To compare the sales of both companies, it is convenient to put their graphs on the **same axes** (see left). The key shows you which company is represented by which kind of bar. Complete the graph.

> A graph that compares two sets of data, like the graph in Question 1 d), is called a **double bar graph**.

e) In which month(s) did Company A sell more than Company B? _____

f) During one month in this period, Company B had several items in their store autographed by a famous athlete. Which month do you think that was? _____

2. Leslie tracked the height of two seedlings. Draw a double bar graph in your notebook or on a computer to show her data.

Day	1	2	3	4	5	6
Height of plant in full sun (cm)	2.0	4.2	6.5	8.8	11.0	14.1
Height of plant in the shade (cm)	1.9	3.6	5.1	6.4	7.9	9.3

3. Students in a Grade 8 class were asked "What is your favourite snack?" at two different times: in October and in December.

   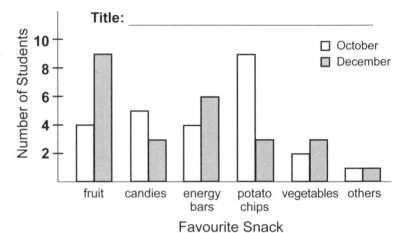

   Title: _____

   a) Add a title to the double bar graph.

   b) What favourite snack was selected by the most students in October?

   _____

   c) What favourite snack was selected by the most students in December?

   _____

   d) How many students chose fruit in October? _____ In December? _____

   e) For which snack was there the biggest change between October and December? _____

   f) How many students responded to the survey question in October? _____ In December? _____

   g) The students did a project on nutrition. Do you think they completed their project in September or November? _____

   Explain. _____

4. A real estate agent sells both houses and condominiums. The double bar graph below shows her sales over the past year.

   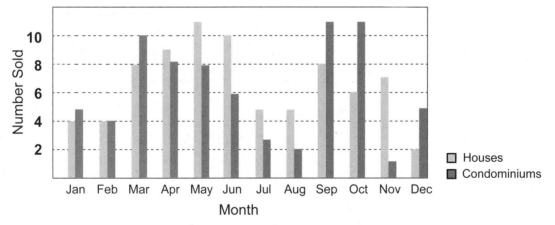

   House and Condominium Sales in 2009

   a) In what month(s) did the agent sell the most houses? _____

   b) In what month(s) did the agent sell the most condominiums? _____

   c) In what month(s) did the agent sell the most total units (houses *and* condominiums)? _____

   d) Next year, the agent wants to go on vacation for a month. In which month would you suggest she take her vacation? _____

   Why? _____

1. The bar graph (left) and the line graph (right) both show the price of CDs on sale.

    Using a ruler, you could draw an arrow across   *Similarily, you could draw a line up from the*
    from the '5 CD' bar to show that 5 CDs cost $25.   *'5 CD' mark and then across to the $25 mark.*

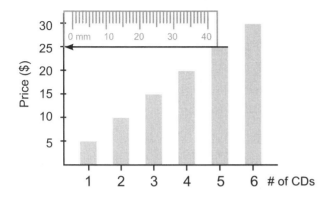   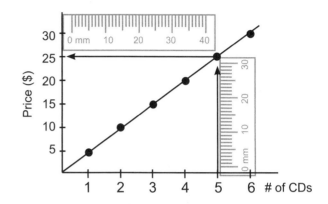

    Draw arrows (using a ruler) on the line graph above to find the cost of…

    a) 3 CDs $ _____   b) 4 CDs $ _____   c) 6 CDs $ _____

2. These graphs show how much money Sally will earn painting houses in the summer.

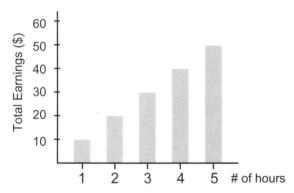   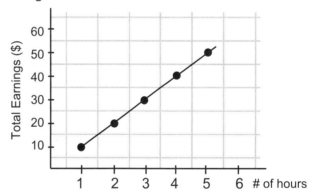

    a) On both graphs, show how much Sally would make for working…

        i) 3 hours   ii) 4 hours

    b) If Sally works $3\frac{1}{2}$ hours, she will make between $ _____ and $ _____.

    c) Draw arrows on the line graph to show how much Sally will earn in $3\frac{1}{2}$ hours.

    d) Extend the line graph to show how much Sally could make in…   i) 6 hours   ii) $\frac{1}{2}$ hour

    e) Explain an advantage of a line graph over a bar graph.

3. Rosa uses a line graph to present data about
    the number of family pets in her class.

    a) Does the advantage of a line graph over a bar graph apply here?
        (Can Rosa find out how many families own 3.5 pets?)

    b) Draw a bar graph to present Rosa's data.

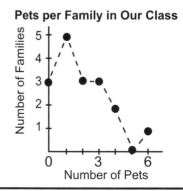

Pets per Family in Our Class

4. This graph shows the cost of parking at a parking lot.

   a) How much will it cost to park for...

      1 hour? _____   4 hours? _____   7 hours? _____

   b) How much will it cost to park for 2.5 hours? _____
      Explain how you figured this out.

      _____

   c) Irene paid $16.75 for parking. How long did
      she park for?

      _____

   d) John parked at the lot at 8:00 a.m. It is 3:55 p.m.
      now. Should he hurry to the parking lot in order
      to pay less? _____ Explain.

   e) After how much time does the cost of parking
      become a flat rate?_____

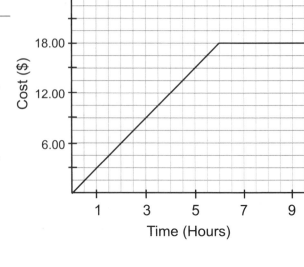

Cost of Parking

5. Scientists measured the body temperature of a lizard
   and presented the data on a line graph.

   a) When did they take the first measurement? _____

      What was the temperature of the lizard at
      that time? _____

   b) Find the temperature of the lizard at these times:

      9:00 _____   9:05 _____   9:10 _____

      9:15 _____   9:20 _____   9:45 _____

   c) In which 5-minute time period between 8:55
      and 9:15 did the temperature of the lizard
      change the most? _____ to _____

      How can you see this from the graph?

      _____

      _____

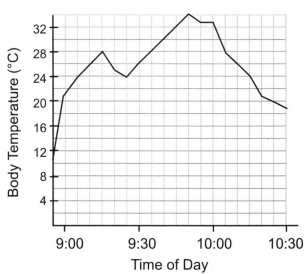

Body Temperature of a Lizard Over Time

   d) At 9:15, a cloud appeared over the lizard and created a shadow.
      What happened to the lizard's body temperature?

   e) How long do you think the lizard stayed in the shadow of the cloud?

   f) What happened to the temperature of the lizard after the cloud moved away?
      How can you see that from the graph?

   g) At some point, the lizard moved into the shade of the mountain and its
      temperature started to drop. How do you see that on the graph? When do
      you think the lizard moved into the shade?

   h) Why do you think the scientists presented their findings using a line graph
      and not a bar graph?

Probability and Data Management 8-3

PDM8-4 Investigating Line Graphs

INVESTIGATION ▶ How is speed reflected in a graph?

Terri goes to a park 1.6 km from her home. She records her distance from home after each 10 minutes of walking.

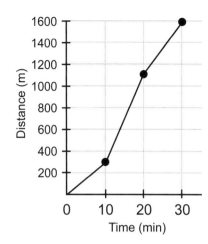

A. Fill in the table.

	1ˢᵗ 10 minutes	2ⁿᵈ 10 minutes	3ʳᵈ 10 minutes
Distance from home after…	*300 m*		
Distance walked in…	*300 m*		

B. During which 10 minutes did she travel…

a) farthest?   1ˢᵗ   2ⁿᵈ   3ʳᵈ   b) fastest?   1ˢᵗ   2ⁿᵈ   3ʳᵈ

C. During which 10 minutes is the graph the steepest?   1ˢᵗ   2ⁿᵈ   3ʳᵈ

D. Compare your answers in parts B and C. What do you notice?

Speed is the ratio of distance travelled to time. Speed can be calculated by dividing distance by time. Speed is measured in kilometres per hour (km/hour), metres per second (m/sec) and similar units.

E. Find Terry's speed in each 10-minute interval.

1ˢᵗ 10 minutes: 2ⁿᵈ 10 minutes: 3ʳᵈ 10 minutes:

___*300 ÷ 10 = 30 m/min*___   _____   _____

F. Compare your answers in parts C and E. What do you notice?

1. a) Find the distance walked and the speed for each graph.

i)
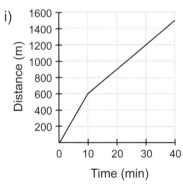

ii)
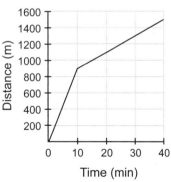

iii)
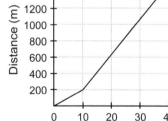

Distance travelled in…

first 10 minutes: _____   first 10 minutes: _____   first 10 minutes: _____
last 30 minutes: _____   last 30 minutes: _____   last 30 minutes: _____

Speed in…

first 10 minutes: _____   first 10 minutes: _____   first 10 minutes: _____
last 30 minutes: _____   last 30 minutes: _____   last 30 minutes: _____

b) Is the graph steeper in the first 10 minutes or in the last 30 minutes?

i) _____   ii) _____   iii) _____

c) Is the graph steeper when the speed is greater or when the speed is smaller?

2. A graph that plots distance versus time will be steeper when the person is walking faster. Circle the interval of time when the person was walking fastest.

a)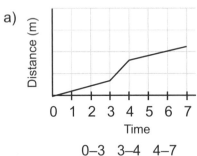

0–3   3–4   4–7

b)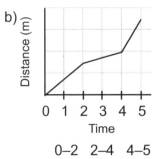

0–2   2–4   4–5

c)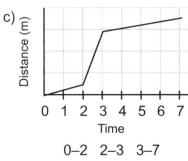

0–2   2–3   3–7

3. Samantha started walking to school and then stopped when she realized it was Saturday. Embarrassed, she ran home. She recorded her distance from home after each minute.

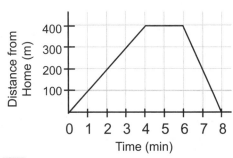

a) How far from home was she after:

1 minute: _____   2 minutes: _____   3 minutes: _____

4 minutes: _____   5 minutes: _____   6 minutes: _____

7 minutes: _____   8 minutes: _____

b) How many minutes was Samantha walking for before she stopped? How long did she stop for?

c) It took Samantha four minutes to walk 400 m. How long did it take her to run the 400 m back home?

d) On any graph that plots distance versus time, what does a horizontal line mean?

e) What would a vertical line mean? Why is this impossible?

4. a) Match the stories to the graphs: which is Graph A and which is Graph B?

____Jeff started <u>walking to school</u>, then <u>ran back</u> home to get his homework, and then <u>ran to school</u>.

____Jane started <u>walking to school</u>, then <u>stopped</u> to play with a kitten, and <u>ran the rest of the way</u>.

A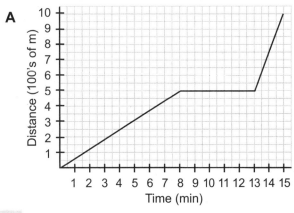

B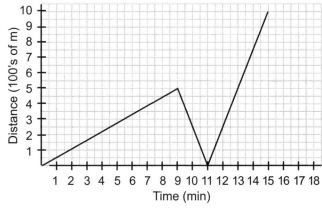

b) How can you tell when the line shows walking and when it shows running?

Probability and Data Management 8-4

1. The chart shows the number of snow shovels a store sells between September and April.

   Complete the line graph. Explain any trends you notice.

Month	# of Snow Shovels Sold
September	4
October	8
November	11
December	17
January	18
February	16
March	3
April	1

Sale of Snow Shovels

2. Graph the data from the Ontario Ministry of Labour on both grids below.

Year	1995	2004	2006	2007
Minimum Wage in Ontario ($/hour)	6.85	7.15	7.75	8.0

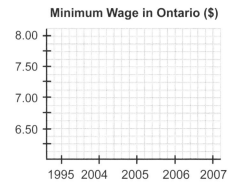

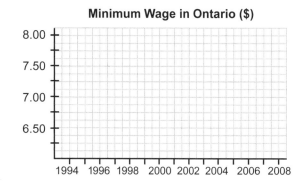

a) Which graph makes it look as if the minimum wage increased at the same rate from 1995 to 2007?

b) Which graph shows that the minimum wage started increasing more quickly in 2004?

c) Which graph best represents the data? What is wrong with the other graph?

3. The data at right shows when the world's population first reached 1 billion, 2 billion, and so on.

   a) Would you use a bar graph or a line graph to present this data? Explain your choice and create the graph.

Population in Billions	1	2	3	4	5	6
Year first reached	1804	1922	1959	1974	1987	1999

Data fom U.S. Census Bureau's Global Profit: 2002

   b) Look at the data on the graph. Is it possible to join the data points with a solid line? Why or why not?

   c) In what year do you think the population will reach 7 billion?

   d) The United Nations predicted that it will take longer to go from 6 to 7 billion than it did to go from 5 to 6 billion. Why might the experts think so?

Two line graphs on the same grid can show a **comparison**. The **key** helps you read the graph. It explains what the different symbols or colours used mean.

4. Josh and his younger brother Mark walked 10 km in a charity walk.

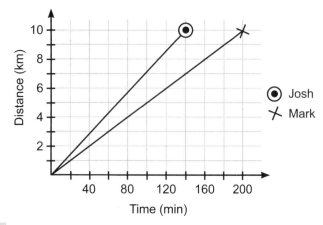

a) How long does it take Josh to complete the walk? _____

b) After 1 hour, how many kilometres has Josh walked? _____

c) After 1 hour, how many kilometres has Mark walked? _____

d) How long does it take Mark to complete the walk? _____

5. Two neighbouring towns began a recycling program in the same year. Here are the results after the first year.

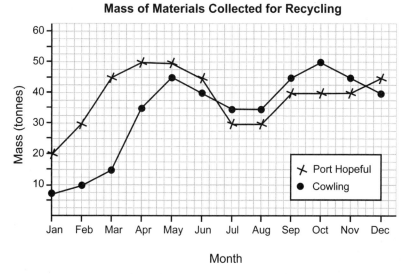

Mass of Materials Collected for Recycling

a) How much did Port Hopeful collect in January?

b) In January, what was the difference between the amount collected by Port Hopeful and Cowling?

c) Which town had the greatest increase:

    i) from February to March?

    ii) from March to April?

d) In Cowling, in which month was there the greatest increase?

e) In which month was there the greatest difference between the two towns in the amount collected?

f) For Cowling, in which month was there no change from the previous month?

g) In April, who collected more, Port Hopeful or Cowling?

h) What is the first month that Cowling collects more than Port Hopeful?

i) Which town do you think conducted the better information campaign before the recycling program started? Why?

j) Can you predict which town's recycling program will be most successful in the next six months? Explain.

6. Create a double bar graph using the data from Question 5 on the computer. Try to answer the questions in Question 5 using the double bar graph. Which graph is more convenient to answer each question?

G8-1 Area of Triangles

1. Find the area of the right triangles.

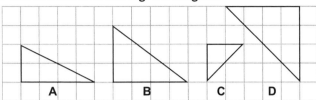

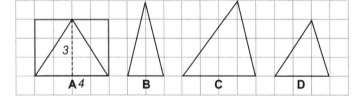
Area of A: _4 × 2 ÷ 2 = 8 ÷ 2 = 4_   Area of B: _____

Area of C: _____   Area of D: _____

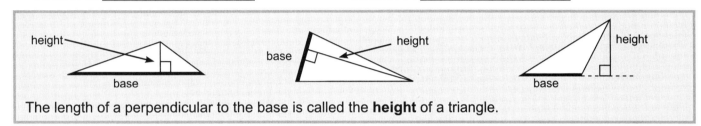

The length of a perpendicular to the base is called the **height** of a triangle.

2. a) Draw a dotted line to show the height of the triangle. Then find the length of the height and the base.

b) Find the area of each triangle by finding half the area of the rectangle that contains the triangle.

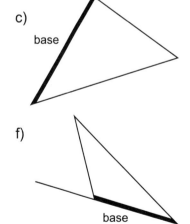

Area of A: _4 × 3 ÷ 2 = 6_ Area of B: _____ Area of C: _____ Area of D: _____

3. Draw the height for each given base in the triangles.

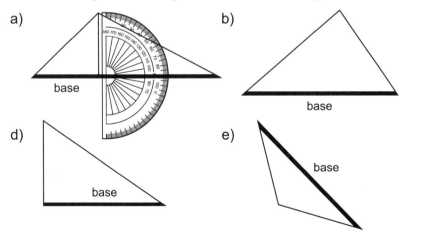

a)

b)

c)

d)

e)

f)

4. The height is given in each triangle. Name the base which is related to the given height.

a)

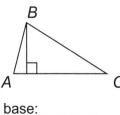

base: _____

b)

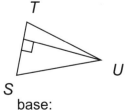

base: _____

c)

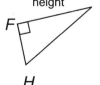

base: _____

d)

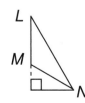

base: _____

5. Jan wants to find the area of a triangle. She cuts the triangle and rearranges the pieces as shown to form a rectangle.

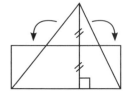

a) What is the width of her rectangle? How is it related to the base of the triangle?

_____

b) What is the height of her rectangle? How is it related to the height of the triangle?

_____

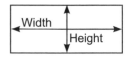

c) Write a formula for the area of the triangle using the base and the height of the triangle from Jan's method.

_____

6. Measure the base and height of each triangle using a ruler. Then find the area.

a)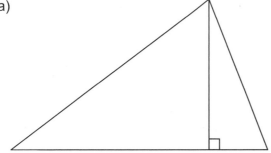

b)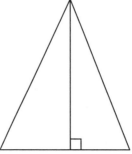

c)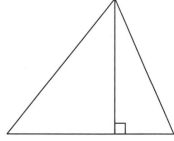

base: _____   base: _____   base: _____

height: _____   height: _____   height: _____

area: _____   area: _____   area: _____

7. a) Measure the lengths of the sides and the heights in this triangle. Mark the measurements on the diagram.

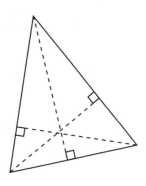

b) Find the area of the triangle three ways, each time using a different side as a base. Did you get the same result?

c) Explain what might cause the results to be different.

8. Find the area of a triangle with the given dimensions.

a) base = 6 cm   b) base = 4 cm   c) base = 6 cm   d) base = 3.2 cm

height = 2 cm   height = 3 cm   height = 4 cm   height = 8 cm

9. On grid paper, draw 3 different triangles with base 4 and height 5. Find the area of these triangles.

G8-2 Squares on a Grid

1. Rotate each line segment 90° ($\frac{1}{4}$ turn) clockwise around point A.

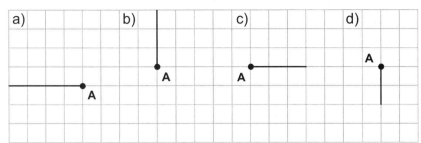

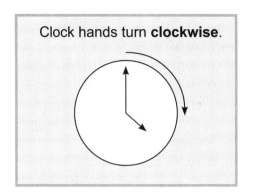

Clock hands turn **clockwise**.

2. Rotate each triangle 90° ($\frac{1}{4}$ turn) counter-clockwise around point O. (Rotate the arrow first.)

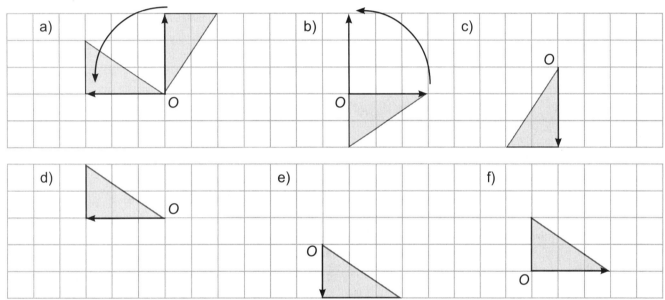

3. Rotate each triangle 90° ($\frac{1}{4}$ turn) clockwise around point O. (Rotate the arrow first.)

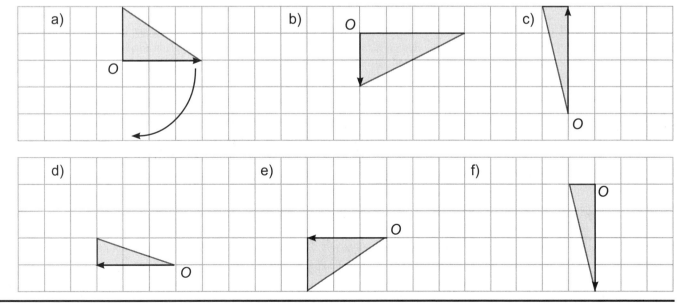

How to rotate a slant line 90° clockwise around *O*

Step 1: Shade a right triangle as shown.	Step 2: Rotate the triangle.	Step 3: Emphasize the line at 90° to the given slant line.
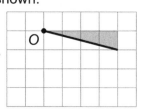	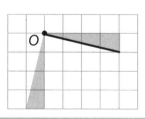	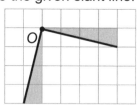

4. a) Rotate these slant lines 90° clockwise around *O*.

   i) 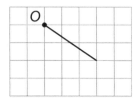 ii) 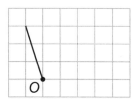 iii)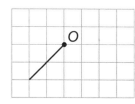

   iv) 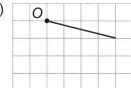 v) 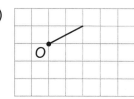 vi)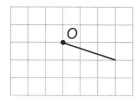

   b) Use a protractor to check that the angle between the given lines and the rotated lines is 90°.

5. Lucy rotates a line segment 90° counter-clockwise around the endpoints three times.

   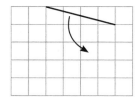

   What do you know about the sides and the angles of Lucy's shape? _____

   _____

   What shape is it? _____

6. Triangle B was made by rotating Triangle A 90° clockwise. Fill in the blanks.

   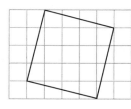

   a) Triangle A has horizontal length __4__ and vertical length __1__.

      Triangle B has horizontal length __1__ and vertical length __4__.

   b) Triangle A has horizontal length ___ and vertical length ___.

      Triangle B has horizontal length ___ and vertical length ___.

   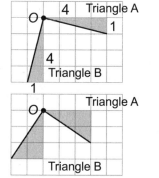

Geometry 8-2

7. Look at your answers in Question 6. If you know the horizontal and the vertical lengths of Triangle A, how can you get the horizontal and the vertical lengths of Triangle B? Check your conjecture with the triangles you drew in Question 4.

_____

_____

_____

8. Create a square using Lucy's method, starting with the given side. Use your conjecture to rotate the sides 90°.

a)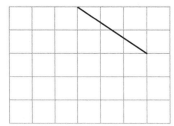
b)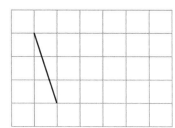
c)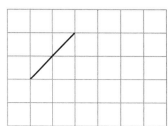

d)
e)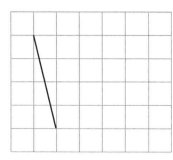
f)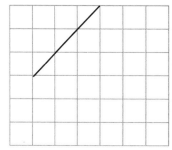

9. Which of the shapes below are squares? Explain how you know.

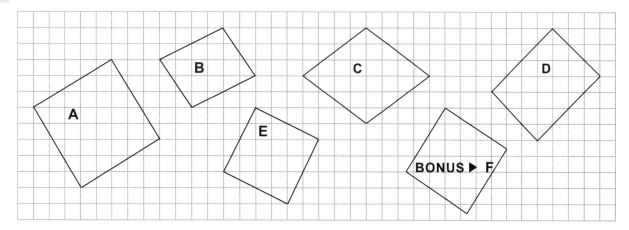

BONUS ▶

a) Which shape in Question 9 is a rhombus but not a square? How do you know?

b) Which shape in Question 9 is a rectangle but not a square? Explain.

G8-3 Length of Slant Line Segments

1. Find the area of each right triangle.

a)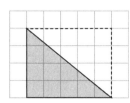

Area = _20_ ÷ 2 = _10_

b)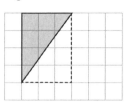

Area = ___ ÷ 2 = ___

c)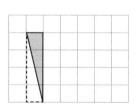

Area = ___ ÷ 2 = ___

d)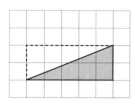

Area = ___ ÷ 2 = ___

2. Find the area of each square by finding the area of 4 right triangles and what is left.

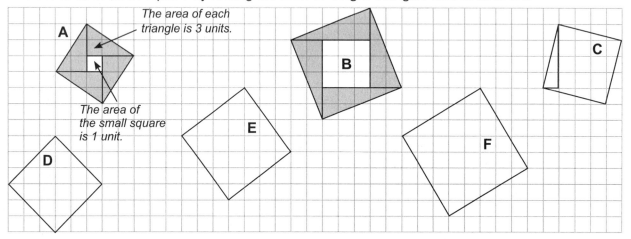

A Area: 4 × _3_ + _1_ = _13_   B Area: 4 × ___ + ___ = ___   C Area: 4 × ___ + ___ = ___

D Area: 4 × ___ + ___ = ___ .   E Area: 4 × ___ + ___ = ___   F Area: 4 × ___ + ___ = ___

3. What is the side length of square E in Question 2? How do you know?

4. Find the side length of each square.

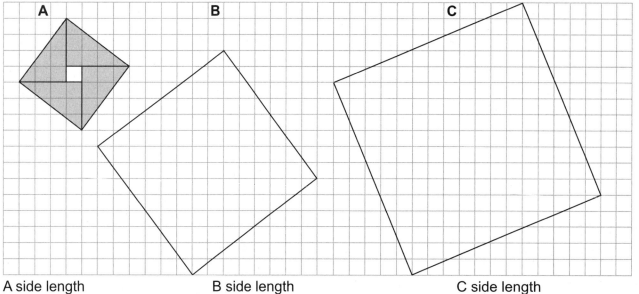

A side length

$= \sqrt{4 \times 6 + 1}$

$= \sqrt{25} = 5$

B side length

$= \sqrt{4 \times \underline{} + \underline{}}$

$= \sqrt{\underline{}} = \underline{}$

C side length

$= \sqrt{4 \times \underline{} + \underline{}}$

$= \sqrt{\underline{}} = \underline{}$

5. Find the side length of each square as a square root. Then estimate the square root.

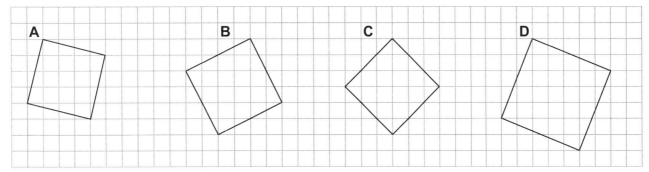

A side length

$= \sqrt{4 \times 2 + 9}$

$= \sqrt{17}$

a little more than _4_

B side length

$= \sqrt{4 \times \underline{} + \underline{}}$

$= \sqrt{\underline{}}$

between ___ and ___

C side length

$= \sqrt{4 \times \underline{} + \underline{}}$

$= \sqrt{\underline{}}$

a little more than ___

D side length

$= \sqrt{4 \times \underline{} + \underline{}}$

$= \sqrt{\underline{}}$

between ___ and ___

6. Draw a square using the line segment as a side and find the area of the square. Then find the length of the line segment.

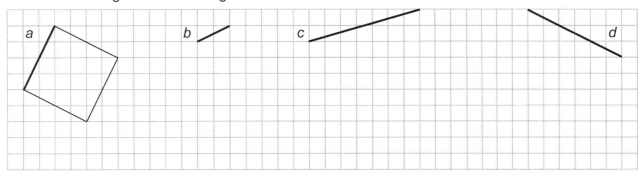

$a^2 =$ _4 × 4 + 4 = 20_

so $a =$ _$\sqrt{20}$_

$b^2 =$ _____

so $b =$ _____

$c^2 =$ _____

so $c =$ _____

$d^2 =$ _____

so $d =$ _____

7. Copy these line segments to 1-cm grid paper and find their lengths by drawing squares. First estimate the length to 1 decimal place using the area of the square. Then measure the length with a ruler to check your estimate.

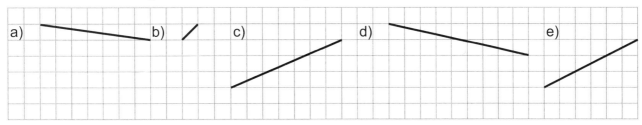

INVESTIGATION ▶

How can you determine the length of the side opposite the right angle in a right triangle?

A. Draw squares on all sides of each right triangle. Calculate the areas and fill in the blanks.

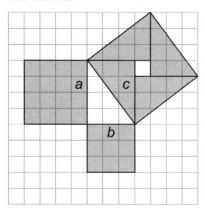 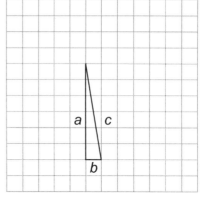

$a^2 = \underline{16}$ $b^2 = \underline{9}$ $c^2 = \underline{4 \times 6 + 1 = 25}$ $a^2 = \underline{\hphantom{xx}}$ $b^2 = \underline{\hphantom{xx}}$ $c^2 = \underline{\hphantom{xxxxxxxx}}$

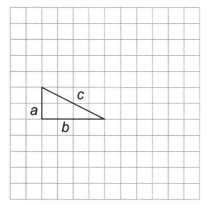 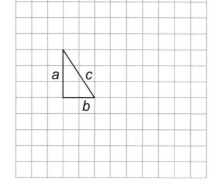

$a^2 = \underline{\hphantom{xx}}$ $b^2 = \underline{\hphantom{xx}}$ $c^2 = \underline{\hphantom{xxxxxxxx}}$ $a^2 = \underline{\hphantom{xx}}$ $b^2 = \underline{\hphantom{xx}}$ $c^2 = \underline{\hphantom{xxxxxxxx}}$

B. Look at the numbers from A. How can you get c^2 from a^2 and b^2? Make a conjecture: If c is the side opposite the right angle in triangle with sides a, b, c, then
$c^2 = \underline{\hphantom{xxxxxx}}$

C. Check your conjecture for two right triangles of your choice.

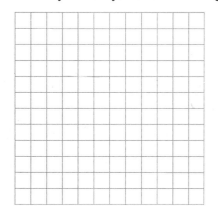 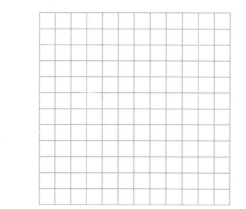

Pythagorean Theorem
If a right triangle has sides a, b, c with c opposite the right angle, then $a^2 + b^2 = c^2$.

---

1. Trace the side c according to the Pythagorean Theorem.

  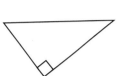 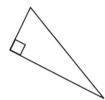

2. What does the Pythagorean Theorem say about each triangle?

a)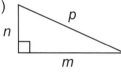
$\underline{n^2 + m^2 = p^2}$

b)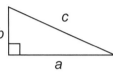
_____

c)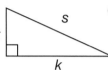
_____

d)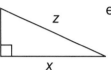
_____

e)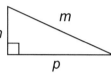
_____

f)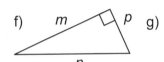
_____

g)
_____

h)
_____

i)
_____

j)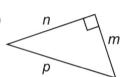
_____

3. Use the Pythagorean Theorem to find the side opposite the right angle.

a)

$\underline{n^2 = 4^2 + 3^2}$

$\underline{\quad = 16 + 9 = 25}$

$\underline{\text{so}\quad n = \sqrt{25} = 5}$

b)
_____
_____
_____

c)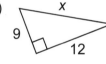
_____
_____
_____

d)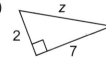
_____
_____
_____

e)

$\underline{b^2 = 5^2 + 3^2}$

$\underline{\quad = 25 + 9 = 34}$

$\underline{\text{so}\ b = \sqrt{34}}$

f)
_____
_____
_____

g)
_____
_____
_____

h)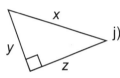
_____
_____
_____

We can use the Pythagorean Theorem to find any side of a right triangle if two sides are given.

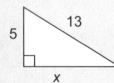

$$5^2 + x^2 = 13^2$$
$$25 + x^2 = 169$$
$$x^2 = 169 - 25 = 144$$
$$so\ x = \sqrt{144} = 12$$

4. What does the Pythagorean Theorem say about each triangle? Write an equation, then find the missing side.

a)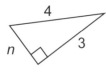

b)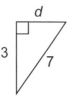

c)

d)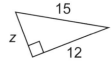

a)
$$n^2 + 3^2 = 4^2$$
$$n^2 + 9 = 16$$
$$n^2 = 16 - 9 = 7$$
$$n = \sqrt{7}$$

5. Find the missing side of the triangle using the Pythagorean Theorem. Then estimate the answer using a number line.

a)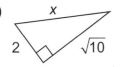

b)

c)

d)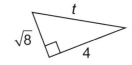

a)
$$2^2 + (\sqrt{10})^2 = x^2$$
$$4 + 10 = x^2$$
$$14 = x^2$$
$$x = \sqrt{14}$$
$$x \approx 3.7$$

```
+--+--+--+--+--+--+--+--+--+--+--+--+--+--*--+--+--+--+--+--+--+--+--+--+--+
0  1  2  3  4  5  6  7  8  9 10 11 12 13 14 15 16 17 18 19 20 21 22 23 24 25
```

6. Find the missing side of the triangle.

a)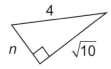

b)

c)

d)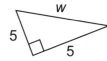

Geometry 8-4

G8-5 Proving the Pythagorean Theorem

Pythagorean Theorem
If a right triangle has sides a, b, c with c opposite the right angle, then $a^2 + b^2 = c^2$.

Figure 1

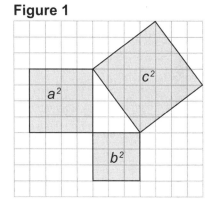

INVESTIGATION 1 ▶ Why does the Pythagorean Theorem work?

A. What does the Pythagorean Theorem say about the areas of squares a^2, b^2, and c^2? _____

_____

B. Figure 2 shows how to create a large square from the right triangle in Figure 1 (Triangle 1) and the two smaller squares.

Do triangles 1, 2, 3, and 4 all have the same area? How do you know?

_____

_____

Figure 2

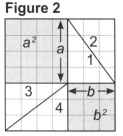

C. Let T represent the area of Triangle 1. Write a formula for the area of the large square using a^2, b^2, and T.

area of large square = _____

D. Create a large square from the smaller squares and four right triangles like the triangle in the figure.

a)

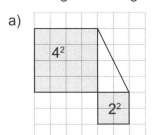

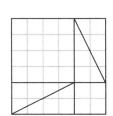

b)

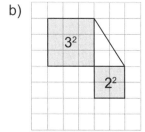

E. Figure 3 shows a different way to create a large square from the right triangle and the largest square in Figure 1.

Do Triangles 5, 6, 7, and 8 in Figure 3 all have the same area? How do you know?

_____

_____

Figure 3

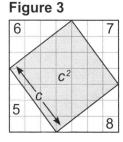

F. Let T represent the area of Triangle 5. Write a formula for the area of the large square in using c^2 and T.

area of large square = _____

G. Create a large square from the square and four right triangles like the triangle in the figure.

a)
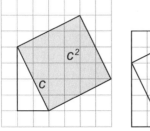

b)
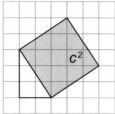

H. Do Triangle 1 in Figure 2 and Triangle 5 in Figure 3 have the same area? _____

I. Compare the formulas you wrote (for the area of the large squares) in parts C and F. How can you derive the Pythagorean Theorem from these formulas?

_____

_____

_____

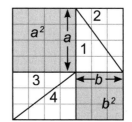
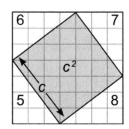

---

1. a) Prove the Pythagorean Theorem for a triangle with sides $a = 2$, $b = 5$, and c.

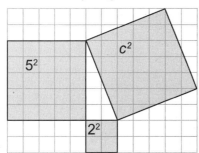
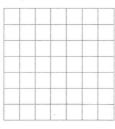
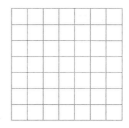

$5^2 + 2^2 = 7^2 - 4 \times$ ____ $c^2 = 7^2 - 4 \times$ ____

b) Find c using the Pythagorean Theorem: $c^2 =$ ___ $+$ ___, so $c =$ _____.

2. Prove the Pythagorean Theorem for a triangle with sides $a = 4$, $b = 2$, and c. Then find c.

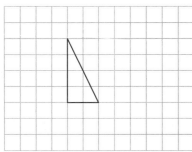
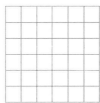
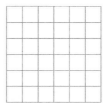

_____ $c^2 =$ _____ $=$ _____

3. Prove the Pythagorean Theorem for a right triangle of your choice.

4. a) In each triangle, $\angle C$ is opposite side c. Find $a^2 + b^2$ and c^2 in your notebook, then look at $\angle C$. Write $<$, $>$ or $=$ in the blanks.

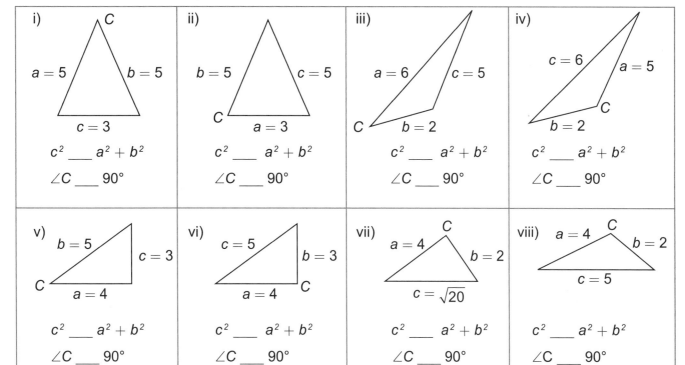

i)

c^2 ____ $a^2 + b^2$

$\angle C$ ____ $90°$

ii)

c^2 ____ $a^2 + b^2$

$\angle C$ ____ $90°$

iii)

c^2 ____ $a^2 + b^2$

$\angle C$ ____ $90°$

iv)

c^2 ____ $a^2 + b^2$

$\angle C$ ____ $90°$

v)

c^2 ____ $a^2 + b^2$

$\angle C$ ____ $90°$

vi)

c^2 ____ $a^2 + b^2$

$\angle C$ ____ $90°$

vii)

c^2 ____ $a^2 + b^2$

$\angle C$ ____ $90°$

viii)

c^2 ____ $a^2 + b^2$

$\angle C$ ____ $90°$

b) Make a conjecture about a triangle with sides a, b, c and angle C opposite the side c:

When $\angle C < 90°$, then c^2 _____ $a^2 + b^2$,

when $\angle C > 90°$, then c^2 _____ $a^2 + b^2$,

when $\angle C = 90°$, then c^2 _____ $a^2 + b^2$.

c) Draw three more triangles and check your conjecture.

5. a) Can there be a triangle with a right angle and an obtuse angle? ____

b) The Pythagorean Theorem applies to right triangles.
In a right triangle, what is the measure of the largest angle? ____

c) In which of the triangles in Question 4 was C the largest angle? _____

d) Why does the Pythagorean Theorem not work for triangles iv) and viii) in Question 4?

e) Triangle v) in Question 4 is a right triangle. Why does c^2 not equal $a^2 + b^2$?

Hint: Look at your answer in c).

f) Why is triangle v) in Question 4 not a counter-example to the Pythagorean Theorem?

INVESTIGATION 2 ▶ Where is the longest side in a triangle?

A. Measure the sides of these triangles. Circle the largest angle and trace the longest side.

a)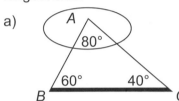

AB = __21__ mm

AC = __29__ mm

BC = __33__ mm

b)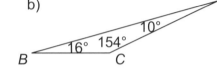

AB = ____ mm

AC = ____ mm

BC = ____ mm

c)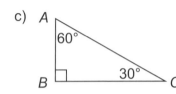

AB = ____ mm

AC = ____ mm

BC = ____ mm

d)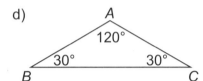

AB = ____ mm

AC = ____ mm

BC = ____ mm

B. Make a conjecture about where the longest side of a triangle is relative to the largest angle:

The longest side of a triangle is always _____ the largest angle.

C. In a right triangle, can there be an angle larger than the right angle? _____

D. Sketch a triangle ABC with $\angle B = 90°$. Which side is the largest? _____

E. Which side is the largest in a triangle DEF with $\angle F = 90°$? Can you tell without sketching $\triangle DEF$?

6. Circle the side that is opposite the largest angle in these triangles.

a) 3 cm, 4 cm, 6 cm   b) 3 m, 7 m, 5 m   c) 1, 2, $\sqrt{5}$ d) 10 km, 10 km, 14 142 m

7. Tegan wants to check whether the triangle at right is a right triangle using the Pythagorean Theorem. She substitutes the lengths of the sides into the formula $a^2 + b^2 = c^2$:

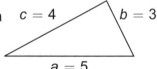

$a = 5, b = 3, c = 4$, so

$a^2 + b^2 = 25 + 9 = 34$, and $c^2 = 16$.

$16 \neq 34$, so Tegan thinks the triangle is not a right triangle. Is she correct? Explain.

_____

8. Order the side lengths from least to greatest. Then use the Pythagorean Theorem to check whether these triangles are right triangles.

a) 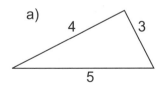   b) 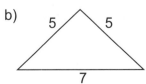   c) 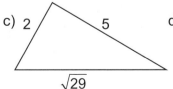   d)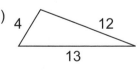

e) 2, 4, $\sqrt{6}$ f) 1, 2, $\sqrt{3}$ g) 2, 4, $\sqrt{20}$ h) $\sqrt{5}$, $\sqrt{3}$, $\sqrt{2}$ i) 2, $\sqrt{5}$, $\sqrt{3}$

G8-6 Problem-Solving — Using a Formula

> When you read a word problem, identify **what you need to find** and **the information you are given**. If you can solve the problem using a **formula**, write the formula.

1. For each of the problems below underline what you need to find and circle the measurements you are given. Then write the formula you are going to use.

   a) A parallelogram has (base 5 cm) and (height 35 mm) What is the area of the parallelogram?

      Formula: _Area of parallelogram = base × height_

   b) A right triangle has short sides 20 cm and 30 cm. What is the length of the longest side?

      Formula: _____

   c) Find the area of a triangle with base 2 m and height 75 cm.

      Formula: _____

> For geometric or measurement problems, it often helps **to make a sketch**. Remember, the sketch does not have to be perfect, but it should include all the information you know.

2. **Problem:** The shortest side of a right triangle is 5 cm long. The middle side is 2 cm longer. What is the length of the longest side?

   a) Underline what you need to find and circle what you are given.

   b) Which formula are you going to use? _____

   c) Which of these sketches will be the most help in solving the problem? Explain your choice.

   A.
   5 − 2 cm

   5 cm

   B.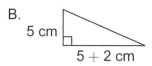
   5 cm

   5 + 2 cm

   C.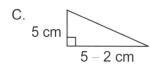
   5 cm

   5 − 2 cm

3. For each problem below:
   • underline **what you need to find**
   • circle **the measurements you are given**
   • **label the sketch** to show the information that you know
   • write **the formula** you are going to use

   Do not solve the problems yet!

   a) In a triangle *ABC*, *BD* is the height, from *B* to the side *AC*. *AD* = 3 cm, *BD* = 5 cm, and *CD* is as long as *AD* and *BD* together. What is the **area** of the triangle?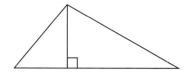

      Formula: _____

   b) In a triangle *ABC*, *BD* is the height, from *B* to the side *AC*. *AD* = 3 cm, *BD* = 5 cm and *CD* is as long as *AD* and *BD* together. What is the **length of the side** *AB* of the triangle?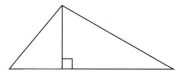

      Formula: _____

When you know what formula you are going to use, look for the values that you need in the word problem. Do you have all the measurements you need to use the formula? Sometimes you will need to do a calculation to **find a value that is not given**.

You will solve the following problem in Questions 4 and 5:

Problem: A parallelogram can be cut into a square and two right triangles. The triangles are as high as the square. The base of each triangle is only half as wide as the square. The height of the square is 8 cm. What is the area of the parallelogram?

4. Judy decides to use the formulas for the area of a square and the area of a triangle to solve the problem.

    a) Judy is using these formulas:

        Area of the square = width × height   Area of a right triangle = base × height ÷ 2

                         = height × height

        What information is not given directly in the problem? _____

    b) Fill in the values Judy needs and mark them on the sketch.

        The height of the square = _____

        The height of each triangle = _____

        The base of each triangle = _____

    c) Area of the square = _____ cm²

        Area of each triangle = _____ cm²

    d) Area of the parallelogram = area of square + _____ × area of each triangle = _____ + _____ = _____

REMINDER▶ area of parallelogram = base × height

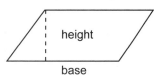

height

base

---

5. Guy decides to use the formula for the area of a parallelogram to solve the problem.

    a) Which value is not given directly in the problem? _____

    b) Fill in the information he needs and mark the information on the sketch.

        The base of parallelogram = _____

        The height of parallelogram = _____

    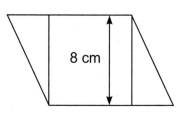

    c) Find the area of the parallelogram. Is the answer the same as in Question 4?

When you substitute data into a formula, **make sure that all the units are the same!** If they are not, convert them before you substitute. Do not forget to write the units in the answer.

Remember: $cm \times cm = cm^2$ and $m \times m = m^2$. Also, $\sqrt{m^2} = m$, and $\sqrt{cm^2} = cm$

You cannot multiply a measurement in metres by a measurement in centimetres!

6. **Problem:** The short sides of a right triangle are called **legs**.
   The longest side is called the **hypotenuse**. A right triangle has
   legs 75 cm and 1 m. What is the length of the hypotenuse?

   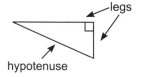

   a) Which units are more convenient—cm or m? Convert all measurements
      to the units you chose.

      leg 1: _____   leg 2: _____

   b) Solve the problem.

7. Solve the problems in Question 3.

8. A right triangle has one leg 30 cm shorter than the other. The longer leg
   is 1.2 m long.

   a) What is the area of the triangle?

   b) What is the length of the hypotenuse of the triangle?

Sometimes you will not have a formula that will give you what you need to find right away. What you need to find might be **part of a related formula**. Use a variable (such as x) to represent the piece of information you do not know in your formula.

9. **Problem:** The length of a rectangle is twice its width. The perimeter of the rectangle
   is 120 cm. How long are the sides of the rectangle?

   a) Underline what you need to find. Circle the information you know.

   b) Perimeter is the sum of the sides of a shape. Write the formula for the
      perimeter of a rectangle in terms of length (**l**) and width (**w**).

      Perimeter of rectangle = _____

   c) Here is a sketch for the problem.
      Mark the width of the rectangle with an x.
      What is the length of the rectangle?

   d) Substitute the length and the width into the formula. _____

   e) Substitute the value of the perimeter into the formula and solve the equation for x.

      $x =$ _____

When you **substitute all the data and the variable** into the formula, you get an equation.
For example, in Question 9:

   Perimeter of a rectangle: 120 cm   width: x cm   length: $2 \times x$ or $2x$ cm

   Equation: $120 = 2x + x + 2x + x$ or $120 = 6x$

10. For each problem below, mark the information you know on the sketch.
Use x for the piece of information that you do not know and mark it on
the sketch. Then write an equation.

a) The area of a rectangle is 15 m². The short side is 3 m long.
What is the long side of the rectangle?

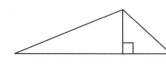

b) The area of a triangle is 3 m². The height is 0.5 m long.
What is the base of the triangle?

c) The shortest side of a right triangle is 30 cm long.
The longest side is 50 cm long. What is the length of the
middle side of the triangle?

11. Compare these two problems:

Problem A: A parallelogram has base of 5 cm and area 30 cm². What is its height?

Problem B: A parallelogram has height of 5 cm and area 30 cm². What is its base?

Do these problems produce different equations? Explain.

12. Fill in the correct units.

a) 3 cm $\times$ 3 cm = 9 _cm^2_   b) 9 cm² $\div$ 3 cm = 3 ____   c) 3 ____ + 3 m = 6 m

d) 3 ____ $\times$ 3 m = 9 m²   e) 9 ____ $\div$ 3 mm = 3 mm   f) $\sqrt{(3\ m)^2 + (4\ m)^2} = 5$ ____

13. Problem: The area of a triangle is 3 m². The height is 30 cm. What is the base of the triangle?

a) Would you convert the measurements for the problem into metres or centimetres? _____

b) Convert the measurements into the units you've chosen: Area = _____ Height = _____

c) Substitute the converted units into the formula for the area of a triangle. Use x for the base.

   Equation: _____

d) Now solve the equation. Do not forget the correct units in the answer!

14. What is wrong with the following "solutions" to Question 13?

a) The equation is $3 \times x \div 2 = 30$, so $x = 30 \times 2 \div 3 = 20$ m.
b) The equation is $30 \times x \div 2 = 3$, so $x = 3 \times 2 \div 30 = 0.2$ m.
c) The equation is $30 \times x \div 2 = 3$, so $x = 3 \times 2 \div 30 = 0.2$ cm.

G8-7 Solving Problems

> **Pythagorean Theorem**
> If a right triangle has sides a, b, c, with c being opposite the right angle, then $a^2 + b^2 = c^2$.

1. Find the missing side. Write the correct units in your answer.

a)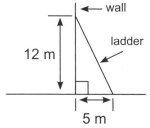
5 m
4 m

b)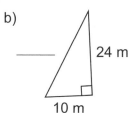
24 m
10 m

c)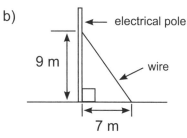
20 mm   15 mm

d)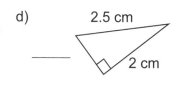
2.5 cm
2 cm

2. a)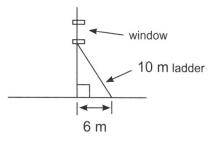

wall
ladder
12 m
5 m

How long is the ladder?

b)
electrical pole
wire
9 m
7 m

How long is the wire?

c)
window
10 m ladder
6 m

How high is the window?

3. Julie cuts a square into two congruent parts and rearranges the parts to make a rectangle. The short side of her new rectangle is 6 cm. What is the area of her rectangle?

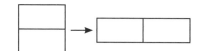

4. A bus window is 80 cm tall, and it has the shape of a parallelogram. The area of the window is 0.96 m². What is the length of the bottom side of the window?

5. a) Three nonzero whole numbers a, b, and c that satisfy $a^2 + b^2 = c^2$ are called a **Pythagorean triple**. Write down the first 15 perfect squares. How many Pythagorean triples can you find?

b) If you multiply or divide each number in a Pythagorean triple by the same number, the result is a Pythagorean triple. Make 3 Pythagorean triples using the numbers 6, 8, and 10.

6. In a rhombus, all sides are the same length and diagonals are perpendicular. If the diagonals are 18 cm and 16 cm, what are the sides of the rhombus?

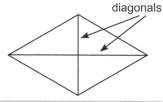
diagonals

> Sometimes you need to apply **the same formula twice**.

7. A straight tunnel passes under a mountain. The mountain is 312 m high and the distance from the summit of the mountain to the entrances of the tunnel is 1270 m and 670 m. What is the length of the tunnel?

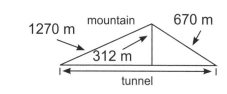
1270 m   mountain   670 m
312 m
tunnel

Sometimes you need to apply **more than one formula** to solve the problem.

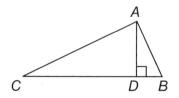

8. In a triangle ABC, side $AB = 10$ cm. AD is the height, and it is 8 cm long. CD is 15 cm.

   a) What is the area of $\triangle ABC$?

      i)   Mark the information you know on the sketch.

      ii) Which formula are you going to use to answer the question?

      iii) Which piece of information in the formula is missing?

      iv) $BC = CD +$ _____. The missing line segment is a side of triangle _____.

      v) Which formula could you use to find BD?

      vi) Find the length of BD and mark it on the sketch.

      vii) Find the area of ABC.

   b) Is ABC a right triangle?

      i)   If ABC is a right triangle, what would the Pythagorean Theorem say about its sides?

      ii) Find AC using the Pythagorean Theorem for $\triangle ABC$.

      iii) Find AC using the Pythagorean Theorem for $\triangle ADC$.

      iv) Did you get the same answer in ii) and in iii)? Explain.

9. A **diagonal** of a quadrilateral is a line segment joining two opposite vertices. A rectangle $ABCD$ has diagonal $AC = 65$ m and side $AB = 42$ m. What is the area of $ABCD$?

10. The area of a rectangle $ABCD$ is 24 m². The side AB is 4 m long. What is the length of the diagonal AC?

11. A park lawn has the shape of an isosceles triangle. The area of the lawn is 400 m². The shortest side of the lawn is 16 m long. What is the length of the two other sides of the lawn?

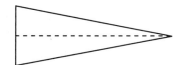

12. A parallelogram is made from two right triangles joined along the longer leg. The sides of the parallelogram are 50 cm and 1.3 m. What is the area of the parallelogram?

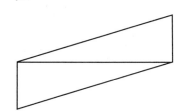

13. John says that he can draw a triangle with sides 5 cm, 12 cm, and 13 cm, and area 30 cm², so that one of the heights will be 10 cm. Is he correct? Explain.

14. A right triangle has short sides of 36 cm and 15 cm. What is the length of the height to the longest side of the triangle?

   Hint: Area of a triangle $=$ base $\times$ height $\div$ 2. Find the area of the triangle in two ways and solve the equation.

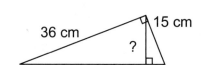

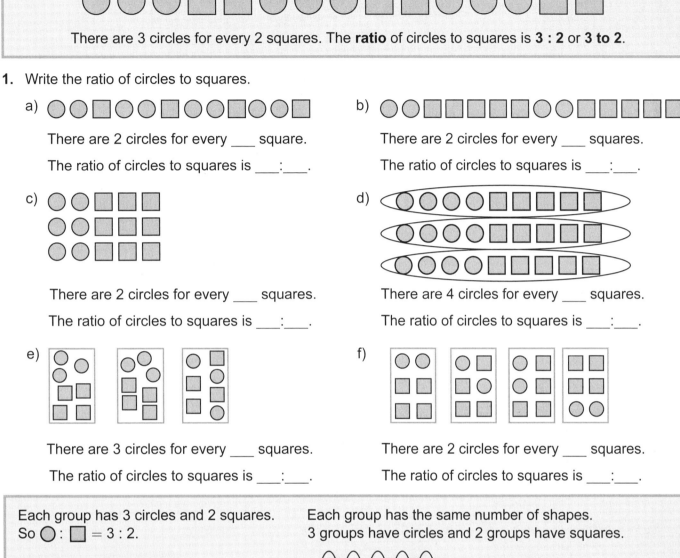

There are 3 circles for every 2 squares. The **ratio** of circles to squares is **3 : 2** or **3 to 2**.

1. Write the ratio of circles to squares.

a)

There are 2 circles for every ___ square.

The ratio of circles to squares is ___:___.

b)

There are 2 circles for every ___ squares.

The ratio of circles to squares is ___:___.

c)

There are 2 circles for every ___ squares.

The ratio of circles to squares is ___:___.

d)

There are 4 circles for every ___ squares.

The ratio of circles to squares is ___:___.

e)

There are 3 circles for every ___ squares.

The ratio of circles to squares is ___:___.

f)

There are 2 circles for every ___ squares.

The ratio of circles to squares is ___:___.

Each group has 3 circles and 2 squares.
So : = 3 : 2.

Each group has the same number of shapes.
3 groups have circles and 2 groups have squares.

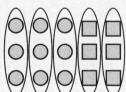

The ratio : is 3 : 2

The two sets have the same total number of circles and squares, so the ratios : are the same!

g)

There is 1 circle for every ___ squares.

The ratio of circles to squares is ___:___.

h)

There are 3 circles for every ___ squares.

The ratio of circles to squares is ___:___.

A **ratio** is a comparison of two or more numbers.
A **part-to-part ratio** compares one part to another part.
    Example: The ratio of squares to triangles is
        2 to 3, or 2 : 3.
A **part-to-whole ratio** compares one part to the whole.
    Example: The ratio of squares to total shapes is 2 to 7, or 2 : 7.

2. a) Write the part-to-part ratios for these shapes.

      i) squares to circles = __4__ : __3__   ii) triangles to circles = ___ : ___

      iii) dark squares to light squares = ___ : ___   iv) light circles to dark circles = ___ : ___

      v) light circles to dark squares = ___ : ___   vi) light shapes to dark shapes = ___ : ___

    b) Write the part-to-whole ratios for the shapes.

      i) circles to all shapes = __3__ : __8__   ii) squares to all shapes = ___ : ___

      iii) light shapes to all shapes = ___ : ___   iv) dark circles to all circles = ___ : ___

      v) light squares to all squares = ___ : ___   vi) dark circles to all dark shapes = ___ : ___

    c) A polygon is a 2-D shape with straight sides. Circle the part-to-whole ratios for the shapes.

      squares to polygons   circles to polygons   triangles to polygons

Part-to-whole ratios can be thought of as fractions.

Example:

The ratio of squares to shapes is 4 : 7, so $\frac{4}{7}$ of the shapes are squares.

The ratio of light squares to all squares is 1 : 4, so $\frac{1}{4}$ of the squares are light.

3. Write the part-to-whole ratios from Question 2 b) as fractions.

    i) ___$\frac{3}{8}$___ of the _shapes_ are _____.   ii) _____ of the _____ are _____.

    iii) _____ of the _____ are _____.   iv) _____ of the _____ are _____.

    v) _____ of the _____ are _____.   vi) _____ of the _____ are _____.

4. Circle the part-to-whole ratios. Underline the part-to-part ratios.

    a) vowels in **band** : letters in **band**   b) vowels in **blog** : consonants in **blog**   c) buses : trucks

    d) school days : days of the week   e) days in January : days in September   f) school buses : buses

5. A part-to-part ratio cannot be thought of as a fraction. Why not?

6. The ratio of circles to triangles is 94 : 93. Are there more circles or triangles? How do you know?

                         Measurement 8-1

ME8-2 Equivalent Ratios

Two ratios are equivalent if they compare the same quantities.

○ ○ ○ ○ □ □ □ □ ○ ○ ○ ○ □ □ □

There are 4 circles for every 3 squares. There are 8 circles for every 6 squares.
The ratio of circles to squares is 4 : 3 or 8 : 6.

4 : 3 and 8 : 6 are **equivalent ratios**.

1. Find two equivalent ratios for each picture.

a)

○ : □ = 3 : ___ = 6 : ___

b)

○ : □ = 1 : ___ = 2 : ___

c)

○ : □ = 2 : ___ = 4 : ___

2. Every word in the phrases below has 2 consonants and 1 vowel.
   Write equivalent ratios for the ratio 2 : 1 by counting all the consonants and vowels.

   a) the dog

   2 : 1 = ___ : ___

   b) the big dog

   2 : 1 = ___ : ___

   c) the dog was wet

   2 : 1 = ___ : ___

   d) the big dog got wet

   2 : 1 = ___ : ___

   e) the big fat dog was dry but got all wet

   2 : 1 = ___ : ___

3. a) Write a word that has 1 consonant for every vowel and a total of...

   i) 2 letters. _____   ii) 4 letters. _____   iii) 6 letters. _____

   b) Write two more equivalent ratios.   1 : 1 = ___ : ___ = ___ : ___

   c) Can you write a 9-letter word that has a ratio of consonants to vowels equal to 1 : 1? Explain.

4. a) Draw 15 circles and squares so that the ratio of circles to squares is 2 : 3.
      Hint: Repeatedly draw 2 circles and 3 squares until you have 15 shapes.

   b) Write an equivalent ratio for 2 : 3 by counting all the circles and squares. 2 : 3 = ___ : ___

To create equivalent ratios, multiply each term in the ratio by the same number.

○ ○ □   ○ ○ □   ○ ○ □   ○ ○ □
               ○ ○ □   ○ ○ □   ○ ○ □
                              ○ ○ □   ○ ○ □
                                             ○ ○ □

2 : 1   =   (2 × 2) : (1 × 2)   =   (2 × 3) : (1 × 3)   =   (2 × 4) : (1 × 4)
2 : 1   =   4 : 2   =   6 : 3   =   8 : 4

5. Starting with the given ratio, write a sequence of four equivalent ratios.

   a) 3 : 4 = _6_ : _8_ = ___ : ___ = ___ : ___   b) 3 : 7 = ___ : ___ = ___ : ___ = ___ : ___

   c) 5 : 8 = ___ : ___ = ___ : ___ = ___ : ___   d) 3 : 10 = ___ : ___ = ___ : ___ = ___ : ___

There are 3 boys for every 2 girls in a class of 20 students.

To find out how many boys are in the class,

write out a sequence of equivalent ratios.

Stop when the terms of the ratio add to 20.

Boys		Girls	Total
3	:	2	5
6	:	4	10
9	:	6	15
12	:	**8**	**20**

12 boys + 8 girls = 20 students, so there are 12 boys in the class.

6. Write a sequence of equivalent ratios to solve each problem.

   a) There are 5 boys for every 4 girls in a class of 27 students.
      How many girls are in the class?

Boys		Girls	Total
5	:	4	9
10	:		

   b) There are 2 red marbles for every 7 blue marbles in a box.

      If the box holds 45 marbles, how many of the marbles are blue?

   c) A recipe for punch calls for 3 L of orange juice for every 4 L of mango juice.
      How many litres of orange juice are needed to make 21 L of punch?

A part-to-part ratio can sometimes be changed to a part-to-whole ratio or fraction.

Example: There are 2 circles for every 5 triangles in a set of circles and triangles.

So there are 2 circles for every 7 shapes.

The ratio of circles to triangles is 2 : 5, so $\frac{2}{7}$ of the shapes are circles.

7. An aquarium has red and blue fish. Change each part-to-part ratio to a part-to-whole fraction.

   a) The ratio of blue fish to red fish is 3 : 2.

   b) The ratio of red fish to blue fish is 3 : 5.

   c) The ratio of blue fish to red fish is 4 : 3.

   d) The ratio of red fish to blue fish is 2 : 7.

8. A team's **win : loss** ratio is **5 : 2**. There are no ties. What fraction of the games did the team win?

9. Tania collects rock and jazz CDs. The ratio **rock CDs : jazz CDs = 4 : 7**.

   What fraction of Tania's CDs are rock CDs?

ME8-3 Solving Proportions

A proportion is an equation that shows two equivalent ratios. Example: $1 : 4 = 2 : 8$

When a proportion has a missing number (Example: $1 : 4 = \_\_\_ : 8$), finding the missing number is called **solving the proportion.**

1. Multiply the first term by the same number the second term was multiplied by.

   a) $4 : 5 = \_\_\_ : 20$ b) $1 : 5 = \_\_\_ : 25$ c) $2 : 5 = \_\_\_ : 20$

   d) $6 : 7 = \_\_\_ : 35$ e) $3 : 4 = \_\_\_ : 16$ f) $2 : 3 = \_\_\_ : 12$

2. Solve the proportion.

   a) $15 : 25 = 60 : \_\_\_$ b) $5 : 9 = \_\_\_ : 45$ c) $3 : 5 = 15 : \_\_\_$ d) $3 : 5 = \_\_\_ : 15$

To create an equivalent ratio with each term a smaller number, divide each term in the ratio by the same number. This is called simplifying the ratio. Example: $40 : 35 = 40 \div \mathbf{5} : 35 \div \mathbf{5}$
$$= 8 : 7$$

3. Simplify each ratio.

   a) $6 : 24 = \_\_\_ : 8$ b) $9 : 21 = 3 : \_\_\_$ c) $60 : 100 = \_\_\_ : 50$ d) $70 : 30 = 35 : \_\_\_$

A ratio is in lowest terms when the numbers in the ratio are as small as they can be.

To write the ratio $30 : 36$ in lowest terms:

Step 1: Find the prime factorizations of 30 and 36. $30 = 2 \times 3 \times 5$

$36 = 2 \times 2 \times 3 \times 3$

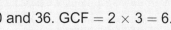 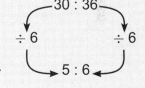

Step 2: Find the greatest common factor (GCF) of 30 and 36. GCF $= 2 \times 3 = 6$.

Step 3: Divide each term in the ratio by the GCF to write the ratio in lowest terms.

4. a) Write the prime factorization of each number.

   i) $10 = $ _____   ii) $12 = $ _____   iii) $30 = $ _____   iv) $75 = $ _____

   b) Find the GCF of each pair.

   i) 10 and 12   ii) 10 and 30   iii) 10 and 75   iv) 12 and 30   v) 12 and 75   vi) 30 and 75

   _____   _____   _____   _____   _____   _____

   c) Write each ratio in lowest terms by dividing both terms by their GCF.

   i) $10 : 12$ ii) $10 : 30$ iii) $10 : 75$ iv) $12 : 30$ v) $12 : 75$ vi) $75 : 30$

   _____   _____   _____   _____   _____   _____

5. Write each ratio in lowest terms.

   a) $25 : 35$ b) $21 : 6$ c) $20 : 12$ d) $14 : 21$ e) $84 : 27$ f) $90 : 75$

6. Write the ratio that is complete in lowest terms. Then find the missing number to make the ratios equivalent.

    a) $8 : 10 = \underline{\ 4\ } : \underline{\ 5\ }$

    so $8 : 10 = \underline{\ 12\ } : 15$

    b) $\quad 4 : 6 = \underline{\ \ \ } : \underline{\ \ \ }$

    so $4 : 6 = 6 : \underline{\ \ \ }$

    c) $\quad 60 : 100 = \underline{\ \ \ } : \underline{\ \ \ }$

    so $60 : 100 = \underline{\ \ \ } : 45$

7. Solve the proportions. Begin by writing the ratio that is complete in lowest terms.

    a) $40 : 50 = \underline{\ \ \ } : \underline{\ \ \ }$
    $= \underline{\ \ \ } : 30$

    b) $70 : 100 = \underline{\ \ \ } : \underline{\ \ \ }$
    $= \underline{\ \ \ } : 30$

    c) $50 : 75 = \underline{\ \ \ } : \underline{\ \ \ }$
    $= \underline{\ \ \ } : 24$

    d) $6 : 24 = \underline{\ \ \ } : \underline{\ \ \ }$
    $= \underline{\ \ \ } : 16$

    e) $11 : 22 = \underline{\ \ \ } : \underline{\ \ \ }$
    $= 5 : \underline{\ \ \ }$

    f) $\underline{\ \ \ } : 7 = \underline{\ \ \ } : \underline{\ \ \ }$
    $= 6 : 3$

    g) $30 : 9 = \underline{\ \ \ } : \underline{\ \ \ }$
    $= 50 : \underline{\ \ \ }$

    h) $\underline{\ \ \ } : 25 = \underline{\ \ \ } : \underline{\ \ \ }$
    $= 4 : 10$

    i) $72 : 18 = \underline{\ \ \ } : \underline{\ \ \ }$
    $= \underline{\ \ \ } : 7$

8. The ratio 3 506 : 5 259 in lowest terms is 2 : 3. What is the ratio 5 259 : 3 506 in lowest terms? How do you know?

   INVESTIGATION ▶ $\dfrac{1}{3}$ of the students are girls. What is the ratio of girls to boys?

   A. i) If there is 1 girl, there are _____ students altogether, so _____ are boys.

   ii) If there are 2 girls, there are _____ students altogether, so _____ are boys.

   iii) If there are 3 girls, there are _____ students altogether, so _____ are boys.

   iv) If there are 4 girls, there are _____ students altogether, so _____ are boys.

   v) If there are 5 girls, there are _____ students altogether, so _____ are boys.

   B. What is the ratio of girls to boys in each case?

   i) 1 : _____   ii) 2 : _____   iii) 3 : _____   iv) 4 : _____   v) 5 : _____

   C. Are the ratios in part B equivalent?

   D. Work backwards to check your work. Start with the ratios of girls to boys you found in part B. What fraction of the students are girls?

   E. What is the ratio of girls to boys in the classes of Ms. X and Mr. Y?

   Ms. X: $\dfrac{2}{5}$ of the students are girls.   Mr. Y: $\dfrac{5}{8}$ of the students are girls.

   F. Whose class from part E has more girls than boys?

   How can you tell from the fraction? How can you tell from the ratio?

ME8-4 Word Problems

> **PROBLEM ▶** In a pet shop, there are 3 cats for every 4 dogs. If there are 12 dogs in the shop, how many cats are there?
>
> **SOLUTION ▶** Write the names of the two things being compared.
>
> | | cats | | dogs |
> |---|---|---|---|
> | | 3 | : | 4 |
>
> Write the quantities under the names, as a ratio.
>
> Re-read the question to determine which quantity is given and which is unknown. Write this information in a new row under the right names.
>
> | | ? | : | 12 |
> |---|---|---|---|
>
> Solve the proportion.
>
> $3 : 4 = ? : 12$
>
> $? = 9$, so there are 9 cats in the shop.

1. Nine bus tickets cost $19. How many bus tickets can you buy with $57?

2. Mike can run 3 laps in 5 minutes. How many laps can he do in 20 minutes?

3. Jared can run 4 laps in 10 minutes. How long will it take Jared to run 6 laps?

4. The ratio of boys to girls in a class is 5 : 6. If there are 20 boys, how many girls are there?

5. Two out of every 5 students at school are in the art program.
   There are 300 students in total. How many are in the art program?

6. Four out of 7 students like rap music. If 280 students like rap music, how many students are there in total?

7. There are 2 rap songs for every 3 rock songs on Will's MP3 player.
   There are a total of 120 rock songs. How many rap songs are there?

8. A muffin recipe calls for 2.5 cups of flour for 12 muffins. Jean wants to make 30 muffins.
   How much flour will she need?

9. The ratio of students in string band to students in brass band is 3 : 4. There are 36 students in the brass band. How many students are in the string band?

10. In a zoo, 2 out of every 3 gorillas are female. There are 15 gorillas in the zoo.
    How many male gorillas are there?

11. There are 3 green chromis fish for every 5 clown fish in an aquarium.

    a) If there are 30 clown fish, how many green chromis fish are there?

    b) If there are 30 green chromis fish, how many clown fish are there?

12. Irene has 64 jazz CDs and 80 rock CDs. Is the ratio of jazz CDs to rock CDs 3 : 4 or 4 : 5?

ME8-5 Circles

All points on a circle are the same distance from
a point called the **centre**. This distance is called
the radius of a circle. The plural of radius is radii.

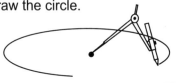

How to construct a circle using a compass,
when given the centre and radius:

Step 1: Set the compass width to the given radius.	**Step 2:** Set the compass point on the centre point.	**Step 3:** Without changing the width of the compass, draw the circle.

1. Construct a circle with centre *O* and radius the length of *AB*.

   a) *A* —————— *B*

   b)
   A
   |
   |
   |
   B

   O

   O

2. a) Construct a circle with center *O* through point *A*.

      Step 1: Set the compass point on point *O*.

      Step 2: Adjust the compass width to distance *OA*.

      Step 3: Draw a circle through point *A*.

      A
      •

      •
      O

   b) Mark any point on the circle and label it *B*.

      Construct *OA* and *OB* using a ruler.

   c) Measure *OA* and *OB*. What do you notice? _____

REMINDER ▶ Types of triangles:

No equal sides — scalene   2 equal sides — isosceles   3 equal sides — equilateral

---

3. a) Construct a circle with centre *A* through point *B*.

   b) Construct a circle with centre *B* through point *A*.

   c) Label one of the intersection points of the circles *C*.
      Construct triangle *ABC*.

      •*A*

      •
      B

   d) What type of triangle have you constructed? Explain.

Measurement 8-5

The **diameter** of a circle is the distance across the circle through the centre.

The radius is half of the diameter.

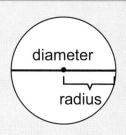

4. Find the radius (circles are not drawn to scale).

a)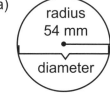

radius _____

b)

radius _____

c)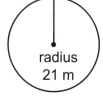

radius _____

d)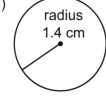

radius _____

5. Find the diameter (circles are not drawn to scale).

a)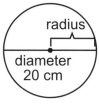

diameter _____

b)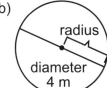

diameter _____

c)

diameter _____

d)

diameter _____

6. Fill in the missing radius or diameter for each circle.

Radius	3 cm	4 cm	12 cm			2.7 cm			r cm
Diameter	6 cm			10 mm	16 m		1 m	1.8 cm	

7. Draw and measure the diameter.

a)

b)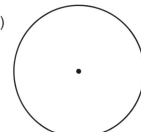

8. Draw and measure the radius.

a)

b)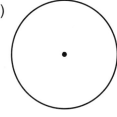

9. Using a ruler and a compass, construct a circle with…

a) radius 5 cm   b) diameter 8 cm   c) diameter 13 cm   d) radius 66 mm

INVESTIGATION ▶

How do different line segments from the centre of a circle compare to the radius?

A. The centre of the circle is point O. Mark a point on the circle and label it Z. Measure OZ. The radius of the circle is _____ cm.

B. Measure the lengths of the line segments from O to all the points inside the circle.

   $OA =$ _____ , _____ , _____ , _____

   Compare the lengths you measured to the radius. What do you notice?

C. Measure the lengths of the line segments from O to the points outside the circle.

   $OE =$ _____ , _____ , _____ , _____

   Compare the lengths you measured to the radius. What do you notice?

D. Draw a circle in your notebook and measure its radius. Mark three points inside the circle and three points outside the circle. Compare the radius to the distances between the centre of the circle and the points you drew. Do you get the same result as in parts B and C?

---

10. A circle with centre O has radius 5 cm.

   a) $OV = 3$ cm. Is V inside the circle, outside the circle, or on the circle?

   b) $OW = 6$ cm. Is W inside the circle, outside the circle, or on the circle?

   c) $OU = 5$ cm. Is U inside the circle, outside the circle, or on the circle?

The Pythagorean Theorem

If a right triangle has sides a, b, c with c opposite the right angle, then $a^2 + b^2 = c^2$.

---

11. Use the Pythagorean theorem to find the distance AB (equal to the length of the line segment AB). Then estimate the square root.

a)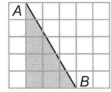

$AB = \sqrt{5^2 + 3^2}$

$\quad = \sqrt{25 + 9}$

$\quad = \sqrt{34}$

$\sqrt{34}$ is slightly

less than 6

b)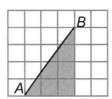

$AB = \sqrt{4^2 + 3^2}$

$\quad =$ _____

_____

_____

_____

_____

c)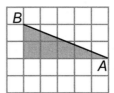

_____

_____

_____

_____

_____

d)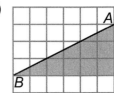

_____

_____

_____

_____

_____

12. **a)** Mark the centre of the circle O. The radius of the circle is _____ squares.

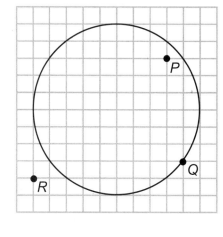

b) Point P is ___inside___ the circle. I expect OP to be _shorter than_ the radius.

Check: $OP = \sqrt{3^2 + 3^2} = \sqrt{9+9} = \sqrt{18}$

c) Point Q is _____ the circle. I expect OQ to be

_____ the radius.

Check: $OQ =$ _____

d) Point R is _____ the circle. I expect OR to be

_____ the radius.

Check: $OR =$ _____

e) Point Q is on the circle and falls on an intersection of the grid lines. Find and mark eleven more such points on the circle.

13. Ariel wants to sketch a circle of radius 6 on grid paper without using a compass. She marks O as the centre of her circle and plots points K, L, M, and N that are on the circle.

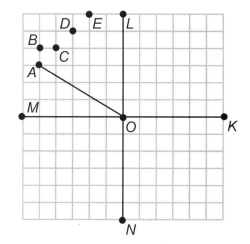

a) Which line segments are the radii of the circle?

_____ , _____ , _____ , _____

b) Which line segments are the diameters of the circle?

_____ and _____

c) Ariel wants to check whether the point A is inside or outside the circle. She finds the distance OA.

$OA = \sqrt{5^2 + 3^2} =$ _____

Is OA more or less than 6? Is OA inside or outside of the circle? _____

d) Use the Pythagorean theorem to find the lengths below. Then decide whether each point is inside or outside the circle.

$OB =$ _____ . Point B is _____ the circle.

$OC =$ _____ . Point C is _____ the circle.

$OD =$ _____ . Point D is _____ the circle.

$OE =$ _____ . Point E is _____ the circle.

e) Sketch a quarter of the circle using the information from d).

f) Using KM and LN as symmetry lines, sketch the rest of the circle on the grid above.

ME8-6 Circumference

The distance around a polygon is called **perimeter**.		The distance around a circle is called **circumference**.	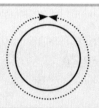

1. A polygon is regular if all its sides and all its angles are equal. This table gives the width (w) and side lengths (s) of different regular polygons.

   a) Find the perimeter (P) of each regular polygon.

   b) Find the ratio of the perimeter (P) to the width (w).

Squares 4 equal sides	width (w) = 1 cm	w = 2 cm	w = 3 cm
	side length (s) = 1 cm	s = 2 cm	s = 3 cm
	perimeter (P) =		
	$\underline{\;1\;cm \times 4 = 4\;\;}$ cm	$P =$ _____	$P =$ _____
	$P : w =$ ___4 : 1___	$P : w =$ _____	$P : w =$ _____
Hexagons 6 equal sides	width (w) = 2 cm	w = 4 cm	w = 6 cm
	side length (s) = 1 cm	s = 2 cm	s = 3 cm
	perimeter (P) =		
	$\underline{\;1\;cm \times 6 =\;\;}$ cm	$P =$ _____	$P =$ _____
	$P : w =$ _____	$P : w =$ _____	$P : w =$ _____
Octagons 8 equal sides	width (w) = 8 cm	w = 4 cm	w = 12 cm
	side length (s) = 3 cm	s = 1.5 cm	s = 4.5 cm
	perimeter (P) =		
	$\underline{\quad\quad} \times 8 =$ _____ cm	$P =$ _____	$P =$ _____
	$P : w =$ _____	$P : w =$ _____	$P : w =$ _____

   c) What do you notice about the ratios $P : w$ in each row?

   d) Divide the perimeter by the width to write each ratio in the form ▨ : 1.

      For a square, $P : w = 4 : 1$. The perimeter of a square is 4 times larger than its width.

      For a hexagon, $P : w =$ ___ :1. The perimeter of a regular hexagon is ___ times larger than its width.

      For an octagon, $P : w =$ ___ :1. The perimeter of a regular octagon is ___ times larger than its width.

INVESTIGATION ▶ What is the ratio of the circumference of a circle
to its diameter (width)?

A. Measure the diameter (the width) of the circles. Estimate the circumference of the
circles by calculating the perimeters of the regular octagons.

a)

b)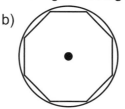

c)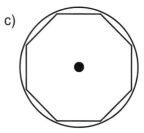

diameter (*d*) __22 mm__

side of octagon __8 mm__

perimeter of octagon __64 mm__

circumference (*C*) __about 64 mm__

diameter (*d*) _____

side of octagon _____

perimeter of octagon _____

circumference (*C*) _____

diameter (*d*) _____

side of octagon _____

perimeter of octagon _____

circumference (*C*) _____

B. Estimate the ratio of the circumference to the diameter of each circle above.
Then divide the circumference by the diameter to write each ratio in the form ▢ : 1.

$C : d \approx$ ____ : ____ = ____ : 1 $C : d \approx$ ____ : ____ = ____ : 1 $C : d \approx$ ____ : ____ = ____ : 1

The ratio of the circumference to the diameter of the circles is about _____

C. Here are the diameters and circumferences of some circles. Find the ratio of circumference to diameter
for each circle. Write each ratio in the form ▢ : 1. What do you notice?

Circle	Circumference (*C*)	Diameter (*d*)	Ratio (*C : d*)
A	15.7 cm	5 cm	3.14 : 1
B	31.4 cm	10 cm	
C	62.8 cm	20 cm	

The actual ratio of circumference to diameter is **the same for all circles**. This number has an infinite
number of digits after its decimal point, so people use the Greek letter π (pronounced "pie") to identify it.

Rounded to 2 decimal places, $\pi \approx 3.14$.

Circumference : diameter $= \pi : 1$, so circumference is π times larger than diameter.

Circumference $= \pi \times$ **diameter** $= \pi \times 2 \times$ **radius** $= \pi \times 2 \times r = 2 \times \pi \times r = 2\pi r$

2. Find the approximate circumference of circles with the given measurements. Use 3.14 for π.

a) diameter = 7 m   b) diameter = 12 m   c) radius = 5 m   d) radius = 4.5 cm

circumference $= \pi \times 7$ m

$\approx 3.14 \times 7$ m $=$ _____

ME8-7 Area of Circles

INVESTIGATION ▶ What is the approximate relation between the radius of a circle and its **area**?

A. Draw a circle with a compass.
Cut out the circle and fold it in half 3 times:

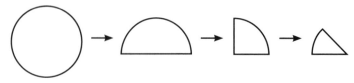

B. Unfold your circle and colour one half of it.
Cut along the fold lines of the circle and rearrange
the pieces, as shown, on top of a sheet of paper:

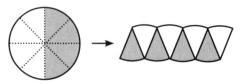

C. Draw a parallelogram around the shape you made.
The area of the parallelogram is **almost equal** to
the area of the circle.

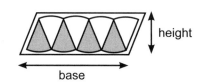

D. Is the **height** of the parallelogram in C. approximately
equal to the radius or the diameter of the circle?

E. What fraction of the circumference is the thick line? Where would
this thick line be if you moved it to the parallelogram? Draw it.

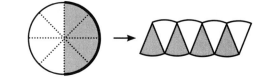

F. How can you get the approximate length of the **base**
of the parallelogram from the circumference of the circle?

G. The formula for the area of a parallelogram is **Area = base × height**. Use your
answers for parts D and F to give the approximate area of the parallelogram:

Area of parallelogram ≈ _____ × _____

          approximate height   approximate base

H. The correct answer for G. is:

Area of parallelogram ≈ radius of circle × the circumference of circle ÷ 2.

Substitute r for the radius and C for the circumference: Area of parallelogram: _____ × _____ ÷ 2.

The circumference (C) of a circle of radius r is $C = 2\pi r$, so

Area of parallelogram   ≈ $r ×$ _____ ÷ 2 $= r ×$ _____ × _____ × _____ ÷ 2

                 $=$ _____ × _____ × _____ × 2 ÷ 2

                 $=$ _____ $× r^2$

The area of the parallelogram is approximately equal to the area of the circle. Mathematicians have
shown that the actual area (A) of a circle is given by the formula $A = \pi r^2$.

1. Find the area of the circles. Use 3.14 for π.

Example: radius 3 m   Area $= \pi r^2 \approx 3.14 × 3^2 = 3.14 × 9 = 28.26$ m^2

a) radius 10 cm   b) radius 5 km   c) radius 7 m   d) radius 3.3 mm
e) diameter 12 m   f) diameter 34 cm   g) diameter 1 m   h) diameter 29 mm

ME8-8 Area, Circumference, and Perimeter

1. Half of a circle is called a **semicircle**. Find the area of the semicircles. Use 3.14 for π.

   a) 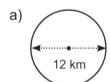 Area of circle $\approx$ _314 cm²_

   Area of semicircle

   $\approx$ _314 cm² $\div$ 2 = 157 cm²_

   b)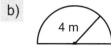

   c)

2. What is the distance around this semicircle?

   a) Circumference of whole circle $= C = 2\pi r \approx$ _____ cm

   b) What fraction of C is the length of the curved side? _____

   length of the curved side $=$ _____ cm

   c) Is the straight side of the semicircle the radius or the diameter of the circle?

   _____

   What is the length of the straight side in terms of r? _____

   d) The distance around the semicircle is about _____ + _____ = _____ cm

   e) The area of a semicircle is half the area of the whole circle. Explain why the distance around the semicircle is not half the distance around the whole circle (circumference).

   f) Find the distance around the semicircles in Questions 1 b) and c).

3. Find the area and the distance around each figure.

   a)
   12 km

   b) 9 cm

   c)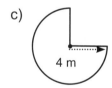
   4 m

   d)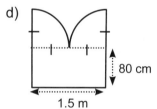
   80 cm
   1.5 m

4. Re-do Question 3 b) by converting cm to m. Compare your answers. How do you convert a measurement in cm² to a measurement in m²?

5. a) The wheels on Karen's bike have diameter 56 cm. What is their circumference?

   b) Karen rotates the wheels at a speed of 3 full rotations in 2 seconds. How far will she go in 10 seconds? In 1 minute? In 1 hour?

   c) Karen's mother can run 10 kilometres in an hour. Will she be able to keep up with Karen on her ride?

   BONUS▶ Karen's father's bike has wheels with diameter 66 cm. If he wants to ride at the same speed as Karen, how many times should the wheels of his bike rotate in 1 hour? In 1 second?

6. a) Find the diameter of each circle (use 3.14 for π).

    i) circumference 5.4 m   ii) circumference 1 m   iii) circumference 360 cm

  b) Find the area of each circle above. Is it more than 1 m² or less than 1 m²?

7. A rotating water sprinkler can spray water a distance of 15 m.

    What area of grass can the sprinkler cover?

8. Fill in the blanks for the shape at right. Use 3.14 for π.

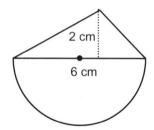

    Area of the triangle: _____

    Radius (not diameter!) of the semicircle: _____

    Area of the semicircle: _____

    Area of the whole shape: _____ + _____ = _____

9. a) The right isosceles triangle in the picture at right has hypotenuse 6 cm.
Using *x* for the length of each of the other sides, write the equation for
the length of the sides from the Pythagorean theorem.

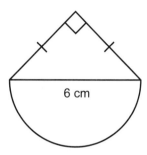

  b) What is the area of the triangle?

  c) A semicircle is constructed on the hypotenuse of the triangle. What is
the area of the semicircle? Leave your answer in terms of π.

10. These shapes were made from quarters or halves of circles and polygons.
Find the area of the shapes. Leave your answer in terms of π.

a) 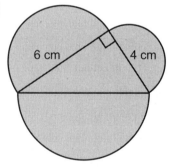   **b)** 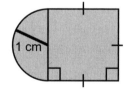   **c)**

11. a) Find the area of each shaded part by subtracting the area of the triangle from
the area of the semicircle or quarter circle. Use 3.14 for π.

    i)   **ii)**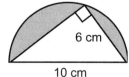

  b) Draw both pictures to scale. Is the area of the shaded part more or less than the
area of the triangle? Does your answer make sense with the picture?

NS8-64 Gains and Losses

1. Write a plus sign (+) if the net result is a gain. Write a minus sign (−) if the net result is a loss.

   a) a gain of $5 __+__

   b) a loss of $3 _____

   c) a gain of $4 _____

   d) a gain of $2 and a loss of $5 __−__

   e) a gain of $3 and a loss of $1 _____

   f) a loss of $3 and a gain of $4 _____

   g) a loss of $6 and a gain of $2 _____

2. Write each sequence of gains and losses using numbers and signs (+ and −).

   a) a gain of $3 and a loss of $5 __+ 3 − 5__

   b) a loss of $2 and a gain of $8 _____

   c) a loss of $4 and a gain of $3 _____

   d) a gain of $6 and a loss of $5 _____

   e) a loss of $5, a gain of $8, a loss of $2, then a gain of $1 ____−5 + 8 − 2 + 1____

   f) a gain of $3, a gain of $5, a loss of $6, then a gain of $2 _____

   g) a loss of $5, a loss of $8, a gain of $10, then a gain of $5 _____

   h) a gain of $4, a loss of $3, a loss of $2, then a gain of $5 _____

3. Decide whether each sequence of gains and losses is a net gain (+) or a net loss (−).

   a) $+5 - 3$ __+__

   b) $+3 - 5$ _____

   c) $-2 + 4$ _____

   d) $-5 + 1$ _____

   e) $+8 - 7$ _____

   f) $+5 - 9$ _____

   g) $-4 + 5$ _____

   h) $-3 + 2$ _____

   i) $-9 + 5$ _____

4. How much was gained or lost overall? Use + for a gain, − for a loss, and 0 for no gain or loss.

   a) $+6 - 5 =$ __+1__

   b) $-4 + 3 =$ _____

   c) $+5 - 5 =$ _____

   d) $-6 + 6 =$ _____

   e) $-3 + 5 =$ _____

   f) $+8 - 12 =$ _____

   g) $+3 + 2 =$ _____

   h) $-4 - 1 =$ _____

   i) $-5 - 2 =$ _____

   j) $-5 + 2 =$ _____

   k) $+5 - 2 =$ _____

   l) $+5 + 2 =$ _____

   m) $+3 - 8 =$ _____

   n) $-6 + 2 =$ _____

   o) $+7 - 2 =$ _____

   p) $-5 + 7 =$ _____

   q) $-4 + 4 =$ _____

   r) $+7 - 7 =$ _____

5. Group the gains (+'s) and losses (−'s) together. Then say how much was gained or lost overall.

   a) $+4 - 3 + 2 =$ __+ 4 + 2 − 3__

   $= $ __+ 6 − 3__

   $= $ __+ 3__

   b) $-3 + 4 - 2 =$ _____

   $= $ _____

   $= $ _____

   c) $-5 + 7 - 3 =$ _____

   $= $ _____

   $= $ _____

   d) $+8 - 5 + 2 =$ _____

   $= $ _____

   $= $ _____

e) $+5-4+6 =$ _____

$=$ _____

$=$ _____

f) $+4-6+3 =$ _____

$=$ _____

$=$ _____

6. Circle all the gains first. Then group the gains (+'s) and losses (−'s).

   Then say how much was gained or lost overall.

   a) $-5-1\left(+3\right)-2\left(+4\right)\left(+6\right)-4 =$ _____ $+3+4+6-5-1-2-4$

   $=$ _____ $+13-12$

   $=$ _____ $+1$

   b) $+6+3-4-5-8+2-1 =$ _____

   $=$ _____

   $=$ _____

   c) $-4+5+6-3-2+8-5+1-4 =$ _____

   $=$ _____

   $=$ _____

When the same number is gained and lost, the two numbers add 0 to the equation, so we can **cancel** them.

---

7. Cancel the numbers that make 0. Then write the total gain or loss.

   a) $-\cancel{3}+4+\cancel{3} =$ _____ $+4$

   b) $-3-2+3 =$ _____

   c) $+5+4-5 =$ _____

   d) $-5-4+5 =$ _____

   e) $-6+7+6 =$ _____

   f) $-5+5+2 =$ _____

   g) $+3+4-4 =$ _____

   h) $-8-5+5 =$ _____

   i) $-5-8+5 =$ _____

   j) $+8-5+2+5-2 =$ _____

   k) $-3+4+2+3-2 =$ _____

   l) $-5+5-6+3-3 =$ _____

   m) $-4-3+2+3-2 =$ _____

   n) $-5-4+4-3+5 =$ _____

   o) $+4-5-4-2+5 =$ _____

   p) $-\cancel{3}+\cancel{2}+4-5-\cancel{2}+\cancel{6}+\cancel{3}-\cancel{6} =$ _____ $+4-5$

   these cancel $=$ _____ -1

   q) $-5+2+6-2+3+4+5-3 =$ _____

   $=$ _____

   r) $+8-11-4+6-2+11-6-4 =$ _____

   $=$ _____

   s) $-4-3+2-7+4+2+3 =$ _____

   $=$ _____

8. Find the mistake in the cancelling. Circle the two numbers that should not have been cancelled.

   $-\cancel{3}+\cancel{4}+\cancel{2}+6-\cancel{2}+\cancel{3}+\cancel{4}-\cancel{7}+\cancel{1} = +6$

NS8-65 Integers

An **integer** is any one of these numbers: ..., –4, –3, –2, –1, 0, 1, 2, 3, 4, ...

Sometimes the numbers 1, 2, 3, 4, ... are written +1, +2, +3, +4, ...

An integer is **less than** another integer if it is **farther left** on the number line.

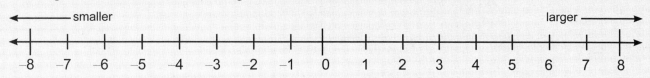

smaller ◄───────

larger ──────►

$$-8 \quad -7 \quad -6 \quad -5 \quad -4 \quad -3 \quad -2 \quad -1 \quad 0 \quad 1 \quad 2 \quad 3 \quad 4 \quad 5 \quad 6 \quad 7 \quad 8$$

1. Write three integers that are less than zero. _____ _____ _____

Integers that are **greater than 0** are called **positive**. Integers that are **less than 0** are called **negative**.

2. Circle the integers that are positive.   +4   7   –3   9   +2   +8   –5   –13

3. Circle the least integer in each pair.

    a) –3 or +5   b) –6 or –3   c) 7 or 5   d) –4 or –6
    e) 7 or –2   f) +8 or +3   g) –5 or –4   h) –7 or –9

4. Write < (less than) or > (greater than) in each box.

    a) +3 ☐ +7   b) –5 ☐ +4   c) 7 ☐ –2   d) –4 ☐ –6   e) –2 ☐ –10

5. Write two integers that are between –7 and –2. _____ and _____

6. Mark each integer on the number line with an X and label it with the correct letter.

    A +5   **B** –3   **C** +7   **D** –4   **E** –6

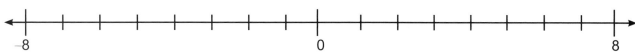

$$-8 \qquad\qquad\qquad\qquad 0 \qquad\qquad\qquad\qquad 8$$

7. Put the integers into the boxes in **increasing** order.

    +5   –3   +10   –7   –2   ☐ ☐ ☐ ☐ ☐

8. Put the temperatures into the boxes in order from warmest to coldest.

    13°C   –18°C   23°C   –17°C   –48°C   ☐ ☐ ☐ ☐ ☐

9. a) If 0 < a < b, mark possible places for a and b on the number line.

    b) Mark –a and –b on the same number line.

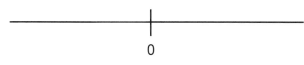

$$0$$

    c) Write the correct symbol (< or >) in each box.

        If 0 < a < b, then 0 ☐ –a ☐ –b.

NS8-66 Adding Integers

A negative integer can represent a loss and a positive integer can represent a gain.

1. Write the gain or loss represented by the integer.

a) –6 _loss of 6_   b) +3 _____   c) –2 _____   d) +7 _____

Any sequence of gains and losses can be written as a sum of integers.

Example: $-3 + 4 - 5 = (-3) + (+4) + (-5)$
$$= (-3) + 4 + (-5).$$

2. Write each sequence of gains and losses as a sum of integers.

a) $+4 - 3 - 5$ ____ $4 + (-3) + (-5)$ ____   b) $-2 + 6 - 3$ _____

c) $+3 + 2 - 7$ _____   d) $+5 - 3 - 4$ _____

e) $-3 + 1 + 5$ _____   f) $-3 + 4 - 2$ _____

3. Write each sum of integers as a sequence of gains and losses.

a) $(+3) + (-4) = \pm 3 - 4$ b) $(+3) + (+4) = $ _____   c) $(-3) + (+4) = $ _____   d) $(-3) + (-4) = $ _____

e) $(+a) + (-b) = $ _____   f) $(+a) + (+b) = $ _____   g) $(-a) + (+b) = $ _____   h) $(-a) + (-b) = $ _____

4. Add the integers by first writing the sum as a sequence of gains and losses.

a) $(+5) + (-2) = $ ____ $+5 - 2$ ____   b) $(-3) + (+4) = $ _____   c) $(-5) + (-4) = $ _____

          $= $ ____ $+3$ ____ $= $ _____ $= $ _____

d) $(+2) + (+6) = $ _____   e) $(-2) + (-9) = $ _____   f) $(-9) + (+7) = $ _____

    $= $ _____ $= $ _____ $= $ _____

g) $(+5) + (-2) + (+3) = $ ____ $+5 - 2 + 3$ ____   h) $(-5) + (+4) + (+2) = $ _____

    $= + $ __8__ $ - $ __2__ $ = $ __+6__ $= + $ ___ $ - $ ___ $ = $ ___

i) $3 + (-5) + (-2) + 6$ j) $(-2) + (-3) + 4 + 1$ k) $4 + 0 + (-5) + (-3)$ l) $3 + 2 + (-2) + (-3)$

Integers that add to 0 are called **opposite integers**.

Example: +3 and –3 are opposite integers because $(+3) + (-3) = +3 - 3 = 0$.

5. Write the opposite of each integer.

a) The opposite of +2 is _____.   b) The opposite of –5 is _____.

c) The opposite of 3 is _____.   d) The opposite of –142 is _____.

BONUS ▶ The opposite of 0 is _____.

6. Add the integers by cancelling the opposite integers.

a) $(+5) + (-5) + (+3) = \underline{\quad +3 \quad}$

b) $(-5) + (+3) + (-3) = \underline{\qquad}$

c) $(+5) + (-3) + (+3) = \underline{\qquad}$

d) $(-3) + (+5) + (-5) = \underline{\qquad}$

e) $(+4) + (-2) + (+2) = \underline{\qquad}$

f) $(+4) + (-4) + (+2) = \underline{\qquad}$

g) $(-6) + 6 + (-3) = \underline{\qquad}$

h) $(+7) + (-7) + (+4) = \underline{\qquad}$

All integers can be written as sums of $+1$s or -1s.

Examples: $3 = (+1) + (+1) + (+1) = 1 + 1 + 1 \qquad -3 = (-1) + (-1) + (-1) = -1 - 1 - 1$

---

7. Write each number as a sum of $+1$s and -1s. Then find the sum by cancelling pairs of $+1$s and -1s.

a) $(+4) + (-2) = \underline{\quad +2 \quad}$

$\quad +1 + 1 + \cancel{1} + \cancel{1} - \cancel{1} - \cancel{1}$

b) $(-2) + (-1) = \underline{\qquad}$

c) $(+3) + (-4) = \underline{\qquad}$

d) $(+4) + (-2) = \underline{\qquad}$

e) $(+2) + (+3) = \underline{\qquad}$

f) $(-2) + (-3) = \underline{\qquad}$

g) $(-3) + (-2) = \underline{\qquad}$

h) $(-3) + (+3) = \underline{\qquad}$

8. Add the integers mentally. Hint: Start by writing $+$ or $-$ to show whether you have a net gain or a net loss.

Remember: Two losses add to a bigger loss. $\quad -7 - 2 = -9$

A gain and a loss cancel each other. $\quad -8 + 6 = -2$

---

a) $(+5) + (-6)$

$=$

b) $(+2) + (-8)$

$=$

c) $(+3) + (+5)$

$=$

d) $(-2) + (-4)$

$=$

e) $(-7) + (+10)$

$=$

f) $(-4) + (+4)$

$=$

g) $(-3) + (-7)$

$=$

h) $(-2) + (-6)$

$=$

i) $(-4) + (-8)$

$=$

j) $(-5) + (+3)$

$=$

k) $(-4) + (-5)$

$=$

l) $(-17) + (+20)$

$=$

9. Decide whether each statement is true or false. If you circle false, give a counter-example.

a) The sum of two negative integers is negative. **T F**

b) If you add a negative integer to a positive integer, the result is negative. **T F**

NS8-67 Adding Integers on a Number Line

To add a negative integer, **move left**.

Example: $(+3) + (-4) = +3 - 4$, so subtract 4 from +3. Start at +3 and move left 4 places.

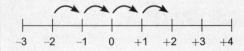

$(+3) + (-4) = (-1)$

To add a positive integer, **move right**.

Example: $(-2) + (+4) = -2 + 4$, so add 4 to -2. Start at -2 and move right 4 places.

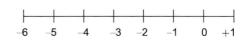

$(-2) + (+4) = (+2)$

1. Use a number line to add the integers.

   a) $(+4) + (-6) = $ _____

   b) $(-3) + (-2) = $ _____

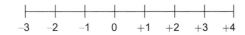

   c) $(+1) + (+2) = $ _____

   d) $(-4) + (+2) = $ _____

   e) $(+4) + (-4) = $ _____

   f) $(-3) + (+3) = $ _____

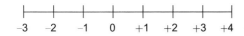

INVESTIGATION ▶ Does adding integers in a different order affect the answer?

A. Draw a number line to add the integers in different orders.

   a) $(-3) + (-5)$ and $(-5) + (-3)$

   b) $(+8) + (-2)$ and $(-2) + (+8)$

   c) $(-3) + (-7)$ and $(-7) + (-3)$

   d) $(-6) + (+2)$ and $(+2) + (-6)$

   e) $(+3) + (-4) + (+2) + (-5) + (+1)$ and $(+3) + (+2) + (+1) + (-4) + (-5)$

B. Look at your answers in part A. Does adding integers in a different order affect the answer?

2. Use a number line to continue the pattern.

   a) $+11, +8, +5, +2,$ _____, _____, _____

   b) $-10, -8, -6, -4,$ _____, _____, _____

NS8-68 Subtracting Integers

Subtraction undoes addition, so to subtract an integer, do the opposite of what you would do to add the integer.

Example: (−5) − (−2)   To add (−2), move ___2___ units to the _____*left*_____ .
                                 To subtract (−2), move ___2___ units to the _____*right*_____ .

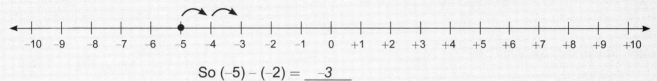

So (−5) − (−2) = ___−3___

1. Use a number line to subtract.

a) (+5) − (−3)

To add (−3), move _____ units _____ .
To subtract (−3), move _____ units _____ .

So (+5) − (−3) = _____

b) (+6) − (+2)

To add (+2), move _____ units _____ .
To subtract (+2), move _____ units _____ .

So (+6) − (+2) = _____

c) (−6) − (+4)

To add (+4), move _____ units _____ .
To subtract (+4), move _____ units _____ .

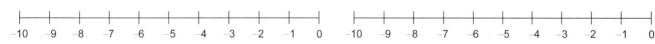

So (−6) − (+4) = _____

d) (−4) − (−3)

To add (−3), move _____ units _____ .
To subtract (−3), move _____ units _____ .

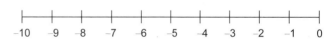

So (−4) − (−3) = _____

e) (+2) − (+5)

To add (+5), move _____ units _____ .
To subtract (+5), move _____ units _____ .

So (+2) − (+5) = _____

f) (+3) − (−1)

To add (−1), move _____ units _____ .
To subtract (−1), move _____ units _____ .

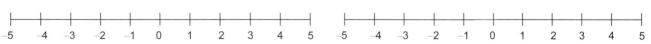

So (+3) − (−1) = _____

g) (−2) − (−3)

To add (−3), move _____ units _____ .
To subtract (−3), move _____ units _____ .

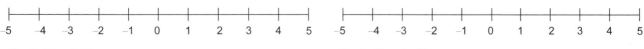

So (−2) − (−3) = _____

h) (−2) − (+3)

To add (+3), move _____ units _____ .
To subtract (+3), move _____ units _____ .

So (−2) − (+3) = _____

2. Would you move **left** or **right** on a number line?

 a) To add +4, move _____ 4 units.

 b) To add −4, move _____ 4 units.

 c) To subtract +4, move _____ 4 units.

 d) To subtract −4, move _____ 4 units.

3. Look at your answers in Question 2.

 a) Subtracting +4 gives the same result as adding _____ so ▢ − (+4) = ▢ + _____ .

 b) Subtracting −4 gives the same result as adding _____ so ▢ − (−4) = ▢ + _____ .

4. Write each difference as a sum and then calculate the answer.

 a) $(-3) - (-4) = (-3) +$ _____   b) $(+2) - (+4) = (+2) +$ _____   c) $(+4) - (-5) = (+4) +$ _____

   = _____   = _____   = _____

 d) $(-3) - (+4) = (-3) +$ _____   e) $(-1) - (+4) = (-1) +$ _____   f) $(+3) - (-7) = (+3) +$ _____

   = _____   = _____   = _____

5. Write the correct integer in the blank.

 a) $x - (-3) = x +$ _____   b) $x - (+7) = x +$ _____   c) $x - (-25) = x +$ _____

6. Subtract by continuing the patterns.

 a) $10 - 4 =$ _____   b) $6 - 4 =$ _____   c) $15 - 4 =$ _____

     $10 - 3 =$ _____ $6 - 3 =$ _____ $15 - 3 =$ _____

     $10 - 2 =$ _____ $6 - 2 =$ _____ $15 - 2 =$ _____

     $10 - 1 =$ _____ $6 - 1 =$ _____ $15 - 1 =$ _____

     $10 - 0 =$ _____ $6 - 0 =$ _____ $15 - 0 =$ _____

   $10 - (-1) =$ _____ $6 - (-1) =$ _____ $15 - (-1) =$ _____

   $10 - (-2) =$ _____ $6 - (-2) =$ _____ $15 - (-2) =$ _____

   $10 - (-3) =$ _____ $6 - (-3) =$ _____ $15 - (-3) =$ _____

   $10 - (-4) =$ _____ $6 - (-4) =$ _____ $15 - (-4) =$ _____

   $10 - (-36) =$ _____ $6 - (-36) =$ _____ $15 - (-36) =$ _____

7. Look at the patterns in Question 6. As the number being subtracted decreases by 1, what happens to the difference? How does $17 - (-15)$ compare to $17 - 0$?

Number Sense 8-68

NS8-69 Subtraction Using a Thermometer

What does 2 − 5 mean on a thermometer?

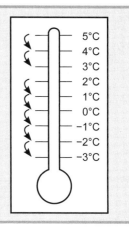

Look at 5 − 2.
If the temperature is 5° and drops 2°, the temperature becomes **5 − 2 = 3°**.

Now switch the 2 and the 5.
If the temperature is 2° and drops 5°, the temperature becomes **2 − 5 = −3°**.

1. Use the thermometer model to calculate each expression.

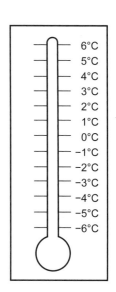

   a) If the temperature is 4° and the temperature drops 3°,
      the temperature becomes 4 − 3 = _____°.

      If the temperature is 3° and the temperature drops 4°,
      the temperature becomes 3 − 4 = _____°.

   b) If the temperature is 5° and the temperature drops 1°,
      the temperature becomes 5 − 1 = _____°.

      If the temperature is 1° and the temperature drops 5°,
      the temperature becomes 1 − 5 = _____°.

   c) 6 − 4 = _____   and   4 − 6 = _____

   d) 5 − 4 = _____   and   4 − 5 = _____

   e) 4 − 1 = _____   and   1 − 4 = _____

   f) 6 − 3 = _____   and   3 − 6 = _____

   g) 6 − 2 = _____   and   2 − 6 = _____

2. a) Look at your answers in Question 1. In general, how does $a − b$ compare to $b − a$?

   _____

   b) Use your answer to part a) to predict 98 − 101: _____

   c) Check your prediction on a calculator. Were you correct? _____

3. Use the thermometer model to subtract.

   a) (−2) − 3 = _____   and   (−3) − 2 = _____   b) (−1) − 4 = _____   and   (−4) − 1 = _____

   c) (−4) − 2 = _____   and   (−2) − 4 = _____   d) (−5) − 1 = _____   and   (−1) − 5 = _____

4. Look at your answers in Question 3.

   How does $(−a) − b$ compare to $(−b) − a$? _____

   How do both of these compare to $a + b$? _____

5. Use the thermometer model to subtract the positive integer from the negative integer. Then change the sign (as you did in Question 2) to subtract the negative integer from the positive integer.

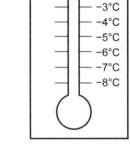

a) $(-2) - 3 = \underline{\ \ -5\ \ }$

    so $3 - (-2) = \underline{\ \ +5\ \ }$

b) $(-1) - 4 = \underline{\hspace{1cm}}$

    so $4 - (-1) = \underline{\hspace{1cm}}$

c) $(-5) - 2 = \underline{\hspace{1cm}}$

    so $2 - (-5) = \underline{\hspace{1cm}}$

d) $(-3) - 4 = \underline{\hspace{1cm}}$

    so $4 - (-3) = \underline{\hspace{1cm}}$

e) $(-4) - 2 = \underline{\hspace{1cm}}$

    so $2 - (-4) = \underline{\hspace{1cm}}$

f) $(-6) - 2 = \underline{\hspace{1cm}}$

    so $2 - (-6) = \underline{\hspace{1cm}}$

6. Copy your answers from Question 5. How can you get the same answer by adding instead of subtracting? Write the correct positive integer in the blank.

a) $3 - (-2) = \underline{\ \ +5\ \ }$

    so $3 - (-2) = 3 + \underline{\ \ (+2)\ \ }$

b) $4 - (-1) = \underline{\hspace{1cm}}$

    so $4 - (-1) = 4 + \underline{\hspace{1cm}}$

c) $2 - (-5) = \underline{\hspace{1cm}}$

    so $2 - (-5) = 2 + \underline{\hspace{1cm}}$

d) $4 - (-3) = \underline{\hspace{1cm}}$

    so $4 - (-3) = 4 + \underline{\hspace{1cm}}$

e) $2 - (-4) = \underline{\hspace{1cm}}$

    so $2 - (-4) = 2 + \underline{\hspace{1cm}}$

f) $2 - (-6) = \underline{\hspace{1cm}}$

    so $2 - (-6) = 2 + \underline{\hspace{1cm}}$

7. In general, $a - (-b)$ gives the same result as $a + \underline{\hspace{1cm}}$.

8. Change the subtraction of a negative integer to the addition of a positive integer.

a) $4 - (-3) = 4 + \underline{\hspace{1cm}}$

     $= \underline{\hspace{1cm}}$

b) $5 - (-5) = 5 + \underline{\hspace{1cm}}$

     $= \underline{\hspace{1cm}}$

c) $6 - (-3) = 6 + \underline{\hspace{1cm}}$

     $= \underline{\hspace{1cm}}$

d) $(-2) - (-1) = (-2) + \underline{\hspace{1cm}}$

     $= \underline{\hspace{1cm}}$

e) $(-3) - (-4) = -3 + \underline{\hspace{1cm}}$

     $= \underline{\hspace{1cm}}$

f) $(-2) - (-5) = -2 + \underline{\hspace{1cm}}$

     $= \underline{\hspace{1cm}}$

> To subtract positive integers, imagine moving down the thermometer.
>
> To subtract negative integers, add their opposites or move up the thermometer.

9. a) $(-3) - 5 = \underline{\hspace{1cm}}$

b) $(-3) - (-5) = \underline{\hspace{1cm}}$

c) $(-2) - (-4) = \underline{\hspace{1cm}}$

d) $4 - 5 = \underline{\hspace{1cm}}$

e) $(-8) - 3 = \underline{\hspace{1cm}}$

f) $4 - (-5) = \underline{\hspace{1cm}}$

g) $2 - 7 = \underline{\hspace{1cm}}$

h) $2 - (-7) = \underline{\hspace{1cm}}$

i) $-2 - (-7) = \underline{\hspace{1cm}}$

j) $(-2) - 7 = \underline{\hspace{1cm}}$

k) $(-7) - 2 = \underline{\hspace{1cm}}$

l) $7 - (-2) = \underline{\hspace{1cm}}$

REMEMBER: **Sums of integers** can be written as sequences of gains and losses.

$$+5 + (+3) = +5 + 3 \qquad +2 + (-5) = +2 - 5 \qquad -3 + (-2) = -3 - 2$$

Differences of integers may also be written as sequences of gains and losses.

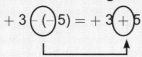

$$+3 - (-5) = +3 + 5 \qquad +2 - (+5) = +2 - 5$$

Taking away a loss
gives a gain

Taking away a gain
gives a loss

$$+ (+ \longrightarrow +$$
$$+ (- \longrightarrow -$$
$$- (+ \longrightarrow -$$
$$- (- \longrightarrow +$$

1. Rewrite each expression as a sequence of gains and losses.

a) $+3 + (-5)$

$= +3 - 5$

b) $-4 - (+2)$

$=$

c) $-5 - (-6)$

$=$

d) $+3 - (-5) + (-4) + (+2) - (+6)$

$=$

2. Simplify each expression and then add to find the result.

a) $+3 + (+2)$

$=$

$=$

b) $-5 + (-3)$

$=$

$=$

c) $+2 - (+3)$

$=$

$=$

d) $-4 - (-6)$

$=$

$=$

e) $-11 - (-6)$

f) $+14 + (-8)$

g) $-3 + (+7)$

h) $-25 - (-5)$

i) $-2 + (-3) + (+4)$

j) $+3 + (-5) + 4$

k) $-9 - (+8) - (-12)$

l) $-4 + 5 - (-6) + (-3)$

3. Draw a number line from -10 to $+10$ and mark a number that is...

A 2 less than 0

B 3 less than 4

C 3 greater than -1

D 5 greater than -2

E halfway between $+2$ and $+6$

F an equal distance from -8 and -2

G the same distance from 0 as -9

H twice as far from zero as -4

4. Solve the puzzle by placing the same integer in each shape.

a) $\square + \square + \square = -6$

b) $\bigcirc + \bigcirc + \bigcirc = -30$

5. If you were to spin the spinner twice and add the two results...

a) What is the highest total you could score? _____

b) What is the lowest total you could score? _____

c) What is the largest possible difference between the two scores?

_____

d) How could you score zero? _____

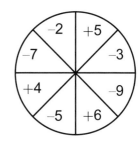

NS8-71 Word Problems

1. In this square, the integers in each row, column, and two diagonals (these include the centre box) add up to +3.

   Fill in the missing integers.

   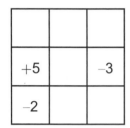

2. The chart shows the average temperatures in winter and summer for three Canadian cities.

   Find the range of average temperatures for each city.

City	Average Winter Temp (°C)	Average Summer Temp (°C)	Range
Toronto	−5	20	
Montreal	−10	21	
Vancouver	−3	23	

3. The chart shows the average temperature on 5 planets.

   a) Write the temperatures in order from least to greatest.

   b) What is the difference between the highest and the lowest average temperature?

   c) Which planet has an average temperature 200°C lower than Earth?

Earth	+20°C
Venus	+470°C
Saturn	−180°C
Mercury	+120°C
Jupiter	−50°C

4. When a plane takes off, the temperature on the ground is 20°C. The temperature outside the plane decreases by 5°C for every 1 000 m it climbs above the ground.

   a) What is the temperature outside the plane when it is 5 000 m above the ground?

   b) What will the temperature outside the plane be when it is 5 400 m above the ground?

5. A cup of hot chocolate has a temperature of +98°C. When Guled adds an ice cube, the temperature decreases by 1°C. Guled writes (+98) + (−7) to find the temperature after adding 7 ice cubes.

   a) How would Guled find the temperature after adding 12 ice cubes? (+98) + _____ = _____

   b) Guled's hot chocolate has 5 ice cubes and a temperature of +93°C. How would Guled find the temperature after **removing** 3 ice cubes?

6. How much did the temperature change in the course of each day?

   Monday _____

   Tuesday _____

   Wednesday _____

   Thursday _____

	Daily Low Temp (°C)	Daily High Temp (°C)
Monday	−8	+2
Tuesday	−10	−8
Wednesday	−4	0
Thursday	−17	−5

REMEMBER: Multiplication is a short form for repeated addition.

Example: $4 \times 5 = 5 + 5 + 5 + 5 = 20$

When you multiply a negative integer and a positive integer, you can think of repeated addition.

Example: $4 \times (-5) = (-5) + (-5) + (-5) + (-5) = -20$

1. Write each product as repeated addition. Then find the answer.

   a) $3 \times (-5) =$ b) $2 \times (-7) =$

   c) $4 \times (-3) =$ d) $4 \times (-2) =$

   e) $5 \times (-6) =$ f) $3 \times (-8) =$

2. Look at your answers in Question 1. How does $a \times (-b)$ compare to $a \times b$?

3. Calculate $a \times (-b)$ by first calculating $a \times b$.

   a) $2 \times 7 = $ _____   b) $3 \times 4 = $ _____   c) $5 \times 6 = $ _____

   so $2 \times (-7) = $ _____   so $3 \times (-4) = $ _____   so $5 \times (-6) = $ _____

   d) $9 \times (-8) = $ _____   e) $8 \times (-7) = $ _____   f) $10 \times (-2) = $ _____

The **distributive law** tells us how multiplication relates to addition and subtraction.

For positive numbers a, b, and c,   Examples:

   $a \times (b + c) = a \times b + a \times c$ $2 \times (3 + 4) = 2 \times 7 = 14$ and $2 \times 3 + 2 \times 4 = 6 + 8 = 14$

   $a \times (b - c) = a \times b - a \times c$ $2 \times (7 - 3) = 2 \times 4 = 8$ and $2 \times 7 - 2 \times 3 = 14 - 6 = 8$

   $(a + b) \times c = a \times c + b \times c$ $(2 + 7) \times 3 = 9 \times 3 = 27$ and $2 \times 3 + 7 \times 3 = 6 + 21 = 27$

   $(a - b) \times c = a \times c - b \times c$ $(7 - 2) \times 3 = 5 \times 3 = 15$ and $7 \times 3 - 2 \times 3 = 21 - 6 = 15$

4. Use the distributive law to rewrite each product.

   a) $2 \times (5 + 3)$ b) $3 \times (4 - 2)$ c) $(5 - 2) \times 3$

   $\quad = 2 \times 5 + 2 \times 3$ $=$ $=$

   d) $(4 + 2) \times 5$ e) $(8 - 3) \times 3$ f) $4 \times (3 - 2)$

   $=$ $=$ $=$

   g) $(9 - 4) \times 2$ h) $(4 + 3) \times 6$ i) $(5 - 5) \times 3$

   $=$ $=$ $=$

INVESTIGATION 1 ▶

Does the distributive law, $a \times (b - c) = a \times b - a \times c$, hold even when $b - c$ is negative?

A. Calculate both sides and then write = (equal) or ≠ (not equal) in the box.

i) $3 \times (2 - 5)$ ☐ $3 \times 2 - 3 \times 5$

ii) $2 \times (4 - 10)$ ☐ $2 \times 4 - 2 \times 10$

iii) $5 \times (1 - 4)$ ☐ $5 \times 1 - 5 \times 4$

iv) $10 \times (2 - 7)$ ☐ $10 \times 2 - 10 \times 7$

B. Choose your own positive integers a, b, and c, with b less than c (so that $b - c$ is negative).

$a =$ _____, $b =$ _____, $c =$ _____

Calculate $a \times (b - c)$ and $a \times b - a \times c$. Does the distributive law hold?

Mathematicians defined multiplication so that the distributive law would hold for negative numbers too.

Here's how to calculate the product of a negative integer with a positive integer. $-3 \times 4 =$?

Step 1: Write the negative integer as a difference between any two positive integers.

$-3 = 2 - 5$, so
$\mathbf{-3} \times 4 = \mathbf{(2 - 5)} \times 4$

Step 2: Use the distributive law.

$= 2 \times 4 - 5 \times 4 = 8 - 20 = -12$

5. Calculate each product of a negative integer with a positive integer by using the distributive law.

a) $(-2) \times 5 = (1 - 3) \times 5$
    $= 1 \times 5 - 3 \times 5$
    $= 5 - 15$
    $= -10$

b) $(-4) \times 7 = (1 - 5) \times 7$
    $= 1 \times 7 - 5 \times 7$

c) $(-3) \times 5 = (0 - 3) \times 5$
    $= 0 \times 5 - 3 \times 5$

d) $(-5) \times 4 = (0 - 5) \times 4$

e) $(-8) \times 3 = (2 - 10) \times 3$

f) $(-8) \times 3 = (0 - 8) \times 3$

6. Which product did you find twice in Question 5? Did you get the same answer both ways? Was one way easier? Explain.

7. Look at your answers to Question 5. How does $(-a) \times b$ compare to $a \times b$?

INVESTIGATION 2 ▶ How does $(-a) \times b$ compare to $a \times (-b)$?

A. Fill in the table. Use your own choice of a and b in the last row of the table.

a	b	$-a$	$-b$	$(-a) \times b$	$a \times (-b)$
2	3	-2	-3	$(-2) \times 3 = -6$	$2 \times (-3) = -6$
4	5				
5	3				

B. Compare the last two columns. What do you notice?

8. Calculate each product.

a) $(-3) \times 7 =$ _____

b) $(-5) \times 4 =$ _____

c) $(-2) \times 7 =$ _____

d) $(-5) \times 8 =$ _____

e) $(-6) \times 3 =$ _____

f) $(-9) \times 8 =$ _____

Since mathematicians defined multiplication with negative integers to satisfy the distributive law, we can use the distributive law to find the product of two negative integers.

$(-3) \times (-2) = (-3) \times (5 - 7)$ ⟵ since $-2 = 5 - 7$
$= (-3) \times 5 - (-3) \times 7$ ⟵ since multiplication distributes over subtraction
$= -15 - (-21)$
$= -15 + 21$
$= +6$

9. Calculate $(-2) \times (-5)$ by replacing -5 by various differences of positive integers.

a) $(-2) \times (-5) = (-2) \times (3 - 8)$
$= (-2) \times 3 - (-2) \times 8$
$= (-6) - (-16)$
$= -6 + 16$
$= +10$

b) $(-2) \times (-5) = (-2) \times (1 - 6)$

c) $(-2) \times (-5) = (-2) \times (0 - 5)$

10. Look at your answers in Question 9. Did you get the same answer all three ways? Was one way easiest? Explain.

11. Follow the steps to multiply negative integers a different way.

a) $(-2) \times (-3)$

   i) Explain why $(-2) \times (3 + (-3))$ equals zero.

   ii) Expand the expression in i) using the distributive law:

   $(-2) \times (3 + (-3)) = $ _____ + _____

   iii) Explain why $(-2) \times 3$ and $(-2) \times (-3)$ are opposite integers.

   iv) $(-2) \times 3 = $ _____

   so $(-2) \times (-3) = $ _____

b) $(-3) \times (-4)$

   i) Explain why $(-3) \times (4 + (-4))$ equals zero.

   ii) Expand the expression in i) using the distributive law:

   $(-3) \times (4 + (-4)) = $ _____ + _____

   iii) Explain why $(-3) \times 4$ and $(-3) \times (-4)$ are opposite integers.

   iv) $(-3) \times 4 = $ _____

   so $(-3) \times (-4) = $ _____

12. Look at your answers in Questions 9 and 11. How does $(-a) \times (-b)$ compare to $a \times b$?

_____

13. Find the products.

a) $(-3) \times (-5) = $ b) $(-4) \times (-9) = $ c) $(-8) \times (-3) = $ d) $(-2) \times (-5) = $

e) $(-4) \times (-8) = $ f) $(-7) \times (-9) = $ g) $(-8) \times (-6) = $ h) $(-5) \times (-11) = $

14. Multiply mentally.

a) $3 \times (-9) = $ b) $-2 \times 2 = $ c) $(-7) \times (-8) = $ d) $4 \times (-6) = $

e) $-6 \times 7 = $ f) $(-9) \times (-4) = $ g) $-4 \times 6 = $ h) $(-9) \times (-9) = $

NS8-73 Dividing Integers

If you know how to multiply negative numbers, then you can divide negative numbers too!

REMEMBER: Since $4 \times 3 = 12$ then $12 \div 3 = 4$ and $12 \div 4 = 3$.

1. Write two division statements from each multiplication statement.

a) $4 \times 3 = 12$

_12 ÷ 3 = 4_

_12 ÷ 4 = 3_

b) $(-4) \times 3 = (-12)$

_(-12) ÷ 3 = -4_

_(-12) ÷ (-4) = 3_

c) $(-4) \times (-3) = 12$

_____

_____

d) $4 \times (-3) = (-12)$

_____

_____

e) $3 \times 2 = 6$

_____

_____

f) $(-3) \times 2 = (-6)$

_____

_____

g) $(-3) \times (-2) = 6$

_____

_____

h) $3 \times (-2) = (-6)$

_____

_____

2. Find the quotients by finding the missing number in the product.

a) _____ $\times 2 = 10$ so $10 \div 2 =$ _____

b) _____ $\times (-3) = (-6)$ so $(-6) \div (-3) =$ _____

c) _____ $\times (-2) = 8$ so $8 \div (-2) =$ _____

d) _____ $\times 2 = 6$ so $6 \div 2 =$ _____

e) _____ $\times 3 = (-15)$ so $(-15) \div 3 =$ _____

f) _____ $\times 4 = (-20)$ so $(-20) \div 4 =$ _____

g) _____ $\times (-3) = 9$ so $9 \div (-3) =$ _____

h) _____ $\times (-6) = (-18)$ so $(-18) \div (-6) =$ _____

3. Look at your answers in Question 2. What is the sign of the quotient in each case?

a) I divided $(+) \div (+)$ in parts __a)__ and __d)__.

The answers were __5__ and __3__.

So $(+) \div (+) =$ _____.

b) I divided $(-) \div (+)$ in parts _____ and _____.

The answers were _____ and _____.

So $(-) \div (+) =$ _____.

c) I divided $(+) \div (-)$ in parts _____ and _____.

The answers were _____ and _____.

So $(+) \div (-) =$ _____.

d) I divided $(-) \div (-)$ in parts _____ and _____.

The answers were _____ and _____.

So $(-) \div (-) =$ _____.

4. Find the following quotients.

a) $(-20) \div 5 =$

b) $(-54) \div (-6) =$

c) $(-72) \div (-9) =$

d) $80 \div (-10) =$

e) $(-16) \div 4 =$

f) $(+30) \div (+6) =$

g) $(-40) \div (-8) =$

h) $(+72) \div 6 =$

5. Use a calculator to find the quotients.

a) $75 \div (-15) =$

b) $(-84) \div (-12) =$

c) $(-78) \div 13 =$

NS8-74 Concepts in Integers

1. The temperature on the surface of Mercury rises or drops at the rate of about 30°C per Earth day. The current temperature is 0°C.

    Answer the questions below using a multiplication <u>or division</u> statement.

    Hint: Think of future time as + and past time as −.

    a) The temperature **rises 30°C** each day.

        What will the temperature be in 3 days?

        $(+30) \times (+3) =$ _____ So the temperature will be _____ °C.

        What was the temperature 3 days ago?

        $(+30) \times (-3) =$ _____ So the temperature was _____ °C.

        When will the temperature be 150°C?

        $(+150) \div (+30) =$ _____ So the temperature will be 150°C in _____ days.

        When was the temperature −120°C?

        $(-120) \div (+30) =$ _____ So the temperature was −120°C _____ days ago.

    b) The temperature **drops 30°C** each day.

        What will the temperature be in 3 days?

        $(-30) \times (+3) =$ _____ So the temperature will be _____ °C.

        What was the temperature 3 days ago?

        _____ × _____ = _____ So the temperature was _____ °C.

        When will the temperature be −210°C? _____ ÷ _____ = _____

        So _____ .

        When was the temperature 360°C? _____ ÷ _____ = _____

        So _____ .

2. Find pairs of integers whose…

    a) sum is −1 and product is −20
    c) sum is +4 and product is −5
    e) sum is −7 and product is +10

    b) sum is +15 and product is −100
    d) sum is −7 and product is +12
    f) sum is −7 and product is −144

3. On three different days, the temperature in Ottawa, Ontario, is exactly halfway between the temperatures in Inuvik, Northwest Territories, and in Tampa, Florida.

    Find the missing temperatures.

Day	Temperature in Inuvik	Temperature in Tampa	Temperature in Ottawa
One	−15°C	25°C	_____ °C
Two	_____ °C	25°C	10°C
Three	−2°C	_____ °C	12°C

4. Decide whether each statement is true or false. If the statement is false, change the statement to make it true.

   a) The sum of two opposite integers is always positive.
   b) $+5$ is opposite to -3 because they have different signs.
   c) A positive integer is always greater than a negative integer.
   d) The product of two integers will be positive when they have the same sign and negative when they do not.

5. a) What is the result when you …

      i) Add any integer x to its opposite?
      ii) Subtract any integer x from its opposite?
      iii) Multiply any integer x by its opposite?
      iv) Divide any integer x by its opposite?

   b) Choose an integer.
      Check your answers to a) by performing the operations in each part on your integer.

6. Multiplication is **commutative**. This means that when you multiply a pair of positive numbers, you get the same answer no matter what order you multiply the numbers in.

   $$4 \times 7 = 7 \times 4 \qquad\qquad 3 \times 8 = 8 \times 3 \qquad\qquad a \times b = b \times a$$

   Is the multiplication of negative numbers commutative? Explain.

7. Lei's golf score was 5 shots above par (par $= 0$). Guled's score was 4 shots below par.

   a) Draw a number line, mark their scores, and find the distance between their scores.
   b) Write a subtraction statement to represent the distance between their scores.

8. Calculate each term in the pattern. What is the 100th term in the pattern? How do you know?

   $(-1) = $ _____

   $(-1) \times (-1) = $ _____

   $(-1) \times (-1) \times (-1) = $ _____

   $(-1) \times (-1) \times (-1) \times (-1) = $ _____

   $(-1) \times (-1) \times (-1) \times (-1) \times (-1) = $ _____

   $(-1) \times (-1) \times (-1) \times (-1) \times (-1) \times (-1) = $ _____

9. Complete the chart for different values of integer a. You can use a number line to help you.

$a = $	$+4$	-3	7	$+1$	-2	0	$+3$
an integer that is the same distance from 0 as a	-4						
an integer that is the same distance from $+3$ as a	$+2$						

   a) How do you obtain the integer that is the same distance from 0 as a? _____

   b) How do you obtain the integer that is the same distance from $+3$ as a? _____

   c) Look for a pattern between the rows in the chart. What do you notice?

10. Write a word problem that requires finding…

   a) $6 \times (-2)$ b) $(-6) \times (-2)$ c) $6 \div (-2)$ d) $(-6) \div (-2)$

G8-8 Introduction to Coordinate Systems

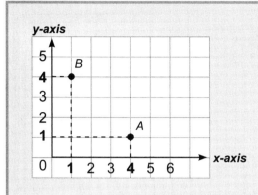

The position of a point on a coordinate grid is identified by an ordered pair of numbers in a bracket.

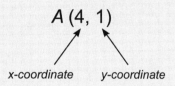

A (4, 1) B (1, 4)

x-coordinate y-coordinate   x-coordinate y-coordinate

The point (0, 0) is called the **origin**.

1. Fill in the coordinates for the given points.

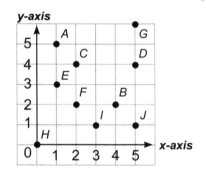

A (_1_ , _5_) B (__ , __)

C (__ , __) D (__ , __)

E (__ , __) F (__ , __)

G (__ , __) H (__ , __)

I (__ , __) J (__ , __)

A grid that has been extended to include negative integers is called a **Cartesian coordinate system**. We use Roman numerals to number the quadrants:
1 = I, 2 = II, 3 = III, 4 = IV.

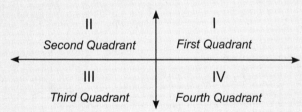

II
Second Quadrant

I
First Quadrant

III
Third Quadrant

IV
Fourth Quadrant

2. a) Label the origin (O) and the x- and y-axes.

b) Label the axes with positive and negative integers.

c) Number the four quadrants (using I, II, III, IV).

d) Which quadrants are these points in?

A (3, 3) _I_ B (–3, –2) ____

C (–3, 3) ____ D (3, –2) ____

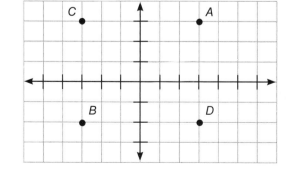

3. In Figure 1, point *A* (2, 3) is in the first quadrant. Its *x*- and *y*-coordinates are both **positive**.

a) Find the coordinates of points…

P (___, ___)   Q (___, ___)

R (___, ___)   S (___, ___)

b) Plot and label.

B (3, 2)   C (1, 4)   D (4, 1)

4. In Figure 1, point *F* (–2, 3) is in the second quadrant. Its *x*-coordinate is **negative** and its *y*-coordinate is **positive**.

a) Find the coordinates of points…

K (___, ___)   L (___, ___)

M (___, ___)   N (___, ___)

b) Plot and label.

G (–3, 2)   H (–1, 6)   I (–4, 1)

5. In Figure 2, point *A* (–2, –3) is in the third quadrant. Its *x*- and *y*-coordinates are both **negative**.

a) Find the coordinates of points…

K (___, ___)   L (___, ___)

M (___, ___)   N (___, ___)

b) Plot and label.

B (–3, –4)   C (–2, –6)   D (–4, –3)

6. In Figure 2, point *F* (2, –3) is in the fourth quadrant. Its *x*-coordinate is **positive** and its *y*-coordinate is **negative**.

a) Find the coordinates of points…

P (___, ___)   Q (___, ___)

R (___, ___)   S (___, ___)

b) Plot and label.

G (3, –4)   H (1, –6)

I (4, –1)   J (1, –2)

Figure 1

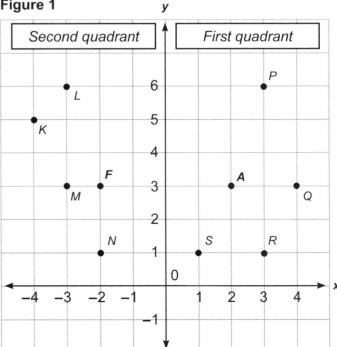

Figure 2

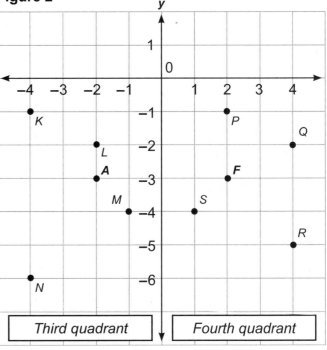

7. In Figure 3, points *B* (2, 0) and *C* (−4, 0) are both on the *x*-axis. The *y*-coordinate of any point on the *x*-axis is **zero**.

a) Find the coordinates of points…

   P (___ , ___)   *Q* (___ , ___)

b) Plot and label.

   A (3, 0)   *M* (−3, 0)

8. In Figure 3, points *D* (0, 2) and *E* (0, −3) are both on the *y*-axis. The *x*-coordinate of any point on the *y*-axis is **zero**.

a) Plot and label.

   G (0, 4)   *H* (0, −1)

b) Find the coordinates of points…

   K (___ , ___)   *L* (___ , ___)

Figure 3

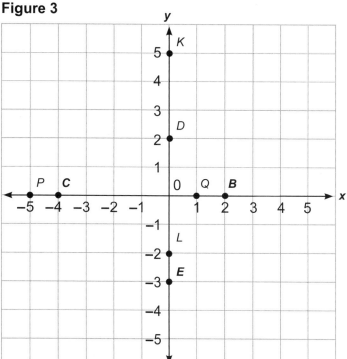

9. a) In Figure 4, find the coordinates of points…

   P (___ , ___)   *Q* (___ , ___)   *R* (___ , ___)   *S* (___ , ___)
   T (___ , ___)   *U* (___ , ___)   *V* (___ , ___)   *W* (___ , ___)

b) Plot and label these points in Figure 4.

   A (3, 4)   *B* (5, −2)
   C (−3, −2)   *D* (−4, 1)
   E (3, 0)   *F* (0, 2)
   G (0, 3)   *H* (−5, 0)

c) Sort the points in Figure 4 by location.

   first quadrant: __*A, Q*_____

   second quadrant: _____

   third quadrant: _____

   fourth quadrant: _____

   on the *x*-axis: _____

   on the *y*-axis: _____

   at the origin: _____

Figure 4

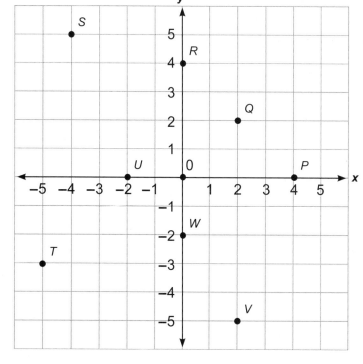

Geometry 8-8

G8-9 Translations

1. How many units right or left and how many units up or down did the dot slide from position *A* to *B*?

a)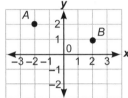

   _4_ units right, _1_ unit down

   A (_-2_ , _2_) *B* (_2_ , _1_)

b)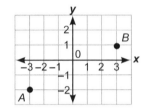

   ___ units right, ___ units up

   A (___ , ___) *B* (___ , ___)

c)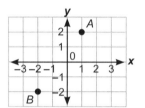

   ___ units left, ___ units down

   A (___ , ___) *B* (___ , ___)

2. Slide the point by the given number of units. The resulting point is called the **image**.

a) 5 units right; 2 units down

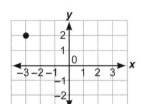

   original point (___ , ___)

   image (___ , ___)

b) 6 units left; 3 units up

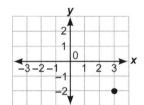

   original point (___ , ___)

   image (___ , ___)

c) 5 units left; 4 units down

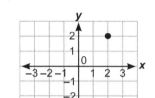

   original point (___ , ___)

   image (___ , ___)

3. Slide the point two units down, then copy the shape. Write the coordinates of the point and its image.

a)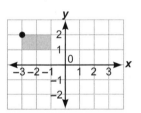

   original point (___ , ___)

   image (___ , ___)

b)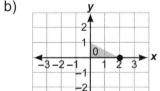

   original point (___ , ___)

   image (___ , ___)

c)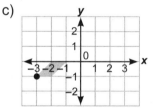

   original point (___ , ___)

   image (___ , ___)

4. Slide each triangle 5 units to the right and 3 units down.

a)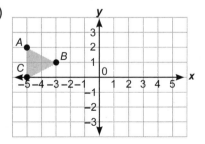

   A (___ , ___) → *A'* (___ , ___)

   B (___ , ___) → *B'* (___ , ___)

   C (___ , ___) → *C'* (___ , ___)

b)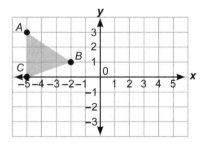

   A (___ , ___) → *A'* (___ , ___)

   B (___ , ___) → *B'* (___ , ___)

   C (___ , ___) → *C'* (___ , ___)

> You can show how a point moves with an arrow: *A* → *A'*

5. a) Describe how point *D* moved to point *D'*:

___4___ units _right_ , _____ units _____

b) Draw an arrow to show where point *A* moved to under the translation.

c) Describe how point *A* moved:

___ units _____ , _____ units _____

d) Did all of the points on the parallelogram move the same amount right and the same amount up? _____

e) Fill in the coordinates of the vertices of the original parallelogram *ABCD* and the image *A'B'C'D'*.

A (__, __) → A' (__, __) B (__, __) → B' (__, __)

C (__, __) → C' (__, __) D (__, __) → D' (__, __)

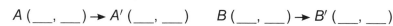

6. Draw a translation arrow from vertex *P* of shape *A* to the corresponding vertex *P'* in *A'*. Then write the coordinates of *P* and *P'*.

a)

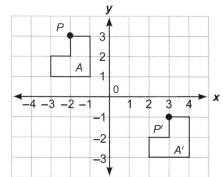

P (__, __)

P' (__↓__, __)

b)

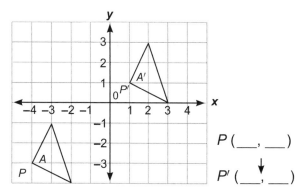

P (__, __)

P' (__↓__, __)

7. Slide the shapes in the grids below using a translation of your choice. Describe how far the shape moved (right/left and up/down) and write the coordinates of *P* and *P'*.

a)

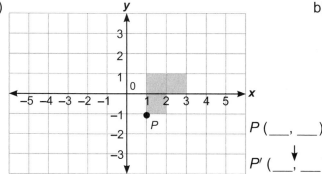

P (__, __)

P' (__↓__, __)

My slide: _____

b)

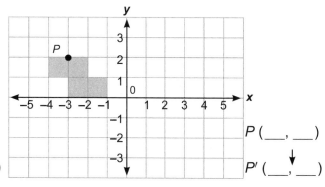

P (__, __)

P' (__↓__, __)

My slide: _____

8. Draw a shape on a coordinate grid. Slide the shape and draw a translation arrow between a vertex and a corresponding vertex of the image. Describe how far the shape moved (right/left and up/down).

9. Draw each shape on a coordinate grid, translate it, and write the coordinates of its new vertices.

a) Square with vertices *A* (1, 1), *B* (1, 3), *C* (3, 3), *D* (3, 1)   Translate 3 units right, 4 units up

b) Triangle with vertices *A* (3, 7), *B* (2, 5), *C* (5, 4)   Translate 4 units right, 3 units down

G8-10 Translations — Advanced

INVESTIGATION ▶ How do coordinates change under translation?

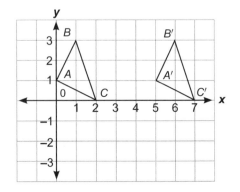

A. Triangle *ABC* slid 5 units to the right. Write the coordinates of its vertices before and after the slide.

before: *A* (__, __)   *B* (__, __)   *C* (__, __)

after: *A′* (__, __)   *B′* (__, __)   *C′* (__, __)

B. Which coordinate changed during the translation, the *x*-coordinate or the *y*-coordinate? _____

C. Look for a pattern: The ____-coordinate increased by ____ .

D. Use the pattern in C. to predict the coordinates of these points after they slide 5 units right.

a) *D* (0, –2) → *D′* (5, –2)   b) *E* (–1, –3) → *E′* (__, __)   c) *F* (–2, 2) → *F′* (__, __)

E. Plot points *D*, *E*, *F* and *D′*, *E′*, *F′* on the grid above to check your prediction.

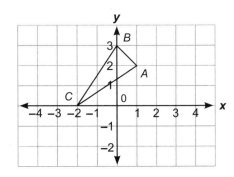

F. Slide triangle *ABC* 3 units right. Compare the coordinates of the vertices before and after the slide.
Complete the algebraic expression for the *x*-coordinate.

Point (*x*, *y*) slides 3 units right to point (_x +___ , _y_)

Check the expression with three other points.

---

1. Slide the point *P* 2 units in the given direction. Write the coordinates of the new point. Which coordinate changed, and by how much?

a) 2 units up

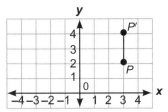

P (3, 2)   *P′* (__, __)

The _y_ -coordinate

_____ increased by 2 _____

b) 2 units down

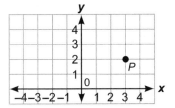

P (3, 2)   *P′* (__, __)

The ____-coordinate

_____

c) 2 units left

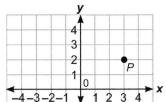

P (3, 2)   *P′* (__, __)

The ____-coordinate

_____

2. Point *Q* (*x*, *y*) slid to point *Q′*. Match the coordinates of *Q′* to the descriptions of translation.

__D__ *Q′* (*x* + 4, *y*)   ____ *Q′* (*x*, *y* – 4)   ____ *Q′* (*x*, *y* + 4)   ____ *Q′* (*x* – 4, *y*)

A. 4 units up   B. 4 units down   C. 4 units left   D. 4 units right

3. A point (*x*, *y*) slides 3 units up and 2 units left. What are the coordinates of the new point? Draw a coordinate system and check your prediction for points (3, 3), (4, –2), (–1, 2), and (–3, –4).

G8-11 Reflections

When a point is **reflected** in a mirror line, the point and the image of the point are the same distance from the mirror line.

The line between the point and the image is **perpendicular** to the mirror line.

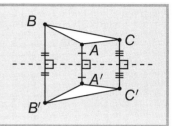

1. Reflect point P using the x-axis as a mirror line. Label the image point P'. Write the coordinates.

a)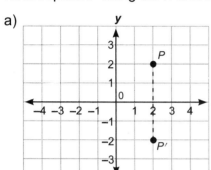

$P(\underline{\ 2\ }, \underline{\ 2\ }) \rightarrow P'(\underline{\ 2\ }, \underline{\ -2\ })$

b)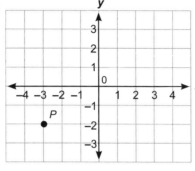

$P(\underline{\ \ }, \underline{\ \ }) \rightarrow P'(\underline{\ \ }, \underline{\ \ })$

c)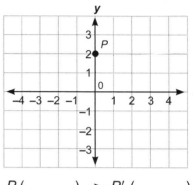

$P(\underline{\ \ }, \underline{\ \ }) \rightarrow P'(\underline{\ \ }, \underline{\ \ })$

2. Reflect points P, Q, and R through the x-axis. Label the image points P', Q', and R' and write the coordinates. Hint: The image of a point on the x-axis through the x-axis is the point itself.

a)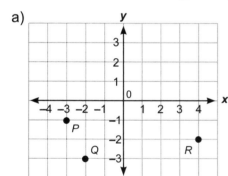

$P(\underline{\ \ }, \underline{\ \ }) \rightarrow P'(\underline{\ \ }, \underline{\ \ })$
$Q(\underline{\ \ }, \underline{\ \ }) \rightarrow Q'(\underline{\ \ }, \underline{\ \ })$
$R(\underline{\ \ }, \underline{\ \ }) \rightarrow R'(\underline{\ \ }, \underline{\ \ })$

b)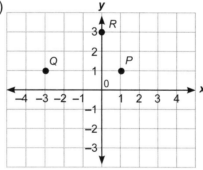

$P(\underline{\ \ }, \underline{\ \ }) \rightarrow P'(\underline{\ \ }, \underline{\ \ })$
$Q(\underline{\ \ }, \underline{\ \ }) \rightarrow Q'(\underline{\ \ }, \underline{\ \ })$
$R(\underline{\ \ }, \underline{\ \ }) \rightarrow R'(\underline{\ \ }, \underline{\ \ })$

c)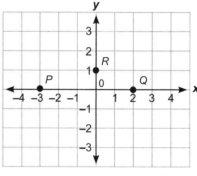

$P(\underline{\ \ }, \underline{\ \ }) \rightarrow P'(\underline{\ \ }, \underline{\ \ })$
$Q(\underline{\ \ }, \underline{\ \ }) \rightarrow Q'(\underline{\ \ }, \underline{\ \ })$
$R(\underline{\ \ }, \underline{\ \ }) \rightarrow R'(\underline{\ \ }, \underline{\ \ })$

3. Look at your answers in Question 2.

a) Which coordinate changed during the reflection through the x-axis?

b) How did the coordinate in a) change?

c) Use your rule in b) to predict the coordinates of these points after reflection through the x-axis.

$D(0, -3) \rightarrow D'(\underline{\ 0\ }, \underline{\ 3\ })$ $E(-1, -4) \rightarrow E'(\underline{\ \ }, \underline{\ \ })$

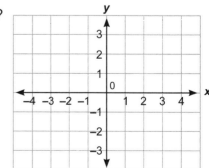

d) Plot points D, E and D', E' to check your prediction.

e) Use your rule in b) to explain why a point on the x-axis does not move when reflected through the x-axis.

4. a) Write the coordinates of vertices *A*, *B*, and *C*.

b) Predict and write the coordinates of the vertices under a reflection through the *x*-axis.

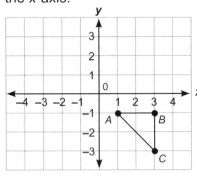 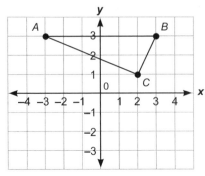 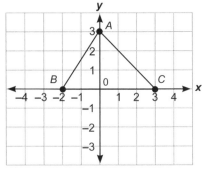

A (__, __) → *A′* (__, __)   *A* (__, __) → *A′* (__, __)   *A* (__, __) → *A′* (__, __)

B (__, __) → *B′* (__, __)   *B* (__, __) → *B′* (__, __)   *B* (__, __) → *B′* (__, __)

C (__, __) → *C′* (__, __)   *C* (__, __) → *C′* (__, __)   *C* (__, __) → *C′* (__, __)

c) Reflect the figure by first reflecting the vertices through the *x*-axis, and check your answers from b).

5. Reflect point *P* using the *y*-axis as a mirror line. Label the image point *P′*. Write the coordinates.

a) 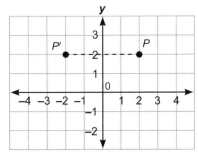 **b)** 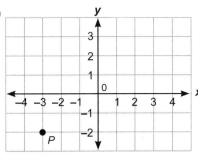 **c)**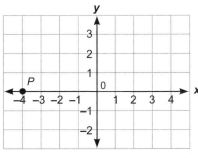

P (_2_ , _2_) → *P′* (_−2_ , _2_)   *P* (__, __) → *P′* (__, __)   *P* (__, __) → *P′* (__, __)

6. Reflect points *P*, *Q*, and *R* through the *y*-axis. Label the image points *P′*, *Q′*, and *R′* and write the coordinates. Hint: The image of a point on the *y*-axis through the *y*-axis is the point itself.

a) 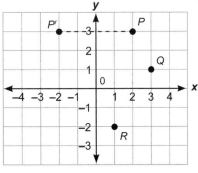 **b)** 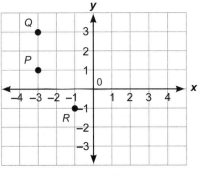 **c)**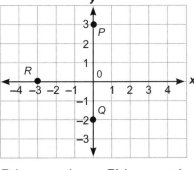

P (_2_ , _3_) → *P′* (_−2_ , _3_)   *P* (__, __) → *P′* (__, __)   *P* (__, __) → *P′* (__, __)

Q (__, __) → *Q′* (__, __)   *Q* (__, __) → *Q′* (__, __)   *Q* (__, __) → *Q′* (__, __)

R (__, __) → *R′* (__, __)   *R* (__, __) → *R′* (__, __)   *R* (__, __) → *R′* (__, __)

7. Look at your answers in Question 6.

   a) Which coordinate changed during the reflection through the *y*-axis? _____

   b) How did that coordinate change during the reflection through the *y*-axis? _____

8. a) Find the coordinates of the vertices of each shape.

   b) Predict and write the coordinates of the vertices under a reflection through the *y*-axis.

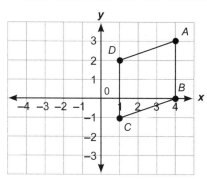 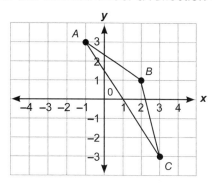 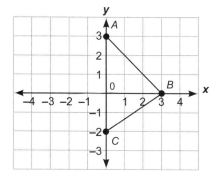

A (__, __) → *A′* (__, __) *A* (__, __) → *A′* (__, __) *A* (__, __) → *A′* (__, __)

B (__, __) → *B′* (__, __) *B* (__, __) → *B′* (__, __) *B* (__, __) → *B′* (__, __)

C (__, __) → *C′* (__, __) *C* (__, __) → *C′* (__, __) *C* (__, __) → *C′* (__, __)

D (__, __) → *D′* (__, __)

   c) Reflect the figure by first reflecting the vertices through the *y*-axis, and check your answers from b).

Two figures are **congruent** if they are the same shape and size.

9. a) Reflect the triangle through the *x*-axis.   b) Slide the triangle 5 units down.

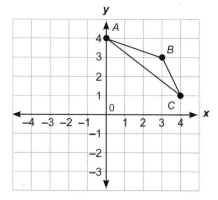 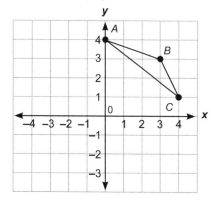

   c) Use parts a) and b) to fill in the table with True or False.

	Reflection	Translation
The original figure and the image are congruent.	*True*	
The original figure and the image face in the same direction.		
The original figure and the image face in opposite directions.		

10. The pairs of triangles below are related by a reflection through the *x*-axis, a reflection through the *y*-axis, or a translation. Without plotting the triangles, say which transformation was used. Then plot the triangles to check your answers.

a) △*ABC* : *A* (3, 1), *B* (3, 4), *C* (5, 2)

△*A′B′C′* : *A′* (−3, 1), *B′* (−3, 4), *C′* (−5, 2)

△*A′B′C′* was obtained from △*ABC* by

_____

b) △*DEF* : *D* (3, −1), *E* (3, −4), *F* (5, −2)

△*D′E′F′* : *D′* (−3, −1), *E′* (−3, −4), *F′* (−1, −2)

△*D′E′F′* was obtained from △*DEF* by

_____

c) △*ABC* from a) and △*DEF* from b).

△*ABC* was obtained from △*DEF* by

_____

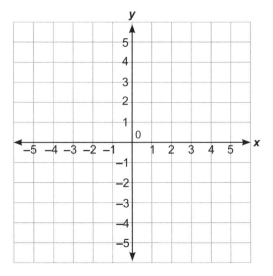

11. a) Reflect △*ABC* through the *x*-axis.

Label the image △*A′B′C′* .

b) Reflect △*A′B′C′* through the *y*-axis.

Label the image △*A″B″C″*.

c) Ying thinks that △*A″B″C″* is obtained from △*ABC* by a translation. Is she correct? Explain why or why not.

_____

_____

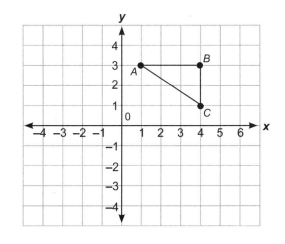

12. a) Reflect *ABCD* first through the *x*-axis, then through the *y*-axis.

b) Reflect *ABCD* first through the *y*-axis, then through the *x*-axis.

c) Did you get the same answer? _____

Explain why this happens using the rules for the change of coordinates for reflections that you developed in Questions 3 and 7.

_____

_____

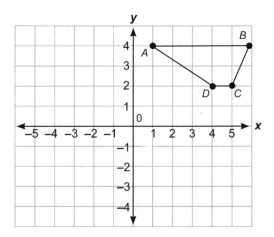

G8-12 Reflections — Advanced

1. Draw a line through P perpendicular to line ℓ. The first one is done for you.

a) 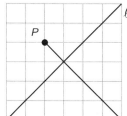 b) 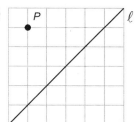 c) 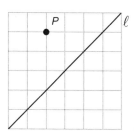 d)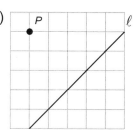

Line ℓ passes through the points
$(1, 1)$, $(2, 2)$, $(3, 3)$, … and $(-1, -1)$, $(-2, -2)$, $(-3, -3)$, ….
It passes through the first and third quadrants.

Example: Reflect point P $(1, 3)$ through mirror line ℓ.

Step 1: Draw a dotted line through point P
perpendicular to line ℓ.
Find the point where the dotted line meets ℓ and label it A.

Step 2: Locate a point P' on the dotted line such that P'
is the same distance from point A as P: $PA = P'A$.

P' is the image of P after reflection through line ℓ.

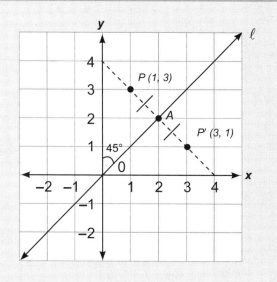

2. Reflect points P, Q, and R through mirror line ℓ. Label the image points P', Q', and R'.

a) 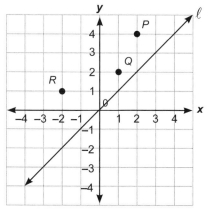 b) 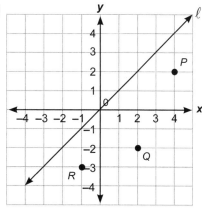 c)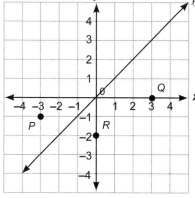

$P (\_\_, \_\_) \rightarrow P' (\_\_, \_\_)$

$Q (\_\_, \_\_) \rightarrow Q' (\_\_, \_\_)$

$R (\_\_, \_\_) \rightarrow R' (\_\_, \_\_)$

$P (\_\_, \_\_) \rightarrow P' (\_\_, \_\_)$

$Q (\_\_, \_\_) \rightarrow Q' (\_\_, \_\_)$

$R (\_\_, \_\_) \rightarrow R' (\_\_, \_\_)$

$P (\_\_, \_\_) \rightarrow P' (\_\_, \_\_)$

$Q (\_\_, \_\_) \rightarrow Q' (\_\_, \_\_)$

$R (\_\_, \_\_) \rightarrow R' (\_\_, \_\_)$

3. Look at your answers in Question 2.

a) Describe how the coordinates of a point change during a reflection through line ℓ.

b) Use the rule you found in part a) to explain why a point on the line ℓ does not change when reflected through the line ℓ.

c) Use the rule from part a) to explain why a point in the second quadrant is reflected into the fourth quadrant. Why do the points in the first and third quadrant stay in the first and third quadrant?

4. a) Find the coordinates of the vertices of each shape.

b) Predict the coordinates of the vertices under a reflection through line ℓ.

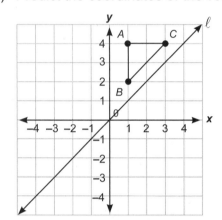 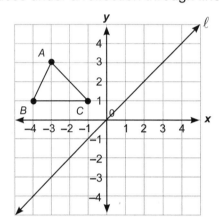 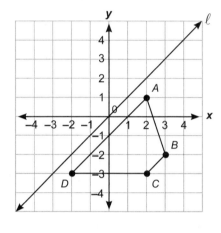

$A\ (\_\_,\_\_) \rightarrow A'\ (\_\_,\_\_)$ $A\ (\_\_,\_\_) \rightarrow A'\ (\_\_,\_\_)$ $A\ (\_\_,\_\_) \rightarrow A'\ (\_\_,\_\_)$

$B\ (\_\_,\_\_) \rightarrow B'\ (\_\_,\_\_)$ $B\ (\_\_,\_\_) \rightarrow B'\ (\_\_,\_\_)$ $B\ (\_\_,\_\_) \rightarrow B'\ (\_\_,\_\_)$

$C\ (\_\_,\_\_) \rightarrow C'\ (\_\_,\_\_)$ $C\ (\_\_,\_\_) \rightarrow C'\ (\_\_,\_\_)$ $C\ (\_\_,\_\_) \rightarrow C'\ (\_\_,\_\_)$

$D\ (\_\_,\_\_) \rightarrow D'\ (\_\_,\_\_)$

c) Reflect the figure by first reflecting the vertices through line ℓ, and check your answers from b).

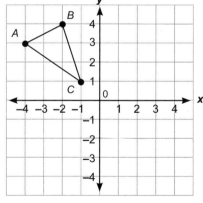

BONUS ▶

a) Reflect $\triangle ABC$ through the x-axis. Label the image $\triangle A'B'C'$.

b) Reflect $\triangle A'B'C'$ through the y-axis. Label the image $\triangle A''B''C''$.

c) Ling thinks that $\triangle A''B''C''$ is obtained from $\triangle ABC$ by a reflection through line ℓ. Is she correct? Explain why or why not using the rule from Question 3 a).

_____

_____

G8-13 Rotations

1. Draw the arrow after each turn. Start by drawing an arc to show where the final arrow should be.

a) 90° clockwise

b) 90° counter-clockwise

c) 90° clockwise

d) 90° counter-clockwise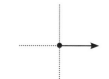

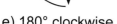
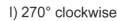

e) 180° clockwise

f) 180° counter-clockwise

g) 180° clockwise

h) 180° counter-clockwise

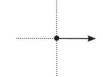

i) 270° clockwise

j) 270° counter-clockwise

k) 270° counter-clockwise

l) 270° clockwise

2. Match each rotation in the left column to a rotation in the right column that produces the same result. Hint: Use your answers from Question 1.

90° clockwise   90° counter-clockwise
180° clockwise   180° counter-clockwise
270° clockwise   270° counter-clockwise

Example: Rotate point *P* 90° clockwise about the origin using a set square.

Step 1: Join *P* and the origin. Mark the direction of rotation.

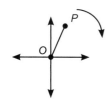

Step 2: Place a set square and draw a line that makes a 90° angle with *OP* in the given direction.

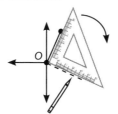

Step 3: Mark *P'* on your line so that *OP* = *OP'*. Use a ruler on the set square or a compass.

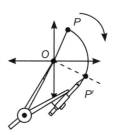

3. Using a set square and a circle instead of a compass, rotate *P* 90° clockwise. Label the image *P'*. Which quadrants are *P* and *P'* in?

a)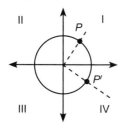

P: Quadrant ___I___

P' : Quadrant ___IV___

b)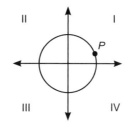

P: Quadrant ____

P' : Quadrant ____

c)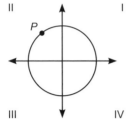

P : Quadrant _____

P' : Quadrant _____

d)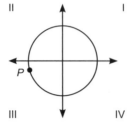

P : Quadrant _____

P' : Quadrant _____

e)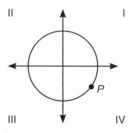

P : Quadrant _____

P' : Quadrant _____

4. Using a set square (or ruler) and a circle, rotate P the given amount clockwise (CW) or counter-clockwise (CCW). Label the image P'. Which quadrants are P and P' in?

> A **straight** angle measures 180°.
>
>
>
> You can use a ruler to rotate a point around the origin 180° (clockwise or counter-clockwise).

a) 180° CW

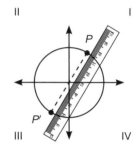

P : Quadrant _____

P' : Quadrant _____

b) 180° CW

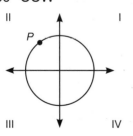

P : Quadrant _____

P' : Quadrant _____

c) 180° CCW

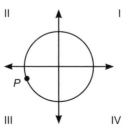

P : Quadrant _____

P' : Quadrant _____

d) 90° CCW

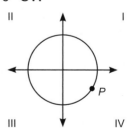

P : Quadrant _____

P' : Quadrant _____

e) 180° CCW

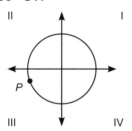

P : Quadrant _____

P' : Quadrant _____

f) 90° CCW

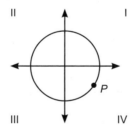

P : Quadrant _____

P' : Quadrant _____

g) 270° CW

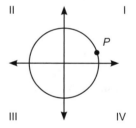

P : Quadrant _____

P' : Quadrant _____

5. a) Cross out the points in the grid that cannot be obtained from P using a clockwise or counter-clockwise rotation around the origin by 90° or 180°. The first one is done for you.

b) Write the amount of rotation needed to obtain the remaining points from P. The first one is done for you.

BONUS ▶ Choose one of the points you crossed out in Quadrant II or IV. Describe both a reflection and a translation that would take P to this point.

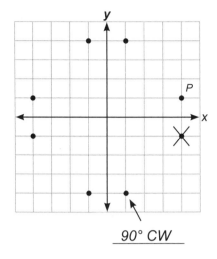

_90° CW_

6. Congruent shapes have equal corresponding sides and equal corresponding angles. Triangles $\triangle OAB$ and $\triangle OA'B'$ are congruent.

a) Which sides and angles in $\triangle OA'B'$ are equal to these sides and angles in $\triangle OAB$?

$OA =$ _____ $OB =$ _____ $AB =$ _____

$\angle AOB =$ _____ $\angle ABO =$ _____ $\angle OAB =$ _____

b) What is the degree measure of $\angle BOB'$? $\angle BOB' =$ _____

c) What is the degree measure of $\angle AOA'$? $\angle AOA' =$ _____ . Explain.

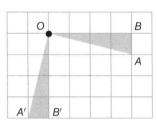

_____

_____

d) Which transformation takes $\triangle OAB$ to $\triangle OA'B'$? _____

7. Point P (4, 1) is obtained by translating the origin 4 units right (horizontally) and 1 unit up (vertically).

Plot these points by translating the origin the given distances.

a) Point A: Horizontal translation: 2 units left

Vertical translation: 1 unit up

A (_−2_ , _1_) Quadrant _II_

b) Point B: Horizontal translation: 3 units right

Vertical translation: 2 units down

B (___ , ___) Quadrant _____

c) Point C: Horizontal translation: 2 units left

Vertical translation: 4 units down

C (___ , ___) Quadrant _____

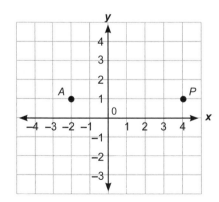

8. Choose one point in each quadrant of a coordinate grid. Describe the translation of the origin that is used to obtain each of the points.

9. Lina wants to rotate point P (2, 3) 90° clockwise around the origin.

a) Which quadrant is P in? _____

b) Which quadrant will the image P' be in? _____

c) Lina shades a right triangle with hypotenuse OP. Rotate her triangle 90° clockwise around the origin. Label the image P'.

d) The triangle before rotation has horizontal length 2 and vertical length 3.

The image triangle has horizontal length ___ and vertical length _____. P' has coordinates (___, ___).

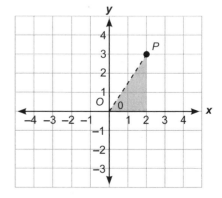

10. Plot the point Q (−4, −2) on the coordinate grid.

a) Use Lina's method to rotate point Q 90° clockwise around the origin. Label the image Q'.

Q is in quadrant _____. Q' is in quadrant _____.

The triangle before rotation has horizontal length ___ and vertical length _____.

The image triangle has horizontal length ___ and vertical length _____. So Q' has coordinates (___, ___).

b) Use Lina's method to rotate point Q (−4, −2) 90° counter-clockwise around the origin. Label the image Q''.

Q'' is in quadrant _____.

The triangle before rotation has horizontal length _____ and vertical length _____.

The image triangle has horizontal length _____ and vertical length _____. So Q'' has coordinates (___, ___).

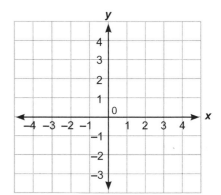

11. Compare the horizontal and the vertical lengths of the image triangles in Question 10. Are they equal? Are points Q' and Q'' the same? Explain.

12. Locate point P (3, 2) in the Cartesian plane. Use Lina's method to rotate P around the origin.

a) 90° clockwise   P' (___, ___)

b) 90° counter-clockwise   P'' (___, ___)

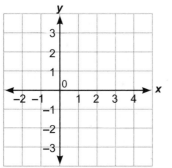

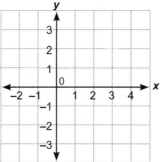

c) Which rotation would take point P' to point P''? _____

13. Locate point *Q* (–3, –2) in the Cartesian plane, then rotate *Q* around the origin.

a) 270° clockwise   *Q′* (___, ___)

b) 270° counter-clockwise   *Q″* (___, ___)

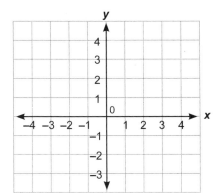

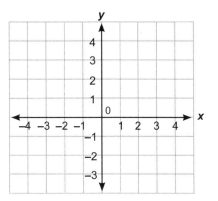

14. Rotate each point *P* around the origin as given using Lina's method. Label the image point *P′*. Fill in the blanks.

a) *P* (–3, 1), 180° clockwise; *P′* (___, ___)

b) *P* (4, –2), 180° counter-clockwise; *P′* (___, ___)

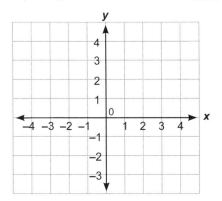

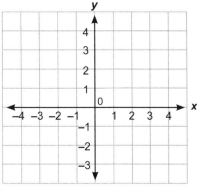

P is in quadrant ____. *P′* is in quadrant ____.

The triangle before rotation has horizontal length ____ and vertical length ____.

The image triangle has horizontal length ____ and vertical length ____.

P is in quadrant ____. *P′* is in quadrant ____.

The triangle before rotation has horizontal length ____ and vertical length ____.

The image triangle has horizontal length ____ and vertical length ____.

15. a) Plot point *P* (4, 2) on the coordinate grid.

b) Rotate *P* 90° clockwise around the origin. *P′* (___, ___)

c) Rotate *P′* 180° clockwise around the origin. *P″* (___, ___)

d) Point *P″* can be obtained by rotating point *P*

_____ clockwise around the origin.

e) Rotate *P″* 270° clockwise around the origin. *P‴* (___, ___)

f) Point *P‴* can be obtained by rotating point *P*

90° + 180° + 270° – 360° = ____ clockwise around the origin.
Explain where each number in this equation comes from.

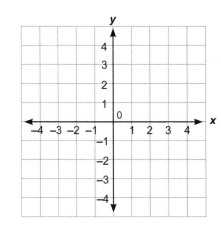

G8-14 Transformations — Advanced

1. Rotate points *P*, *Q*, and *R* around the origin. Label the image points *P'*, *Q'*, and *R'*.

   a) 90° counter-clockwise

   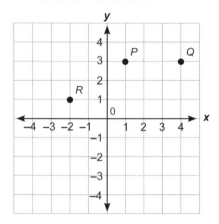

   P (__ , __), *Q* (__ , __), *R* (__ , __)
   P' (__ , __), *Q'* (__ , __), *R'* (__ , __)

   b) 270° counter-clockwise

   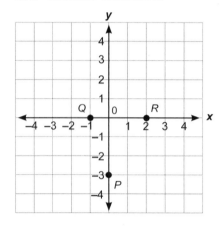

   P (__ , __), *Q* (__ , __), *R* (__ , __)
   P' (__ , __), *Q'* (__ , __), *R'* (__ , __)

   c) 180° counter-clockwise

   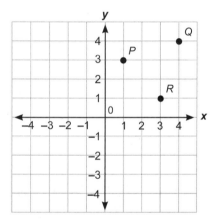

   P (__ , __), *Q* (__ , __), *R* (__ , __)
   P' (__ , __), *Q'* (__ , __), *R'* (__ , __)

   d) 270° counter-clockwise

   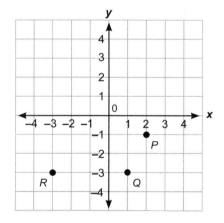

   P (__ , __), *Q* (__ , __), *R* (__ , __)
   P' (__ , __), *Q'* (__ , __), *R'* (__ , __)

2. Rotate the figure around the origin by first rotating the vertices.

   a) 90° clockwise

   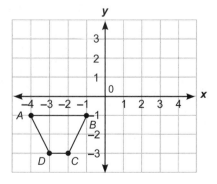

   b) 90° clockwise

   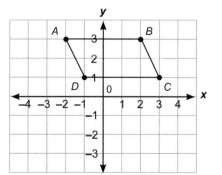

3. Rotate the figure around the origin by first rotating the vertices.

a) 180° clockwise

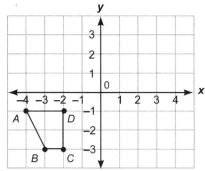

b) 180° clockwise

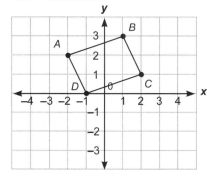

4. a) Write the coordinates of the points in 3 a) and b) in the table.

3 a)	original figure	A (__ , __)	B (__ , __)	C (__ , __)	D (__ , __)
	image figure	A′ (__ , __)	B′ (__ , __)	C′ (__ , __)	D′ (__ , __)
3 b)	original figure	A (__ , __)	B (__ , __)	C (__ , __)	D (__ , __)
	image figure	A′ (__ , __)	B′ (__ , __)	C′ (__ , __)	D′ (__ , __)

b) What do you notice about the coordinates of the images $A'B'C'D'$?

_____

_____

5. a) Plot these points in the Cartesian plane.

$A(-1, -2)$, $B(-1, -4)$,

$C(-3, -4)$, $D(-4, -2)$

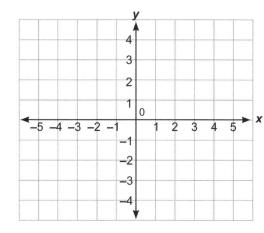

b) Predict the coordinates of the vertices of the image of $ABCD$ under a 180° clockwise rotation.

A′ (__ , __)   B′ (__ , __)
C′ (__ , __)   D′ (__ , __)

c) Rotate $ABCD$ 180° clockwise to check your answer.

Geometry 8-14

6. Which transformation changes triangle *A* into…

triangle *B*? _____

triangle *C*? _____

triangle *D*? _____

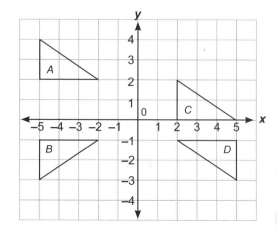

7. Draw a mirror line for the reflection.

A (___, ___)   *B* (___, ___)   *C* (___, ___)

A′ (___, ___)   *B′* (___, ___)   *C′* (___, ___)

Which coordinate does not change in the reflection, the
x-coordinate or the *y*-coordinate? Explain.

_____

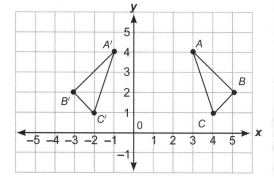

8. Find two different points *F* and *G* so that △*DFE* and △*DGE*
are congruent to △*ABC*. (Two figures are congruent if they
have the same size and shape.)

F (___, ___)   *G* (___, ___)

△*DFE* was obtained from △*ABC* by

_____

△*DGE* was obtained from △*ABC* by

_____

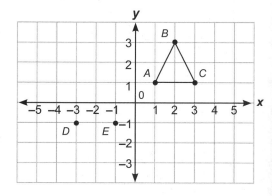

9. Design your own transformations.

a) I rotate *ABCD* _____ degrees clockwise.

A′ (___, ___) *B′* (___, ___)

C′ (___, ___) *D′* (___, ___)

b) I translate *A′B′C′D′* ____ units ____
(up/down) and ____ units ____ (right/left).

A″ (___, ___) *B″* (___, ___)

C″ (___, ___) *D″* (___, ___)

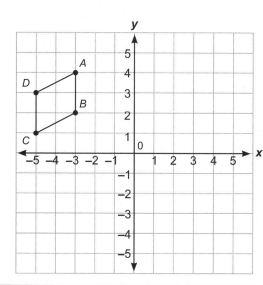